BORN FROM LAMENT

BORN FROM LAMENT

The Theology and Politics of Hope in Africa

Emmanuel Katongole

WILLIAM B. EERDMANS PUBLISHING COMPANY
GRAND RAPIDS, MICHIGAN

Wm. B. Eerdmans Publishing Co.
2140 Oak Industrial Drive N.E., Grand Rapids, Michigan 49505
www.eerdmans.com

23 22 21 20 19 18 17   1 2 3 4 5 6 7

ISBN 978-0-8028-7434-4

Library of Congress Cataloging-in-Publication Data

A catalog record for this book is available from the Library of Congress

How could we tire of hope?
—so much is in bud . . .
there is too much broken
that must be mended

too much hurt we have done
to each other
that cannot yet be forgiven . . .

So much is unfolding that must
complete its gesture,

so much is in bud

—Denise Levertov

Contents

Acknowledgments

I owe a deep debt of gratitude to the many people and institutions that have made the writing of this book possible. The Kroc Institute for International Peace Studies at Notre Dame University, where I serve as professor of theology and peace studies, provided generous research funding. I am particularly grateful to Scott Appleby, the former director of the Institute, now dean of the Keough School of Global Affairs, for his interest in and support of my work. A major part of the research was funded by a grant from the Kellogg Institute for International Studies at Notre Dame. I am especially grateful to Sharon Schierling for her support, and to Paulo Carozza (the director) and the entire staff of the Kellogg Institute. I wrote the initial draft of *Born from Lament* during a semester-long leave from Notre Dame, which I spent as a fellow at the Center for World Catholicism and Intercultural Theology at De Paul University. I am grateful to Bill Cavanaugh, the director of CWCICT, for the generous Fellowship and for the hospitality and support throughout my time at De Paul. To my friends Michael Budde and Stan Ilo, you made my stay and my period of writing at De Paul both stimulating and delightful. Thank you for your interest in this work and for your feedback on ideas and sundry sections, as well as the final draft of the manuscript. And to Francis, Karen, and Anna, I have nothing but gratitude and admiration for your dedicated support and servant leadership. To Fr. Ken Simpson and the community of St. Clement Church, Lincoln Park, thank you for hosting me and for welcoming me (again) into your parish community.

During my research time in Eastern Congo, a number of people provided hospitality and support, for which I am extremely grateful. Thank you, Katho and Feli (Bungishiabaku), and your family for your hospitality and for introducing me to the troubled history of Bunia and Nyankunde, and for various insights on reading Jeremiah in an African context. To David Kasali and Kaswera in Beni, and the staff at the Université Chrétienne Bilingue du Congo (UCBC): Daniel, Honaree, Chris; Fr. Jose Minaku, SJ; and the other Jesuits at Alifajari in Bukavu; my various guides and translators in Bunia, Beni, Butembo and Bukavu—thank you all for your generosity and assistance. To all my research assistants at Notre Dame, especially Kyle Lembelet, and to my assistants, translators, and transcribers in Eastern Africa: Sylvestre Kimbese (and the CRS network), Augustine Baganda, Josephine Nabakooza, Jessica Shewan, Rebecca Camp and especially the team of students from UCBC who carried out various interviews and collected lament songs, poems and stories through UCBC's Institute for Integrated Research under the guidance of Jonathan Shaw and Laura Lysen, a big thank you to you all.

The final version of *Born from Lament* has benefited from the critical feedback of many people for which I am grateful. I am particularly grateful to Stanley Hauerwas, Michael Budde, Jeff Goh, Jay Carney, Stan Ilo, and Kyle Lembelet for their comments on the draft and recommendations for improvement. I am also grateful to the critical and constructive feedback from the students in the Fall 2014 and Fall 2015 graduate seminars, which were organized around the research and content of *Born from Lament*. I am lucky to have Judith Heyhoe as my editorial assistant. Without her many hours of editorial scrutiny and labor, *Born from Lament* would not have attained this level of readability. The same debt of editorial gratitude extends to my editors Michael Thomson, Reinder VanTil, and Jenny Hoffman at Eerdmans.

My final and biggest gratitude is for all the people whose stories and work are discussed in *Born from Lament*, especially Jeff Opiyo, Fr. Paul Peter Abim, Sr. Rosemary Nyirumbe, David Kasali and Maggy Barankitse. I am grateful for your willingness to share your stories and for your patience and ever-gracious response to my requests for interviews, for information, and for answers to my many questions and inquiries. My gratitude extends beyond your availability to answer my questions, to the many ways in which your life and work provides a far more compelling argument than any scholar can provide about the gift and work of hope in Africa. That is why getting to know you in the process of researching your stories (and coming to claim you as my friends) is a rare and a most precious gift.

To you and to the memory of Christopher Munzihirwa and Emmanuel Kataliko, *Born from Lament* is dedicated.

Notre Dame, Indiana
December 11, 2016
(Third Sunday of Advent—"Rejoice . . . again I say, Rejoice")

On Arguing and Wrestling with God in Africa

"What kept you going?" I asked her.

This was in January 2008, at the ranch on the lake resort near Kampala. I was moderating a plenary session with Angelina Atyam at a gathering of the African Great Lakes Initiative. Angelina had just shared with the audience the story of the abduction of her daughter (together with 139 other girls) by the Lord's Resistance Army in 1996. She had told the audience how in the aftermath of the abduction, the parents of the abducted girls met regularly for prayer, fasting, and advocacy for the release of their children. Through these weekly meetings the parents had come to "receive the gift of forgiveness"—a gift that deepened their advocacy and led to the formation of the Concerned Parents' Association. The decisive moment in Angelina's advocacy came when the rebel leaders, seeking to buy her silence, offered to release her daughter if she would stop the advocacy and publicity campaign. She turned down the rebels' offer. She would only stop the advocacy if the rebels released all the abducted girls, for she had told them "every child is my child." The rebels refused Angelina's demand. She walked back home without her daughter, who remained in the bush for seven years and seven months—until she escaped.

"Why did you not accept the rebels' offer?" I asked her.

"There was no way," she said, "that I would ever be content to have my own daughter back knowing that all the girls were still suffering in the bush. How could I explain it to the other parents? We had all become one family and all the children were my children."

"Did you *know* that your daughter would ever be released or escape?" I asked her.

"No," she answered, "but I continued to trust that one day I would get her back."

"How did you deal with the fact that you had 'sacrificed' your own daughter?" I inquired.

"It was terrible," she said. "I cried a lot. My family turned against me, but there was nothing I could do. I found support in other parents. . . . We had work to do. I traveled from one community to another . . . and spoke a lot on the radio."

"What kept you going?"

"Every Saturday I washed and put out Charlotte's clothes on the line to dry, and every day I set a place for her at the table and prayed for her. . . . I prayed a lot. Many nights I was not able to sleep and I would sit up and argue with God. It was actually on this particular night, seven years and seven months after the girls were abducted that I spent the whole night wrestling with God and asking God many questions. That was the night that my daughter escaped from the rebels."

I reconstruct this conversation with Angelina Atyam because it helps to explain how and why I started working on this book. In my earlier work, *The Sacrifice of Africa* (2009), I discussed the story of Angelina and the Concerned Parents' Association (CPA) together with two other initiatives: Paride Taban's Holy Trinity Peace Village and Maggy Barankitse's Maison Shalom. This was part of an argument for the need and possibility of a new foundation for politics in Africa. Within this broad argument, I noted that CPA, Holy Trinity Peace Village, and Maison Shalom provide the much-needed theological critique and interruption of the politics of violence that wantonly sacrifice millions in Africa. Thus, Angelina's politics of forgiveness represented an alternative form of politics, one that is committed to saving and serving the very lives that are often wasted within the power struggles of Africa's political modernity.

But while I was able, in *The Sacrifice of Africa*, to locate Angelina's (and the other activists') advocacy within the broader political history of Africa, and narrate their advocacy as a theopolitical imagination committed to the invention of a new future in Africa, I was left with a nagging feeling that I had not fully captured the tragic nature of Angelina's story (as well as the other stories). Even though their stories were impressive, and offered a good exemplification for the kind of political theology I was calling for, it was not exactly clear how such a tragic sacrifice like Angelina's could turn out, as I implied, to be a unique "sacrifice" (in its original Latin sense of *sacra facere*—to make sacred), thus a reflection of God's redemptive suffering. And what did this say about the nature and shape of hope in the midst of suffering in general, Africa's turbulent history in particular? This limitation became particularly evident to me in the final months of completing *The Sacrifice of Africa*, as I realized that the faith activists I had profiled—Angelina, Taban, and Maggy—shared a major characteristic. Their agency and activism was born in and through the experience of suffering and social dislocation. I was particularly struck by the capacity of the faith activists to embrace, hold, and transform the experience of personal and communal suffering and tragedy into energy, commitment, and advocacy for nonviolent alternatives. I was not sure how to account for this transformation. At the same time, I noted that their agency and nonviolent activism was forged at a unique intersection between, on the one hand, a sense of not knowing (the future) and, on the other, trust (even confidence) that the future would turn out all right; between resistance and innovation, between a courageous "No" to a culture of war, tribalism, and corruption, and a daring "Yes" to nonviolent alternatives in the midst of war.

Even as I became aware of this nexus of the nonviolent agency of the activists as I finished working on *The Sacrifice of Africa*, I did not have either the time or the resources to attend more fully to the internal logic of that intersection. But I was beginning to feel that, without getting *inside* this intersection, the full extent of their theological agency would remain somewhat opaque. It was not sufficient to simply note the matrix of Christian agency in the midst of suffering and point to the theological notion of lament as the discipline that made it possible; a more theoretical framework was needed to explain it. How, I wondered, was one able to remain and sustain agency within such a painful space of anguish? What kept one going? What carried a person forward through the dark nights of not knowing? I was particularly interested to know what, for someone like Angelina, the relationship between her and God looked and felt like, and the kind of prayer that constituted that relationship. More specifically, when Angelina said, "I argued a lot with God" and "I wrestled with God," I was curious to know what the content and shape of that arguing or wrestling was. And what was the relationship between the arguing and wrestling and the work that needed to be done—work that took the form of fiery and compassionate advocacy on behalf of the abducted children, which included Angelina's willingness to sacrifice her own daughter? These questions were pointing to the need for a full-fledged investigation regarding the nature and grounds of hope in the midst of suffering. More specifically, the questions pointed to the need to explore in depth the biblical and theological notion of lament and its relationship to hope. For I was beginning to sense that the notion of lament held the key to a full explication of the nature and reality of hope in the midst of Africa's turbulent history.

I was also convinced that an investigation into the notion and practice of lament would have far-reaching theological and political implications. The political dimensions of the investigation became even more evident after I read Jason Stearns's *Dancing in the Glory of Monsters: The Collapse of the Congo and the Great War of Africa*. This was in the summer of 2012. I had just accepted a position at Notre Dame's Kroc Institute for Peace Studies and was thinking about how I would teach a doctoral seminar in theology and peacebuilding. As I put together a list of books I considered Stearns's book and its vivid and moving chronicle of the Congolese Civil Wars, which began in 1996 in the wake of the Rwanda genocide, and which left millions displaced from their homes, over 5.4 million dead, and tens of thousands of women raped.

Stearns not only sheds light on the key actors, their complex calculations, motivations and agency during the war; he also provides a number of testimonies and stories of ordinary people caught up in the fighting. Reading *Dancing in the Glory of Monsters* confirmed a number of conclusions I had reached in *The Sacrifice of Africa*. For in many ways, one could see in *Dancing in the Glory* the full outworking, more than a hundred years later, of the effects of King Leopold's brutal legacy in the Congo. But the book also raised a number of crucial questions with respect to the nature and possibility of hope in Africa, for Stearns ends his chronicle on a note of despair about Congo's future, given its "lack of visionary, civic-minded leadership" (328).

I was bothered by that conclusion: not only did it easily perpetuate the image of a "hope-less" continent, but also, even more substantively, it did not square with my own experience. In my interactions via the Great Lakes Initiative, I had come to know—either personally or through their stories—a number of civic-minded Christian leaders, including Congo leaders such as Munzihirwa, Kataliko, Daphrose, Kasali, Katho and many others, and while it's true that such leaders were not "political" in the sense that Kagame, Kaguta, and Kabila were, in their work with the congregations and the local communities they exhibited an exceptional sense of civic engagement. Stearns's conclusion led me to want to investigate the stories of these and similar leaders in order to get a better sense of their agency in the context of Congo's violent social history. I was particularly curious to see whether, and to what extent, their social engagement was born, nurtured, and sustained at the dynamic intersection of lament and hope.

In the summer of 2013, I spent three weeks in Eastern Congo, during which I visited four towns—Bunia, Beni, Butembo, and Bukavu—trying to get a general sense (through interviews and workshops) of "ordinary" people's experience during the Congo Wars, but also investigating the stories of David Kasali, Christopher Munzihirwa, and Emmanuel Kataliko. That summer research proved to be exceptionally fruitful on a number of fronts. First, the research confirmed the innovative, diverse, and far-reaching civic engagement of those three leaders. Second, I came back from Eastern Congo more determined to tell their stories, if for no other reason than to prove Stearns wrong regarding the general lack of visionary civic leadership. Third, my research also confirmed the rich theological matrix of convictions, practices, and reasons out of which the activists operated. Fourth, my research revealed that at the heart of their innovative and nonviolent civic engagement, and also somehow the reason for it, was a deep sense of grief, anguish, and suffering.

A grant from the Kellogg Institute at Notre Dame provided the means for me to follow up the initial visit to Congo with more extended research that, with the aid of assistants and help from the Institute for Integrated Research at the Université Chrétienne Bilingue du Congo (UCBC), allowed me to carry out extensive interviews with local communities, churches and individuals, and to collect poems, songs and artistic pieces from Eastern Congo and Northern Uganda that express the communities' lament. Poring over these laments and comparing them to the biblical laments (the book of Lamentations and the psalms of lament) led me to see them not as cries of despair but as multilayered performances through which a community's suffering, mourning and hope are articulated. The laments provided insight into the cultural moorings of hope in the midst of Africa's multiple dislocations and proved to be an invaluable resource for a theological conversation about hope in Africa.

The grant also allowed me to hold a workshop with eight Christian activists, who have led or have been involved in initiatives of nonviolent change from across the Great Lakes Region of Eastern Africa. The workshop not only allowed me to capture (listen to) their stories, but also to share findings from my research and test out some of the emerging themes and see if and to what extent these conclusions were reflected in their own experiences. Framing the workshop through the reading and discussion of the book of Lamentations proved to be exceptionally fruitful as the leaders not only were immediately able to identity with the plight and lament of Daughter Zion but also welcomed a biblical/theological framework. In fact, reading the book of Lamentations together offered them both language and an opportunity to talk about their own practice of arguing and wrestling with God. Moreover, it was clear from their individual and collective sharing that the arguing and wrestling with God was not only a one-time historical event that birthed their activism, it was an ongoing practice that sustains their nonviolent activism. It was at the heart of their agency. Thus the workshop confirmed the connection between lament and hope.

Born from Lament is a distillation of what I have learned through this research. It is an extended argument for this deep connection between lament and hope. In 1 Peter 3:15, the author exhorts the Christians of his day, who found themselves imperiled by various tribulations and suffering, to "always [be] prepared to make a defense to anyone who asks you for a reason for the hope that is in you; yet do it with gentleness and respect." This is exactly what I plan to do in *Born from Lament*—to give an account of hope in Africa through the portraits of select Christian activists for nonviolent change from the East African region. Even though all the portraits are from the East Africa Great Lakes Region, my use of portraiture as a theological method involves an assumption that, in these particular and localized portraits, the reader will be able to discover general themes and patterns that resonate across much of sub-Saharan Africa. It is for this reason that—even though I am fully aware of the many philosophical, ideological, and methodological questions related to the concept of "Africa"—I retain "Africa" in the title of the book.

The central argument of this book is that, in the midst of suffering, hope takes the form of arguing and wrestling with God. If we understand it as lament, such arguing and wrestling is not merely a sentiment, not merely a cry of pain. It is a way of mourning, of protesting to, appealing to, and engaging God—and a way of acting in the midst of ruins. Lament is what sustains and carries forth Christian agency in the midst of suffering. *Born from Lament* seeks to display the practice of lament as the work of hope in its theological and practical dimensions in the context of Africa's turbulent social history. The argument is developed in five parts. Each part is framed by a biblical lens, which helps to locate the agency of the Christian nonviolent activists within a scriptural and theological journey. While there is an inherent logic to the parts—thus they should be read sequentially—each section stands on its own as a fully integrated argument. In the end, the sections operate as different portraits of the same argument, with each section providing a different theological/biblical perspective and its practical dimensions on the inner connection between lament and hope. Accordingly, there is no strict need to read the parts sequentially; but it is important to read all the chapters within a section together. In this way, the reader can see more clearly the connection between the scriptural/theological argument and its social, political, and practical display through the portrait of a faith activist.

Part One ("A Hope-less Continent?") serves as an extended introduction and lays out the context, motivations, and methodology of the study. In Chapter 1, I discuss Jason Stearns's *Dancing in the Glory of Monsters*. Doing so allows me to rehearse and reexamine some of the key conclusions of my own

The Sacrifice of Africa, as well as to highlight the individual, social, and communal unraveling under way in the wake of Congo's violence. Using Congo as a mirror, I raise in this chapter questions about the possibility and the nature of hope in Africa more generally, and argue that theological language and analysis is needed to engage a conversation about hope. Chapter 2 picks up this conclusion and notes that a theological conversation about hope is exactly what has been missing in most accounts of Africa. As a result, the assessment of Africa's prospects tends to swing between the extremes of pessimism and optimism. The much-needed and urgent theological task, the chapter argues, is to respond to Peter's exhortation to "always be prepared to give an account of the hope that is in you." I analyze the theological, ecclesiological, and epistemological implications of the exhortation as a way to highlight the connection between suffering and hope, of which the first letter of Peter constantly reminds us, by referring to the suffering and death of Christ, on the one hand, to his resurrection, on the other. The exhortation to "give an account of hope" also points to the central role that "story" needs to play in a theology of hope for Africa. In this book I adopt Sara Lawrence-Lightfoot's method of portraiture as the unique form of narrative able to capture a movement of hope in Africa in its complex ecclesiological, theological, and practical dimensions.

Part Two ("Soundscapes of Lament") argues that the starting point of any discussion of hope is the valley of lament. Chapter 3 explores the book of Lamentations in order to locate the cry of lament in the context of Jerusalem's destruction. What emerges from this discussion is a clear parallel between the destruction of Jerusalem and the violent dislocations in Africa. What also emerges is a comprehensive vision of lament as a complex set of practices or disciplines—a way of *seeing, standing,* and *wrestling* or *arguing* with God, and thus a way of hoping in the midst of ruins. In Chapter 4, I trace this multilayered practice of lament through songs, dances, poems, prayers, and artistic expressions from Eastern Africa, and I highlight both the cultural and theological significance of the laments as sites within which the memory and the striving, pain, and hope of a suffering people are articulated.

In Part Three ("The God of Lament"), I develop another portrait of lament as a way of turning in and toward God in the midst of suffering. Chapter 5 examines the psalms of lament in the Hebrew Scripture and highlights the fact that the God who is encountered in such psalms is often hidden and silent in the face of the people's pleas. The chapter also argues that the silence of God cannot be interpreted as an indication of a God who does not care. On the contrary, the "silence" of God reflects a deeply caring God (grounded in the covenant relationship) and may itself point to a rich theological mystery of a

God who is not only moved, but hurts and suffers with God's suffering people. By drawing attention to the work of scholars such as Jürgen Moltmann, David Tracy, and Gustavo Gutiérrez, I make explicit the connection between the God of lament and the incarnate and "crucified God," a God who responds to "an excess of evil with an excess of love." What these writers confirm is that, far from leading to resignation or further "theoretical" exploration, the notion of a "crucified God" pushes Christians into *theopraxis*, the passionate advocacy with and on behalf of God's "crucified peoples" in history. In Chapter 6, I show that it is the reality of a crucified God that lies behind the passionate, pastoral, and practical engagement of Emmanuel Kataliko in Bukavu and Sr. Rosemary Nyirumbe in northern Uganda.

In Part Four ("The Peace of Lament"), I examine the prophetic laments of the prophets (Jesus and Jeremiah) in Chapter 7 as a way to explore the peace-building dimension of prophetic lament. I note that the laments of Jesus and Jeremiah are a critique of both the political and the religious institutions of their day, pointing to God's covenant with Israel, which was founded on an intimate knowledge of and relationship with God as the key to peace. The overall argument of this section is to present lament as an epistemology—a unique way of knowing—and as participation in the revolutionary nonviolent vision of society. The story of Archbishop Christopher Munzihirwa of Bukavu (Chapter 8) provides a concrete exemplification of the kind of prophetic critique and knowledge that is available only to "eyes that have cried." The overall thrust of the section is to argue that lament not only has far-reaching political implications but also is a fundamental critique and reframing of politics from a thoroughly theological viewpoint—an argument that is carried over in the last section. To set the stage for this argument, Section IV concludes with a chapter (Chapter 9) on the "costly loss" of lament, which both notes the loss of lament and responds to a critique raised by Melissa Snarr that lament is mere "spirituality" that stops short of full political engagement.

Part Five ("The Politics of Lament") explores why and how lament is a decisive form of political agency and engagement that takes many forms. The theoretical (and theological) framework of the argument in Chapter 10 is shaped around the story of Rachel's weeping at the beginning of Matthew's Gospel (Matt. 2:17–18). The context here is the slaughter of the innocents, which Matthew now presents as a "fulfillment" of Jeremiah 31:15–22. The surprising thing here is that, in the midst of Rachel's weeping, the text ends with the promise that "the Lord has created a new thing on the earth" (Jer. 31:22). The image of Rachel's weeping thus "explodes" with rich sociopolitical and practical implications in the African context, which I explore in the last three chapters.

In Chapter 11, I argue that the logic found in Rachel's weeping is similar to the logic of the promise of a "new thing" that drives the work of the Kasalis and the Congo Initiative. In Chapter 12, I use the story of Maggy Barankitse to explore the gendered dimension of Rachel's cry as a mother crying for her children. Rachel is instructed (in Jer. 31:21) to set up "road markers" for a new future, and Maggy is doing something like this through Maison Shalom in Burundi and beyond. The conclusion from this portrait of Maggy's life and work is to confirm that Maison Shalom is born in lament, deepened through lament, and carried forth through lament as Maggy meditates daily on the cross but also regularly revisits the gravesite of her lament so as "to see more clearly the future." In the last chapter (Chapter 13), against the story of the slaughter of the innocents in Matthew's Gospel (which is the immediate context that evokes Rachel's memory), I make explicit the connections between courage, hope, and martyrdom by using the stories of a select group of martyrs from East Africa. This chapter argues that martyrs provide the most decisive and clearest example of hope, and their memory, like Rachel's memory of her children, is a form of resistance (against "cheap hope") and struggle to transform the structures of violence, poverty, and marginalization into "an excess of love."

The overall effect of my inquiry is not only to confirm the inner connection between lament and hope, but also to display the rich theological, ecclesiological, and practical implications of this matrix of Christian agency in the context of Africa's troubled history. Therefore, what I trust emerges here is a better appreciation of the meaning and practice of lament in general, and of the dynamic reality and nature of hope in Africa in particular, and that it illustrates what a response to Peter's exhortation "to give an account of hope" might look like in our time. But I am also confident that the study confirms that responding to Peter's exhortation in Africa calls for a narrative theological approach or method—a unique style of storytelling through which one is able to trace the logic of Christ's suffering-death-resurrection in the lives and work of Christian activists in the nonviolent search for a new future in Africa. By offering different portraits of hope in the midst of Africa's social turmoil, I invite readers to enter into the theopraxis of lament, to enter into its internal logic, and to learn from the inside an account of the hope that animates improvisational and transformative nonviolent activism in East Africa. Such an account must be located in the midst of Africa's social histories of war, violence, and multiple dislocations. Since the Congo is an example of—in fact, a metaphor for—the devastation and suffering in Africa, attending to Congo's recent history confirms the deep sense of trauma in whose ruins a conversation about hope becomes not only relevant but extremely urgent. Jason Stearns's *Dancing in the Glory of Monsters* is therefore a good place to start a theological conversation about hope in Africa.

PART ONE

A Hope-less Continent?

CHAPTER 1

The Possibility and the Nature of Hope in Africa

We are living on top of our dead.

Pastor Philippe

A Landscape of Lament

Few books about Congo's recent history are as moving as Jason Stearns's *Dancing in the Glory of Monsters*. If Congo is a huge and complex country, its recent history is even more complex and difficult to grasp. In the last twenty-five years, this second largest nation in Africa, the size of Western Europe and a quarter the size of the United States, has been the center of a series of wars and fighting that have left over 5.4 million dead, millions displaced from their homes, tens of thousands of women raped,[1] and its 67 million people among the world's most impoverished. At a certain point, the numbers stop making any sense, and all one is left with are media images of red-eyed and gun-wielding militias roaming the African jungle, raping and killing in the most outlandish way imaginable. If, for many in the West, these images confirm the long-held suspicion of Africa as a "dark continent" (Joseph Conrad's "heart of darkness") that lies beyond the pale of reason and/or humanity, for many Africans, especially those in countries such as the Central African Republic (CAR), Sierra Leone, Southern Sudan, Liberia, Burundi, Rwanda, and Uganda, the images are eerily familiar.

But what is going on? What explanation, what rationale might there be for

1. See Sara E. Casey et al., "Care-Seeking Behavior by Survivors of Sexual Assault in the Democratic Republic of Congo," *American Journal of Public Health* 101 (June 2011): 1054-56.

the fighting in the Congo and the senseless violence it has unleashed? Perhaps, if one were to make sense of the violence in the Congo, one might be able to see the connections with similar cases of fighting and violence in the other parts of Africa. For, in many ways, Congo is a mirror of the violence in postcolonial Africa; or, to use Frantz Fanon's famous image, Africa has the shape of a pistol, and Congo is the trigger.[2] Yet, Congo is not merely a symbol. It has a long, contingent, and singular history of violence, and part of the challenge of trying to make sense of the contemporary topography of violence in the Congo is this complex history. How does one make sense of a conflict (or better, conflicts) that at its height involved the armies of nine countries, multiple groups of UN peacekeepers, and twenty armed groups?

In *Dancing in the Glory of Monsters*, Stearns attempts to unravel the many interlocking strands of this complex tale of Congo's recent turmoil, which is helpful on at least two levels. First, concerning historical reconstruction, Stearns provides a vivid and moving chronicle of the Congolese civil wars, which began in 1996 in the wake of the Rwanda Genocide and ended Mobutu's thirty-one-year reign and installed Desire Kabila. He covers Kabila's tumultuous and short-lived time as president, his assassination, and the installation of his son, Joseph Kabila, and the young Kabila's first few years in office. Stearns not only sheds light on the key actors, their complex calculations, motivations, and agency during the war; even more important, he locates the fighting within the context of Congo's political history.[3]

2. Jason K. Stearns, *Dancing in the Glory of Monsters: The Collapse of the Congo and the Great War of Africa* (New York: PublicAffairs, 2012), 45. The quote is from Franz Fanon's *The Wretched of the Earth*.

3. For its breadth, grasp and accessibility, *Dancing in the Glory of Monsters* has received a number of positive reviews. Adam Hochschild thinks it is "the best account so far: more serious than several recent macho-war-correspondent travelogues, and more lucid and accessible than its nearest competitor, Gérard Prunier's dense and overwhelming *Africa's World War: Congo, the Rwandan Genocide, and the Making of a Continental Catastrophe* (see http://www.nytimes.com/2011/04/03/books/review/book-review-dancing-in-the-glory-of-monsters-the-collapse-of-the-congo-and-the-great-war-of-africa-by-jason-k-stearns.html?=all&_r=0 [accessed January 27, 2015]). John Le Carré notes that "no serious educated reader of DRC contemporary political history can overlook the wealth of information and insight . . . [brought] forth in weaving an intricate narrative of politics outside conventional political science frame as may be the case of DRC in the aftermath of the Rwandan genocide" (http://www.amazon.com/Dancing-Glory-Monsters-Collapse-Africa-ebook/dp/B0076M4VDC [December 3, 2015]). I tend to agree with this positive assessment even though I am aware that other reviewers find Stearns's book somewhat shallow. Van de Walle, for instance, finds Stearns's account lacking "the sweeping historical detail of Gerard Prunier's *Africa's World War* or the careful examination of the underlying ethnocultural sources of the conflict of René Lemarchand's

The second level on which I find Stearns's book helpful is in terms of the personal testimonies and close-up portraits of ordinary people caught up in the fighting. By way of these stories, one is able to glimpse the depth of suffering, as well as the national, communal, and individual trauma under way in the wake of the violence.

By taking time to explore these two aspects of Stearns's work, I will be able to highlight why and how this kind of violence is thinkable within the context of Congo's political imagination. Accordingly, reflecting on *Dancing in the Glory of Monsters* provides an opportunity to rehearse some of the key conclusions of *The Sacrifice of Africa*, where I located the ongoing performance of violence within the imaginative landscape of modern Africa. But reflecting on the social and personal trauma of both the agents and the victims of the violence in the Congo raises deep theological questions. How can one even begin to think about hope and what hope would look like in the context of Africa's ongoing realities of war, violence and social disruption? The story of Congo serves as a good theological starting point.

Making the Violence in the Congo Thinkable

In *Dancing in the Glory of Monsters*, Stearns seeks to move beyond the standard picture of the fighting in the Congo as "a morass of rebel groups fighting over minerals in the ruins of a failed state" (327). Accordingly, his goal is not simply historical reconstruction, but to explain the fighting as an expression of political violence. Rather than simply narrating what happened next, he sets out to inquire into "what kind of political system produced this kind of violence" (6). To this end, at various places in his historical reconstruction, he provides enough analytical anchors that help to locate the violence within Congo's political history. What he notes about the Congo rings true for other African countries. For as Michela Wrong notes, Congo is in many ways "a paradigm of all that was wrong with post-colonial Africa,"[4] even though as a case of "negative excellence" Congo seems to embody within its history the faults of any normal African state and pitch them one frequency higher. Capturing

The Dynamics of Violence in Central Africa." Stearns is more concerned with the "perceptions, motivations, and actions of an eclectic mix of actors in the conflict" (Nicolas van de Walle, "Review: *Dancing in the Glory of Monsters: The Collapse of the Congo and the Great War of Africa*," *Foreign Affairs* [May-June 2011]).

4. Michela Wrong, *In the Footsteps of Mr. Kurtz: Living on the Brink of Disaster in Mobutu's Congo* (New York: HarperCollins, 2001), 10.

some of Stearns's observations about the Congo helps to confirm some key conclusions of *The Sacrifice of Africa*.

Institutional Weakness of the State

Without trying to reduce the causes of the fighting to one factor, Stearns points to the institutional weakness of the Congolese state as a major factor. Stearns begins by locating this institutional weakness of the state within Congo's political history, looking first at how King Leopold "killed or mutilated hundreds of thousands and pushed millions of others to starvation or death from disease" (70). Second, within the history of the Belgian colonial administration and the subsequent postcolonial politics of Mobutu's dictatorship, Stearns observes that

> since 1970 until today, the Congolese state has not had an effective army, administration, or judiciary, nor have its leaders been interested in creating strong institutions. Instead they have seen the state apparatus as a threat, to be kept weak so as to better manipulate it. This has left a bitter Congolese paradox: a state that is everywhere and oppressive but that is defunct and dysfunctional. (126)

What Stearns's narrative makes clear, and what is important to keep in mind, is that the Congolese state's dysfunctional nature does not reflect a "failed state." There is also nothing culturally "African" or "Congolese" about it. As Stearns rightly notes, "the lack of responsible politics is not due to some genetic defect in Congolese DNA, a missing 'virtue' gene, or even something about Congolese culture. Instead, it is deeply rooted in the country's political history" (215). Congo operates just the way it was meant to from the very start of its contact with and inception into modern Western history. Its institutional weakness is part the legacy of its unique story.

> [Modern Congo] was the victim of one of the most brutal episodes of colonial rule, when it was turned into the private business empire of King Leopold; under his reign and the subsequent rule by the republican Belgian government, the Congo's remaining customary chiefs were fought, co-opted, or sent into exile. Religious leaders who defied the orthodoxy of the European-run churches faced the same fate: the prophet Simon Kimbangu died after thirty years in prison for his anticolonial rhetoric. (215)

Mobutu just continued the same manipulative "taming" of the state institutions and turned them into personal fiefdoms. He did so not only for private gain but also in order to prevent any challengers to his power from emerging, a policy that effectively ended up eroding that very power in the process (126).

Anyone familiar with recent developments in Africa will immediately recognize this pattern of "taming" and "eroding" of political institutions by African leaders bent on extending their stay in power (witness, e.g., the attempts at constitutional amendments to allow for a "third term" and other clientalist representation). As I noted in *The Sacrifice of Africa*—and what Stearns helps to illuminate with respect to Congo—this institutional weakness of the state is not an incidental glitch that can be repaired by some technical and ethical education; it is part of the social imagery of Africa's modernity—the way modern Africa was *imagined* from the very start.

"Fighting" and the Politics of the Belly

While the fighting in the Congo may have started with an ideology or set of ideologies, in the end it came to reflect and confirm the self-serving *la politique du ventre*, as various national forces and local militias fought for control of Congo's rich mineral and natural resources. In 1996, Rwanda led an invasion of the Congo, ostensibly because it needed to destroy the *Interahamwe*-controlled refugee camps that continued to pose a threat to Rwanda. However, the most significant aspect of this first Congo war, apart from the speed with which it succeeded in toppling Mobutu's regime, was the international coalition it was able to piece together in order "to liberate Congo" from Mobutu's dictatorship. Led by Rwanda, the coalition brought together Ugandan, Congolese, and Angolan fighters, and had the support of Burundi, Zambia, and Zimbabwe. This united front seemed to represent "the heyday of African Renaissance." However, no sooner had Kabila come to power than the coalition began to crack and, with the assassination of Kabila, to break apart. Congo would become the theater of "Africa's World War" as various former partners found themselves on different sides of the fighting. Even the two closest allies, Uganda and Rwanda, would eventually fight it out in Kisangani. What the infighting revealed is that while the genesis might have been steeped in ideology, greed and plunder had become the main motives for conflict in the region. "Within several years, the Congo was to become the graveyard for the lofty rhetoric of African leadership as preached by Mbeki" (56).

It is within this unique chemistry of a struggle for power and plunder, especially evident in the proxy war between Kigali and Kinshasa, that one can see how the entire country became increasingly militarized. This was especially true of eastern Congo, where local Mai Mai militias formed in protest of Rwandan occupation. Without providing any training, Kinshasa dropped tons of weapons and ammunition at various airports in the jungles of eastern Congo for the Hutu militia as well as for Mai Mai groups (250).

> However, as the country became more militarized, discontented and unemployed youth joined militias and set up roadblocks to tax the local population. Family and land disputes, which had previously been settled in traditional courts, were now sometimes solved through violence, and communal feuds between rival clans or tribes resulted in skirmishes and targeted killings. (250–51)

The Rassemblement Congolais pour la Démocratie (RCD), the Congolese Rally for Democracy, Rwanda's main allies in the east, responded in kind. In both South and North Kivu, governors created local militias, "[b]ut instead of improving security, these ramshackle, untrained local militias for the most part just exacerbated the suffering by taxing, abusing, and raping the local population" (251).

It is within this context that one has to understand the ethnic dimension that the fighting in eastern Congo would soon take on. Here Stearns's analysis is lacking. For it is misleading to suggest that "if the fiercest ideology of ethics that can be found in the country is ethnic, that is because no other institution has been strong enough for the people to rally around" (216).[5] Though such an observation may be descriptively true, it does not take into full account the way in which, within the unique nexus of the politics of plunder and power, ethnic identification has not been a stable and unchanging form of *social* identification, but rather is one that is constantly manufactured, reproduced, and recruited as the elites fight for political spoils. "Congolese rebel politics since the 1960s has been either an elite or an ethnic affair, or—most often—a mixture of both" (232).[6]

5. See, e.g., the review by Harry Verhoeven. This limitation might be connected to "the absence of interaction with theoretical models": "So, overall, are his reflections on ethnicity which is seen as some kind of residue that does nasty things to people but that remains neither defined, nor linked consistently to other concepts or analytical categories" ("Review," *African Arguments*, Aug. 2, 2011: http://africanarguments.org/2011/08/02/when-an-african-giant-falls -apart-review-of-dancing-in-the-glory-of-monsters-the-collapse-of-the-congo-and-the-great -war-of-africa-by-jason-stearns/ (accessed Jan. 27, 2015).

6. Mobutu continued the colonial (Belgian) policy of creating ever-new customary rulers

Anyone familiar with African politics will easily recognize a similar pattern and logic within the endless regimes of "fighting" and the reproduction of militia rebels. Whereas the fighting might often be couched in lofty ideologies of "liberating" our people, quite often it is neither liberation nor even the capture of state power that is at stake. Just as in the Congo, the armed groups "are not so much about controlling territory as about controlling civilians, who are brutalized in order to obtain resources and as retaliation for attacks by their rivals" (329). This not only redefines the notion of "sovereignty"; it also points to a social context where millions of young, vulnerable, unemployed youths become an easy target for either recruitment or abduction into the militia forces.[7]

Illusory Salvation

That a number of young people found themselves easily drawn into the fighting in the Congo is perhaps not surprising. Mobutu's thirty-two years in power had not only destroyed the country but had left millions of Congolese, the youth especially, without any viable options for the future. For many young people, fighting gave them a sense of purpose. In this respect, Stearns's interactions and interviews with some of the young former combatants are quite illuminating. Hundreds of street children, unemployed youths, and pupils were recruited, and each was given one hundred dollars—five times the monthly rent for a house. But even more importantly, the new recruits were told that they were being enlisted to fight Mobutu, who had ruined the country and had made people corrupt and tribalistic. They were fighting to liberate their country and to establish a new future of democracy and development. In order to do that, they were instructed in various ways of confronting and killing the enemy. Kizito, a young boy ("Kadogo") who was recruited into the "rebellion" by Kabila in 1996, captures the significance of what was being offered him. "It was obvious to me. . . I had no future in Bukavu. They were offering me a future. . . . It was like a dream. I was so excited" (144–45).

But as Stearns's narrative follows Kizito's story, the promised future soon turns into a nightmare as the young recruits, trained in various modes of

---

(chiefs), co-opted by the state, who have no real political power, but whose presence in the community was more ceremonial and symbolic. In this way, there was always an "ethnic" or "tribal" dimension to Congo's society.

7. For more on "sovereignty" with respect to the Lord's Resistance Army, see E. Katongole, *The Sacrifice of Africa: A Political Theology for Africa* (Grand Rapids: Eerdmans, 2011).

combat, fight and kill their way through the jungle. In fact, Stearns devotes an entire chapter, "This Is How You Fight," to a description of how the recruits were turned into soldiers. In one particularly gripping narrative, Stearns provides a glimpse into the effect of the violence on the recruits. At the end of the day, when the exhausted fighters retired to their tents to sleep, Kizito was not able to sleep. And he was not the only one. "At night Kizito would hear kids in the other tents sobbing and reciting bible verses" (149).

What Kizito's experience confirms is the gradual embeddedness of the trauma of violence in the minds of the young fighters, which confirms the blurring of the categories of victim-perpetrator with regard to child soldiers such as Kizito. This, of course, is related to the creativity and ongoing reproduction of violence even within so-called "post-conflict" countries in Africa. Reflecting on the story of Morris, a child soldier who had fought in both the Liberian and Sierra Leone wars, John and Angela Lederach note that, even though the violence had ended, it continued to plague Morris's mind as he tried to begin a new life in the refugee camp:

> It is so hard. You have this weapon. I do not mean a weapon like just a gun, but your mind, your mind is the weapon. All you have in your mind is violence. You have been living in violence for so long and at any moment with any person you can take this weapon out. It does not matter where you are. It is *embedded* in you. And it is creative. You can do unimaginable things, terrible things with this creativity, because you have seen so much violence.[8]

What both Kizito and Morris confirm is that the promised future (liberation, democracy, development, peace), to the extent that it is premised on fighting and violence, cannot but lead to a deeper entrenchment of violence in the individual and social imagination. But far from securing peace and liberation, fighting sooner or later becomes an end in itself as it institutionalizes a culture of violence that everything and everyone are drawn into. The "senseless" fighting in the Congo, in its many violent mutations, reflects and perpetuates a culture of violence in which no one is a winner—everyone is a loser. This is one key conclusion of Stearns's *Dancing in the Glory of Monsters*. Toward the end he recounts the story of Pastor Philippe of Kisangani, whose three children were killed in the fighting. Asked who was to blame for his

8. John Paul Lederach and Angela Jill Lederach, *When Blood and Bones Cry Out: Journeys through the Soundscape of Healing and Reconciliation* (Oxford: Oxford University Press, 2010), 19 (emphasis added).

children's deaths, Pastor Philippe responded in a way that summed up the causes and agonizing consequences of the Congo wars: "There are too many people to blame. Mobutu for ruining our country. Rwanda and Uganda for invading it. Ourselves for letting them do so. None of that will help bring my children back" (248).

The Depth of the Loss

If *Dancing in the Glory of Monsters* provides a framework for making the fighting thinkable on the macro level, Stearns also provides descriptions of and testimonies to events, massacres, and developing violence that allow the reader to see the extent and effects of the violence at the micro level. The stories are too many to summarize, but one can get a glimpse of the depth of the personal and social trauma accompanying the violence through the various attempts by survivors to try to put into words the pain and loss that is too deep for words. The survivors use different images and metaphors to express the inexpressible, metaphors such as "we are living on top of our dead" (244),[9] and "we carry the grief around with us" (101).[10]

The more closely one looks at the metaphors and images that the fighters used to express the ineffable, the more one realizes that what has been lost through the violence, and what is mourned, is not just the loss of loved ones. The sentiments point to a loss that is far deeper: it is the loss of an anchor for the future, of community, and eventually a loss of humanity.

Loss of Future

In a number of vignettes, the survivors of the massacres lament the lack of a place to bury and/or mourn the dead: "No one has even so much as put a memorial plaque there. You can still see the charred remains. We have nowhere to mourn our dead" (106).[11] What these and similar sentiments point to is

9. Pastor Philippe, talking about his second child.

10. "They didn't give us time to bury our dead. . . . We do not even have tombs to go to mourn our dead, we carry the grief around with us" (Alex, a Munyamulenge boy giving a narrative of the massacre, in 1996, of 153 people from his community, including the husband and children of the prophetess Mariam).

11. Neno Lundila, pastor of the Malkai wa Ubembe church in Abala, where 103 of his congregation, including his two wives and six children, were massacred in October 1996.

not simply the lack of a "place" to bury the dead, but a more elemental sense of dislocation. As a result, there can be no closure, as the words of one elder who lost his wife and two children in the massacre at Kasika told Stearns: "We are still living through the massacre.... There has been no justice, not even a sign or a tree, or a monument in the honor of those who died that day" (262).

Such grief over the lack of a place to bury the dead goes deep within the African tradition, where the ancestors, the living dead, provide a narrative anchor and direction for the future. A proper funeral and the remembrance of the dead connect the living to the world of those who have gone before. Thus the lament of the village elder quoted above. A similar sentiment is captured by the words of the groundskeeper at Kasika, where more than a thousand villagers were killed, including three nuns, the priest, and a catechist: "We never had [a chance] to give them a proper burial ... we have nothing to remember them by. It is a shame.... There are hundreds buried like this" (252). Regarding his son who was killed during the fighting in Kisangani, Pastor Philippe said: "I saw him bleed to death in front of me. I buried him in my compound, right next to Sophie.... There was no time for a proper funeral. Actually, you can find hundreds of bodies buried in people's gardens around the city for the same reason. We are living on top of our dead" (244).

But Pastor Philippe's words "we are living on top of our dead" also point to a cosmological disorientation. Though the world of the dead may be seen as connected to the world of the living, there exist clear boundaries that separate them. Now, in the ongoing violence, the boundaries have become blurred. The entire country has become one big graveyard.

Loss of Community

Behind the different expressions of lament, there is grieving for the loss of community. This is especially true when leaders such as the priest and nuns, but also the chief (*omwami*) in Kasika, have been massacred. The role of traditional chief in Congo is very important, especially in rural communities where government reach is minimal. Recognized by the constitution, the *omwami* plays an intermediary role between state and community, mediating conflicts (e.g., over land) and settling local disputes. But the significance of the chiefs goes beyond their function: they embody the community and provide a vital link, a relationship like a glue between the land, ancestors, and community. Those relationships ensure a sense of both communal and individual identity, as well as a sense of belonging and stability. In a society defined by communitarian relationships and communal belonging, the chief *is* the community. Killing the chief is like killing the community and everything the community stands for.[12] Thus the lament of a village community: "You do not kill the *omwami* during the war. Killing him is like killing all of us" (256). A similar sentiment lies behind the lament of the groundskeeper at Kasika at the killing of the priest: "The priest had just begun blessing the host. . . . Then they told the priest to kneel down and pray. And [they] shot him in the back of his head. . . . They killed them all. They killed our Father. He was such a good man. His poor father went crazy afterwards—he was all we had. . . . Animals!" (255–56).

Loss of Humanity

The groundskeeper at Kasika referred to the killers as "animals," thereby signifying that in carrying out these indescribable brutalities, the rebels had gone outside the pale of humanity. How, then, does one explain not only the carrying out of so many massacres, but also the often bizarre way in which the killings are done. In describing the massacre at Kasika, Stearns notes:

> The way the victims were killed said as much as the number of the dead; they displayed a macabre fascination with human anatomy. . . . The chief's heart had been cut out and the wife's genitals were gone. . . . It was not enough to kill their victims; they disfigured and played with their bodies. They disemboweled one woman by cutting her open between her anus and vagina, then propped up the dead body on all fours and left her with her buttocks facing upwards. . . . They would kill the priests, rape the nuns, rip babies from their mother's womb, and even twist the corpses into origami figures. (257)

As one parishioner who witnessed the massacre noted: "We had seen people killed before. . . . But this was worse than killing. It was like they killed them, and then killed them again. And again" (257). What that parishioner's

12. David Muwazé, "Spate of Village Chief Killings Hits Northeast DR Congo," *The Observers*, January 17, 2014: http://observers.france24.com/content/20140117-village-chief-killings-congo-kivu (accessed Dec. 2, 2015). Muwazé writes: "Here, village chiefs are the symbol of the state and of stability. They make sure people respect the rule of law, look after their people's well-being, and contact the security forces if there are any problems. . . . People here have total confidence in the authority and the wisdom of their chiefs. If their chief is killed, they are lost, and feel unsafe. Their only solution is to leave the village."

words point to is the fact that the killing had moved beyond any utilitarian/logical framework and had become pathological. It had lost any moral compass, and operated within a register below human. One can also hear the lament of the loss of humanity in Maria Umutesi's description of the women during the 2,000-kilometer journey through the forest, in which they were preyed on by armies, warlords, and bandits during the first Congo war: "Old fleshless grandmothers even though they weren't even thirty . . . they had lost all their womanly attributes. . . . We only knew they were women because they looked after the children" (131).[13]

The loss of humanity also somehow explains the widespread phenomenon of rape, captured by the lament of a woman: "Baba, all of us, all of us here have been raped. Every single one of us" (263). A 2011 study in the *American Journal of Public Health* indicates that 1,152 women were raped every day during that conflict—a rate equal to forty-eight per hour.[14] The study, carried out by three public health researchers from the International Food Policy Research Institute at the State University of New York at Stony Brook and the World Bank, showed that 12 percent of all Congolese women had been raped at least once, and 3 percent of Congolese women across the Congo were raped between 2006 and 2007 alone. The factors behind the widespread rape and violence against women in Congo are complex. The common explanation given is that rape is simply a "weapon of war."[15] While there is truth in that statement, Maria

13. For a full account of her story, see Maria Beatrice Umutesi, *Surviving the Slaughter: The Ordeal of a Rwandan Refugee in Zaire* (Madison: University of Wisconsin Press, 2004).

14. The study is cited by Jo Adetunji: "Forty-eight Women Raped Every Hour in Congo, Study Finds," *The Guardian*, May 12, 2011: http://www.theguardian.com/world/2011/may/12/48 -women-raped-hour-congo (accessed Apr. 8, 2014).

15. Kenneth Omeje, "Understanding the Diversity and Complexity of Conflict in the Africa Great Lakes Region," in *Conflict and Peacebuilding in the African Great Lakes Region*, ed. Kenneth Omeje and Tricia Redeker Hepner (Bloomington: Indiana University Press, 2013). According to Human Rights Watch, soldiers used rape systematically as a weapon because women are viewed as symbolic representatives of their community. To rape such a woman is to terrorize and dehumanize her entire community (*The War Within the War: Sexual Violence against Women and Girls in Eastern Congo* [New York: Human Rights Watch, 2002]); Janie Leatherman talks about rape as a genocidal tool (*Sexual Violence and Armed Conflict* [Cambridge: Polity, 2011], 90); and Sara Meger frames it as a political tool that is meant to destabilize existing social structures ("Militarized Masculinities and the Political Economy of Wartime Sexual Violence in the Democratic Republic of Congo," in *Engaging Men in the Fight against Gender Violence: Case Studies from Africa*, ed. Jane Freedman [New York: Palgrave Macmillan, 2012], 40–42; see also Karie Cross, "Mapping Exercise: Gender and Grassroots Perspectives," unpublished term paper for Professor John Lederach's class at the Kroc Institute for International Peace Studies, University of Notre Dame, 2014.

Baaz and Maria Stern are correct in saying that such explanations are a limited explication of the violence: such accounts ascribe a rational—and utilitarian—dimension to the rape, which is often missing from the reality on the ground. "'Rape as a weapon of war' narrative does not match the empirical messiness of war. . . . Congolese military units are scarcely ever disciplined enough to use anything, much less rape, in a systematic fashion."[16]

However, what Baaz and Stern fail to point out is that rape does not only reflect disorder and military structural fragility, quite often—and this is the case for Congo—the widespread phenomenon of rape, including rape with extreme violence (REV), represents a "new pathology."[17] This is confirmed by the gang rape of eighty-year-old Mama Mburano, in Luvungi, by a group of rebels who could have been the age of her own grandsons. "Grandsons, get off me," she cried as she tried to repel the attackers.[18] It is, in fact, the same pathological space that communities now exist in when rapists continue to live among those they have raped, when they "are our own children who joined the mai mai" (263).

Thus, behind the grief within these stories is also a deep sense of uncertainty and silent questioning: *How* does one live within this strange space where the rapists are one's children and grandchildren? *What* kind of existence is this? *What* kind of human beings are we now? *Who* are we as individuals and as a community?[19] Can there be a future? And if so, of what kind?

16. Maria Eriksson Baaz and Maria Stern, *Sexual Violence as a Weapon of War: Perceptions, Prescriptions, Problems in the Congo and Beyond* (London: Zed Books, 2013), 10; see also Karie Cross, "Mapping Exercise," 4. I am grateful to Karie Cross for this section.

17. Denis Mukengere Mukegwe and Cathy Nangini, "Rape with Extreme Violence: The New Pathology in South Kivu, Democratic Republic of Congo," *Plos Medicine* 6, no. 2 (December 2009): http://www.ncbi.nlm.nih.gov/pmc/articles/PMC2791171/ (accessed Feb. 2, 2015).

18. See Jacob Onyumbe, "Why Must I Go about Mourning," *Duke Divinity Magazine* 12, no. 2 (2013): https://divinity.duke.edu/community-student-life/divinity-magazine/spring-2013/why-must-i-go-about-mourning (accessed Dec. 2, 2015).

19. For my reflection on similar questions following the Rwanda Genocide, see E. Katongole, "Justice, Forgiveness, and Reconciliation in the Wake of Genocide: The End of Words," *The Other Journal*, August 16, 2012: http://theotherjournal.com/2012/08/16/justice-forgiveness-and-reconciliation-in-the-wake-of-genocide-the-end-of-words/ (accessed Dec. 2, 2015). In her moving memoir, *Mighty Be Our Powers: How Sisterhood, Prayer, and Sex Changed a Nation at War: A Memoir* (New York: Beast Books, 2011), Leymah Gbowee narrates a number of "inhuman" experiences during the war in Liberia that confirm that, through the war experience, people found themselves "in another world"; they had crossed a line (see, e.g., 33, 53).

"Narrative Wreckage" as the Foundations Are Destroyed

Trauma Healing and Its Limits

The personal stories and testimonies of the agents and victims of Congo's wars in *Dancing in the Glory of Monsters* touched me on a number of levels. First, they offered a glimpse into the inexpressible grief and suffering within Congo's wars. Second, they allowed me to see the generative nature of violence: with the progression of the fighting, the violence not only metastasized and spread like a cancer into the whole body politic; it took on increasingly bizarre, pathological forms. Third, they exposed the illusory promises of fighting and war as a means to peace/liberation. Rather than securing those ends, Congo's wars simply succeeded in embedding violence within the individual and social imagination, from whence it continued to haunt its victims and perpetrators alike. Fourth, they led me to see how the effects of violence are far deeper than the loss of lives, homes, and security. And last, they led me to see that violence not only tears apart individuals and communities; it shatters the very foundations of human and social existence. The overall effect of these insights was to confirm Congo as a mirror through which I was once more seeing the reality and effects of political violence in sub-Saharan Africa.

But if *Dancing in the Glory of Monsters* brought me to these insights, it also raised a number of troubling questions about social healing in general—and about the church in particular. The questions revolved around a Bible verse that had lodged in my mind in the course of reading *Dancing in the Glory of Monsters*: "If the foundations are destroyed, what can the righteous do?" (Ps. 11:3). As I struggled with this verse in the context of Congo's story, I kept wondering: How does one live within the narrative wreckage, where all anchors of the past and bridges to the future are destroyed? How does one live, and what does life look like, in the midst of ruins? How does one repair the shattered foundations of social and personal existence in the wake of war? What is social healing?

To be sure, these and similar questions had started to form in my mind in 2009, when I visited Congo for the first time. I had traveled to Goma to meet with some of the leaders in the Great Lakes Initiative and to explore the possibility of holding the next GLI gathering in Goma. There had been a lull in the fighting between the Congolese army and Nkunda's CNDP rebels. The town was teeming with people, newly returned refugees from the fighting and the volcanic eruption of Mount Nyiragongo in 2002. Thus the refugee camps on Goma's outskirts were still full. During my conversations and meetings with the leaders, I was constantly confronted with the language of "trauma" and the need for "healing"; so I visited one such trauma healing program, the Daphrose and Gratia Counseling Center. Here Daphrose and her husband, Katavo, talked about their work with children and youth, many of whom had seen their parents, friends, and community leaders killed. They also talked about other trauma healing centers in Goma and in Eastern Congo, and about different methodologies of trauma healing.[20]

I returned from the visit with a deeper appreciation of the work of the Daphrose and Gratia Counseling Center, as well as that of other programs that seek to provide resources that help individuals "cope" with the traumatic effects of violence. But I also returned with a number of unanswered questions. For instance, in the face of the profound shattering challenges, I began to wonder whether the language of "healing" (as in the phrase "trauma healing") is not misleading, especially if it conjures up an image of being "fixed up." Trauma does not simply go away. There is no way to put an end to the pain of Mama Mburano.

I was also aware that most trauma healing programs target the individual, with the goal being personal healing. Yet the violence had shattered entire communities and affected whole generations. What kind of healing, if any, is possible in the context of such social or collective and transgenerational trauma? What does social healing look like in Congo and other countries in Africa when their whole social history is stitched through by periods and layers of violence?[21] If social healing is the "reconstruction of communal re-

20. E.g., Ushindi Center, Trauma Healing Institute (Isiro) and the Global Gratitude Alliance (Bukavu) for survivors of sexual violence, and many other centers using such methods as counselling, narrative theater, drama, etc.

21. A full-fledged study of the collective/cumulative trauma in Congo that assesses the physical, structural, and pyscho-social violence since King Leopold's brutal rule, Belgian colonialism, struggle for independence, Mobutu's thirty-two years, and the more recent Congo wars, is still to be undertaken. Most studies of trauma in the Congo focus on sexual violence during the recent Congo wars. What is needed is a study along the lines of Judy Atkinson's *Trauma Trails, Recreating Song Lines: The Transgenerational Effects of Trauma in Indigenous Australia* (North Melbourne: Spinifex, 2002). I totally agree with Atkinson about the need for "greater understanding of community trauma and communal responses to trauma, which must include greater comprehension of 'the nature and effects of continuing and recursive violence and the interplay between multiple traumata.'" Most important is the need to recognize the "political context of trauma and its effect and the fact that structural violence such as that inherent in oppressive systems has potentially severe and continuing posttraumatic effects" (Atkinson, 57, quoting M. A. Simpson, "Bitter Waters: Effects on Children of Unrest and Oppression," in *International Handbook of Traumatic Stress Syndrome*, ed. J. P. Wilson and B. Raphael [New York: Plenum Press, 1993], 601).

lations after mass violence . . . through initiatives that *rehumanize* broken relationships, rebuild trust, normalize daily life and restore hope,"[22] how does this "rehumanization" take place? Through what concrete practices?

Turning in and around God

If these and similar questions had been on my mind, they took on a more persistent and even haunting character in light of Jason Stearns's book. But they also took on a decidedly theological character via the psalmist's persistent question: When the foundations are destroyed, what can the righteous do? The psalmist's question is about rehumanizing, that is, rebuilding the shattered foundations of social and human existence in the wake of violence. But since the task of rebuilding is at the same time one of "re-creating" the foundations, I began to see why a theological lexicon is necessary, particularly in the wake of the devastation like the one witnessed in *Dancing in the Glory of Monsters*. Re-creation requires God, since both "creation" and "re-creation" are thick theological categories that point to God and God's ongoing work of "reconciling all things," which offers the gift of "new creation," not simply as a future promise but as a present reality.[23]

This also seems to be the direction in which the psalmist (in Ps. 11) is pointing. He is feeling overwhelmed, surrounded by enemies ("the wicked"), who bend their bows and set their arrows to shoot at him from all sides. He feels he has nowhere to hide or to stand. That is when he cries out: "When the foundations are destroyed, what can the righteous do?" One would expect that he would be given very concrete advice on what he needs to do. Instead, the psalmist turns to God—to "[t]he Lord . . . in his holy temple, the Lord . . . on his heavenly throne," who "tests the righteous" and everyone on the earth (Ps. 11:4–5).

Once I made the connection between social healing and re-creation, I

---

22. Lederach and Lederach, *Blood and Bones*, 7.

23. To the extent that most transitional justice mechanisms lack a theological component, they do fall short of this sense of "re-creation." See Laurel E. Fletcher, "Violence and Social Repair: Rethinking the Contribution of Justice to Reconciliation," *Human Rights Quarterly* 24 (2002): 573–639: http://scholarship.law.berkeley.edu/cgi/viewcontent.cgi?article=1544& context=facpubs. For a more recent attempt to present "reconciliation" as the unique religious contribution to social repair that reflects the overlapping consensus of different religious traditions, see Daniel Philpott, *Just and Unjust Peace: An Ethic of Political Reconciliation* (Oxford: Oxford University Press, 2012).

began to be more interested in the nature of the psalmist's turning to God. How can and does one turn to God, I wondered, when the foundations are destroyed? What does the turning look like in the midst of the violent destruction and shattering of the foundations of human and social existence? What words and what kind of language does one use to express the ineffable? What kind of prayer is possible for someone like Anna Mburano?

The questions had led me to the doorstep of the theological practice of lament as a form of turning toward God in the midst of ruins. Lament, I began to see, was a way of dwelling amid ruins. It was only then, I must confess, that I began to glimpse the possibility of hope with regard to Congo. For reading *Dancing in the Glory of Monsters* had pushed me close to despair, just as it had for Stearns.[24] But in light of the connections that I was beginning to make, I could see how even in the midst of such unimaginable violence (as in Congo) there might be a way of speaking about hope. Not hope as a consolation but as the anguished discipline of turning to and around God. I began to trace this anguished movement in the lives of the Christian activists I knew from Congo—Kataliko, Kasali, Katho, Mike Upio, Daphrose, Bishop Djomo, and others—and to see that their agency did indeed bear the logic of this turning toward God in the midst of ruins. The nonviolent advocacy and forms of repair they were involved in emerged out of this crucible, and was once the gift of their anguished lament. In their lives and agency I could see evidence of the claim that even in the midst of inscrutable violence, God is always planting seeds of hope (Isa. 43:19), seeds that bear the promise and evidence of God's re-creation.

Given Africa's ongoing social turmoil, this fact can, very easily and very often, be missed—thus the image of a "hope-less" continent. Accordingly, in the light of *Dancing in the Glory of Monsters*, I saw more clearly that a most pressing theological task is to give an account of Africa's hope. Such an account would need not only to make explicit the connections between lament and hope; it would also need to explicate the inner logic that confirms that the turning toward God (which lament is) is at once a discipline and a gift; it is at once something that one does but is also the gift through which the shattered foundations of our social and human existence that are threatened by violence are re-created.

24. See, e.g., Stearns's conclusion: "Perhaps the most nagging, persistent problem I have witnessed . . . is the lack of visionary, civic-minded leadership" (*Dancing in the Glory of Monsters*, 328). Stearns's conclusion seems inevitable in the absence of a theological grammar and of an appreciation of a notion and praxis of lament.

However, as I looked at the literature about, and coming out of, Africa, it soon became clear that no such theological account exists. As a result, popular conversations about Africa have tended to swing between pessimism and optimism, while theological accounts have been dominated by prescriptive recommendations for the need to have hope. Few, however, have fully embraced Peter's recommendations to "give an account" or "make a defense" of hope (1 Pet. 3:15). The result is that theology has either remained silent in the wake of devastations like those in Congo, or it has had very little to offer other than adding its own optimistic prescriptions for a better future. Either way, the peace that the church represents and offers in places like Congo—and in Africa as a whole—is never fully explicated. These are huge claims, and they involve significant theological, ecclesiological, and methodological claims about hope in general, about Africa's hope in particular. These are claims that need to be justified and unpacked, and it is to this task that I now turn.

CHAPTER 2

The Need and Urgency of a Theology of Hope

*Always [be] prepared to make a defense to anyone who asks you for
a reason for the hope that is in you.*

1 Peter 3:15

The absence of a dynamic conversation about hope in Africa is at once surprising and unfortunate. It is surprising given that Africa finds herself at the intersection of, on the one hand, endless cycles of war, violence, poverty, and other social challenges, and, on the other hand, dynamic expressions of Christian faith. In *The Sacrifice of Africa*, I used the image of "coffins and churches" to depict this odd intersection. One would imagine that at this nexus of a distressed and massively Christian continent an animated and sustained conversation about hope would be generated; but that has not been the case. There may be a number of reasons for this absence, among them the fact that Christian theology and practice have tended to readily and uncritically surrender the diagnosis and prescription for what is going on to the secular disciplines of politics, economics, and sociology. Locating Christian practice and theology neatly within these analyses means that the Christian difference becomes framed primarily in *spiritual* terms, which tends to reduce theological discussions of hope to nothing more than forms of private spiritual encouragements, motivations, and consolations. The effect is that, in the absence of a dynamic conversation about hope, public sentiments and discussions about Africa—even within Christian circles—tend to reflect the current political and economic moods, and thus to swing between optimism and despair.

Suspended Between Pessimism and Optimism

Nowhere is this swing in mood more reflected than in *The Economist*. Little more than fifteen years ago, the magazine ran a cover story that depicted Africa as a "hopeless" and dying continent.[1] More recently, in a March 2, 2013, special edition, its cover story depicted Africa as a "hopeful continent"—a mood shared by many economists, who increasingly speak of Africa as a "rising'" giant and seek to project "Africa's next boom."[2] Notice that the 2000 portrayal of a continent mired in poverty, disease, rape, cannibalism, government-sponsored thuggery, and wars declared that such factors were "not exclusively African—brutality, despotism and corruption exist everywhere—but African societies, for *reasons buried in their cultures* seem especially susceptible to them."[3] The 2013 issue of *The Economist* did not see any contradiction in the earlier report; in fact, it seemed to justify it, noting that they had "rightly labeled the Continent 'hopeless' back in 2000." Now, however, there were positive indications that "things seem too good to be true," and that gains had "been made in reducing malaria deaths, HIV infections, increasing cell-phone connectivity, tripling GDP, lengthening life expectancy."[4] It is not clear what happened in little over a decade to those "reasons buried in their cultures" that had made Africa, in the eyes of *The Economist*, a hopeless continent in 2000.

In the absence of a historical account and sufficient social analysis, it may not be clear what is hopeful about this new Africa. It is not that I have a problem with the positive projection for Africa. I want to believe it—and for a better reason than that it just happens to be Africa's turn to rise.[5] Moreover, I would like to see how factors like "rising education levels and new African leadership, expanded global investment"—the markers of Africa's "next boom"—play out in places like Eastern Congo, Burundi, and South Sudan.

1. "The Hopeless Continent," *The Economist*, May 13, 2000.

2. Charles Robertson, "Africa's Next Boom," Ted Talk, June 2013: https://www.ted.com /talks/charles_robertson_africa_s_next_boom?language=en (accessed Dec. 2, 2015).

3. "Hopeless Africa," *The Economist*, May 11, 2000: http://www.economist.com /node/333429 (accessed Dec. 2, 2015).

4. "A Hopeful Continent," *The Economist*, Feb. 28, 2013: http://www.economist.com/news /special-report/21572377-african-lives-have-already-greatly-improved-over-past-decade-says -oliver-august (accessed Dec. 2, 2015).

5. The economic positivism is particularly evident in Robertson's depiction of Africa's "next boom." That Africa is rising, Robertson notes, should not be surprising. "Everybody grows. GDP growth knows no religious, ethnic, climate or continental barriers. It is just a matter of when the inevitable happens. This happens to be Africa's turn" (Robertson, "Africa's Next Boom").

Part of the challenge, of course, is one of terminology. The economic status of Africa is described as either "hopeless" or "hopeful." But what is hope? What is the difference or relationship between hope and rising GDPs? Do Christians in the so-called developed countries have more hope than their brothers and sisters in the global south? And what is the difference between hope and optimism? What difference does religion, Christianity in particular, make in the way one understands and names hope? How do Christian practice and language inform a conversation about hope? If these and similar questions are obscured in conversations that depict Africa as a "hopeless" continent, they are equally obscured in recent depictions of Africa as a "hopeful" continent.

Dayo Olopade's *The Bright Continent: Breaking Rules and Making Change in Modern Africa* provides a good illustration.[6] Olopade, a Nigerian-American journalist, sets out across sub-Saharan Africa to find out how ordinary people are dealing with the challenges they face every day. She discovers what to her is an unexpected, almost incredible Africa: resilient, joyful, and innovative, a continent of do-it-yourself change-makers and impassioned community leaders. She traces this spirit of creativity, resilience, and innovation born from African difficulty, which she calls *Kanju*, through five registers or maps: the family, technology, commerce, nature, and youth.

There is a good deal that is positive in *The Bright Continent*, which offers a refreshing departure from the usual staple of pessimistic portrayals of the "dark" continent. Moreover, Olopade rightly complains about the "formality bias" within Western governments, developments, aid agencies, and analyses that tend to focus on the so-called formal sectors (government, civil service, public sector units, banking, etc.) and thus miss the creativity, resourcefulness, and leadership in the so-called informal sector, where most of the *Kanju* happens. Accordingly, Olopade's account is populated not with the usual statistics of economic projections, but with stories of ordinary African innovators: a Nigerian who turned his low-budget, straight-to-VHS movies into a multi-million-dollar film industry known as Nollywood; a Malawian who helped transform cast-off American computers into touchscreen databases that allow hospitals across Malawi to process patients in seconds.

My one surprise is that religion failed to make it onto Olopade's list as one of the areas where *Kanju* resilience and innovativeness are at work. Even though she rightly notes that "countless Africans . . . have depended upon

6. Dayo Olopade, *The Bright Continent: Breaking Rules and Making Change in Modern Africa* (Boston: Houghton Mifflin Harcourt, 2014). Hereafter, page references to this work appear in parentheses within the text.

religious organizations to backstop state failure" (76), she does not pay sufficient attention to the religious/cultural grammar that seems to pervade and drive everything.[7] With typical secularist slight, she dismisses religion from serious consideration with a quick reference to its destructive side, pointing to the "prosperity gospel," and the pastors who extract tithes from their congregants in exchange for salvation, as the reasons that keep many devout African Christians in poverty (77). While I totally agree with her assessment of the prosperity gospel, to dismiss religious consideration from the discussion of a continent that seems to be "incurably religious" is to perpetuate a version of the same formality bias that she seeks to overcome. Of course, part of the challenge may be that religious scholars have themselves not offered convincing accounts for why journalists (such as Olopade), economists, and other social scientists should take religion seriously.

At any rate, my aim in noting this surprising lacuna in Olopade's analysis is not to dismiss her work; rather, it is to point to her work as a confirmation of the need for accounts that take religion seriously and are therefore able to display the innovation and creativity within this pervasive cultural grammar. Moreover, her work presses the question of the nature and distinctiveness of Christian hope even more urgently. What is the difference between *Kanju* and Christian hope? Is Christian hope nothing more than "strategies of survival" (22), nothing more than "resilience," which has "deep neurobiological roots" and which some academics call "hardiness," or "grit" (26)? Is Christian hope nothing but "uncomplaining dynamism and perseverance" in the face of difficulties (27)?

If these and similar questions about the nature, possibility, and distinctiveness of Christian hope in Africa are pressing, official church statements and theological discussion about Africa have not offered much insight. For the most part, rather than narrate or explicate the reality of hope in Africa, theological discussions about Africa's future tend to simply state or prescribe hope. The postsynodical Apostolic Exhortation *Africae Munus* (2011) and the theological reconstructions of Kä Mana and Samuel Kobiah provide good illustrations.

7. On religion as the cultural grammar that shaped and drives everything in Africa, see Laurenti Magesa, *What Is Not Sacred? African Spirituality* (Maryknoll, NY: Orbis, 2014).

On Prescribing Hope: The Theological Problem

In the postsynodical Apostolic Exhortation entitled *Africae Munus*, which followed the second Synod on Africa (2009), Pope Benedict notes the various experiences of trauma and suffering in Africa. The document describes Africa's "anthropological crisis,"[8] which arises out of not only Africa's painful memory of fratricidal conflicts between ethnic groups, the slave trade, and colonization[9] (which have left Africa painfully scarred); it is also the result of numerous serious and looming threats. Comparing Africa to the paralytic in Mark's Gospel (Mark 2:1–12), *Africae Munus* calls on the church to mobilize spiritual energies and material resources to relieve Africa's heavy burden, and so to open Africans to the fullness of life in Christ.[10]

The exhortation offers various recommendations, addressed to various sections of the church, to stand in solidarity and creativity,[11] to remove various obstacles to Africa's healing, and to seek reconciliation. Reconciliation, the exhortation notes, "overcomes crises, restores the dignity of individuals and opens up the path to development and lasting peace between peoples at every level."[12] But while the exhortation offers recommendations to various constituents of the church and invites everyone to seek reconciliation, justice, and peace, it does not offer narratives of real life. To be sure, *Africae Munus* mentions different areas in which the church has made practical contributions to African society—education, health care, and social communications—but it does not offer stories to back up or display these contributions or show what the projected reconciliation might concretely look like on the ground. In the end, the pope's claim to "see grounds for hope in Africa's rich intellectual, cultural and religious heritage" remains more of a stated hope than a narrated one.[13]

I am, of course, aware that the form and genre of an Apostolic Exhortation is not the place for stories that declare convictions and exhortations; but *Africae Munus* is representative of the prescriptive impulse within much of theo-

---

8. *Africae Munus,* §11: http://w2.vatican.va/content/benedict-xvi/en/apost_exhortations /documents/hf_ben-xvi_exh_20111119_africae-munus.html.

9. *Africae Munus,* §9.

10. In *Ecclesia in Africa* (1995), Pope John Paul II had compared Africa to the man who fell among brigands, and thus called on church and society to be a good Samaritan to Africa: http://w2.vatican.va/content/john-paul-ii/en/apost_exhortations/documents/hf_jp-ii _exh_14091995_ecclesia-in-africa.html.

11. *Africae Munus,* §98.

12. *Africae Munus,* §21.

13. *Africae Munus,* §9.

logical reflection on Africa. Many of these contributions note the need for the church to contribute to political and social advancement in Africa, and even explicitly see this contribution as part and parcel of the church's ministry of hope; however, the hope is often more projected or prescribed than narrated. Take the case of Kä Mana's theology of reconstruction, which, on the whole, I find compelling. In *Christians and Churches of Africa Envisioning the Future*, Kä Mana notes that all African theology should be at the service of the ministry of hope, which "constitutes the essential principle of their intelligibility as a contribution to the problem of salvation in Africa."[14] Thus, the goal must be

> the creation of a visionary, creative and resourceful society for the struggle against all the negative forces that Africa is suffering from, the debilitating powers of sorcery, witchcraft and witch beliefs, and the social-political and economic powers that are embodied in the harmful and sterile institutions and social structures, whether local or international.[15]

For Kä Mana, therefore, the reconstruction of Africa requires "a change of mentality" and "social economic politico-energies," and it is here that Christian faith and theology can play a key role in mobilizing these energies and requirements and thus become a transformative force for a "better future" in Africa.

For all his positive recommendations for an African theology of reconstruction, Kä Mana does not offer any indications of how the "change of mentality" concretely happens or even how it might already be under way via theological praxis. And what is hopeful about the "struggle against the negative forces" in Africa? Does the hope lie in the assured success of the struggle? What provides the logic, focus, and energy for this struggle? In the absence of answers to these and similar questions, Kä Mana's "better future"—the telos of his reconstructive theology—cannot but appear as mere optimism, which is simply announced and not accounted for or narrated:

> We Africans who are witnessing the beginning of a new millennium with many anxieties and great hope, are ourselves carriers of a powerful energy of rebirth, of renaissance, re-creation, reconstruction, regeneration and renewal, namely, Christ himself as the heart of a new creativity in the vitality

14. Kä Mana, *Christians and Churches of Africa Envisioning the Future: Salvation in Jesus Christ and the Building of a New African Society* (Akropong-Akuapen, Ghana: Regnum Africa, 2002), 102–3.

15. Kä Mana, *Christians and Churches of Africa*, 102–3.

of our being, in the spiritual, symbolic and material resource, which today should be used for building a new society.[16]

A similar projection of hope is evident in Samuel Kobia's *The Courage of Hope: The Roots for a New Vision and the Calling of the Church in Africa*. In this powerful and well-written book, the former leader of the National Council of Churches in Kenya and former secretary-general of the World Council of Churches analyses the ongoing legacy of slavery, colonialism, civil war, corruption, poverty, HIV/AIDS, and other deadly diseases on the African continent. Given this legacy he asks, "How are we to live authentic lives in the face of untold suffering and apparent social nihilism within the continent?"[17] Inspired by Tillich's *The Courage to Be*, Kobia proposes *The Courage of Hope* as both a spiritual (strength of the heart) and intellectual (strength of mind) condition through which African peoples affirm themselves, their life and their community, in spite of the strong odds, anxieties, and conditions that militate against this essential self-affirmation (4).

Kobia's analyses of Africa's historical and social conditions is rich and in a number of places quite perceptive. I find his analysis of the conditions and contradictions within Africa's nation-state modernity particularly illuminating. For instance, he rightly notes that the postcolonial state has remained a device of control and manipulation by those in power, thus perpetuating the colonial legacy: "The colonial regime primarily designed the state as an instrument of manipulation and control of the movement of people and goods to create and secure wealth. Thus, the process of statecraft was essentially a process of corruption not only of indigenous institutions but also of the general polity" (55). He locates Africa's endless civil wars, ethnic violence, and corruption within this legacy of the modern nation-state, which gained international legitimacy in the family of nations globally, but not locally: "The horrifying events of genocide and massacres in Africa today can be traced and related to a precolonial design of the state and how juggling ethnic identities became the means for managing political clientelism and manipulating national resources at the behest of the colonial regime" (66).

While I find Kobia's analysis illuminating, his recommendations for the churches to be "agents of hope" are quite standard. Churches, he writes, must

16. Kä Mana, *Christians and Churches of Africa*, 105.

17. Samuel Kobia, *The Courage of Hope: The Roots for a New Vision and the Calling of the Church in Africa* (Geneva: World Council of Churches, 2002), 2. Hereafter, page references to this work appear in parentheses within the text.

"assist change through democratic and non-violent means" (161); denounce corruption and educate the electorate on participatory democracy (161); overcome ethnic divisions; develop capacities for ethical discernment, advocacy, and programs that link processes at grassroots levels to national and regional levels (171–73); and in the face of HIV/AIDS, become "sanctuaries of life"—places of solace and compassion for the ailing and dying children of Africa (79ff.).

These recommendations are, of course, very much needed, but they provide no inner explication for what it means for the church to "dare to hope" and the kinds of "reasons" that shape the church's courage to hope. Or, to put it differently, in the face of HIV/AIDS, which has devastated entire families and communities, how does the church reason her way into hope? And hope for what? In other words, Kobia does not provide a *theological* account of hope, and in the absence of such an account, hope devolves into merely a "can-do spirit" or optimism: "When people act out of hope, they become forward looking; they are liberated from captivity to the past and fear of a tomorrow that is no better than yesterday. They acquire positive attitudes that free them from reliance on the past as a place of retreat" (4).

But what difference does being a Christian make to this forward-looking attitude? And what would such a positive attitude have to say to Pastor Phillipe, Mama Mburano, and the other women suffering in the Congo? As I noted in the preceding chapter, the various laments depicted by Stearns in *Dancing in the Glory of Monsters* point to a more fundamental dislocation: the loss of future, loss of community, loss of humanity—the destruction of the very foundations of what it means to be human. Rebuilding such foundations requires much more than a "can-do spirit." It requires, at least from a Christian point of view, an explicit engagement with God. But what does such an engagement look like, and how do we make sense of it? Answering these and similar questions requires not only an explicit theological grammar, but one that is able to adequately respond to Peter's invitation to "always be prepared to give an account." By attending to the theological, ecclesiological, and methodological dimensions of Peter's call, we can highlight the need and urgency, as well as the form that a theology of hope in Africa needs to take.

An Account of Hope: 1 Peter 3:15

> In your hearts honor Christ the Lord as holy, always being prepared to make a defense to anyone who asks you for a reason for the hope that is in you; yet do it with gentleness and respect. (1 Pet. 3:15)

Thus writes Peter in his first letter. The letter is addressed to Christian communities located in five provinces of Asia Minor, including areas evangelized by Paul (Acts 16:6–7; 18:23). Peter encourages Christians there to remain faithful to their standards of belief and conduct in spite of threats of persecution. Three dimensions of Peter's letter stand out and speak directly to the character of Christian hope and bear direct relevance to a conversation about hope in Africa.

God's New People

The first dimension is ecclesiological, that is, it points to the reality of the church as God's new people. Two major themes run through Peter's letter, themes that might seem contradictory: the high dignity and boundless joy of being a Christian and the tremendous cost and suffering. No other book in the New Testament refers as often to the suffering of Jesus and at the same time is so filled with a spirit of joy as 1 Peter. The themes of life and death, suffering and praise, pain and hope are interwoven and run together throughout. This is evident immediately, in the opening salutation that speaks of hope in distress: "Blessed be the God and Father of our Lord Jesus Christ! According to his great mercy, he has caused us to be born again to a living hope through the resurrection of Jesus Christ from the dead. . . . In this you rejoice, though now for a little while, if necessary, you have been grieved by various trials" (1:3, 6).

The reason those being addressed are to rejoice (even in the midst of tribulations) is their *new* identity and the *new* life they have received: "You have been born again, not of perishable seed but of imperishable, through the living and abiding word of God" (1:23). The Christians to whom Peter is writing are scattered in remote parts of the empire, cut off from the mainstream of the Roman empire and viewed with suspicion, if not open hostility. This is why Peter addresses them as "exiles" and as "aliens and sojourners." What keeps them grounded and going in their sojourn existence is the reality of their identity as God's new people, who have been called out of darkness into God's wonderful light and therefore are "a chosen race, a royal priesthood, a holy nation, a people for his own possession" (2:9).

What these observations confirm is that at the heart of Peter's letter is a clear ecclesiological identity and vision of the church as God's new people. Accordingly, Peter's exhortations are addressed not simply to individual Christians but to the community of those born anew, who must maintain good conduct among the Gentiles, "so that when they speak against you as evildoers, they may see your good deeds and glorify God on the day of visitation" (2:12). It is in view of their ecclesial identity and calling in the world that Peter exhorts them to "always [be] prepared to make a defense to anyone who asks you for a reason for the hope that is in you" (3:15). Peter makes repeated appeals to Christ's resurrection and the hope that it foregrounds (1:3–5). For Peter, therefore, the suffering, death, and resurrection of Christ (1:19; 2:21–25; 3:18) serve as the rationale behind the hope that the church herself is as God's new people who, through their new birth of baptism (1:3, 23–25; 3:21) have taken on this pattern of Christ's life. If we are to follow Peter's logic—if, on the one hand, it is Christ's suffering and death and, on the other, resurrection and new birth that lie at the heart of Christian hope, then hope becomes the very essence and identity of God's new people.

But Peter's exhortation to "be prepared to give an account of hope" also points to the need for very concrete practical displays of where Christians might have seen the logic of Christ's death and resurrection at work in the world and in their lives. It calls not merely for a statement but for a display of this logic of death—resurrection as something tasted, touched, and experienced. As he notes, "you have tasted that the Lord is good" (2:3). In this respect, for Peter, as for the author of the letter to the Hebrews, hope is the very essence of faith, "the assurance of things hoped for, the conviction of things not seen" (Heb. 11:1). Reflecting on this text, Pope Benedict XVI, in the encyclical entitled *Spe Salvi*, confirms this close link between faith and hope; but he also points out that by describing faith as "the proof of what is hoped for," the author of Hebrews confirms that hope is not merely a sentiment.

> It gives us something. It gives us even now something of the reality we are waiting for, and this present reality constitutes for us a "proof" of the things that are still unseen. Faith draws the future into the present, so that it is no longer simply a "not yet." The fact that this future exists changes the present; the present is touched by the future reality, and thus the things of the future spill over into those of the present and those of the present into those of the future. (*Spe Salvi*, §7)

Therefore, as important as the need for a logic of hope is (a logic that places it within the narrative of Christ's death and resurrection), it is not enough—in fact, cannot be realized—without another equally important task: the need to tell where and how Christians have concretely experienced this in their lives, where and how they have seen something of that logic of death and resurrection at work in the world. This is what calls for stories that display Christian hope. Thus, to "give a reason for the hope that is in you" is at the same time an invitation to display the concrete, practical, and lived reality of that hope. It is in this respect that hope is essentially different from optimism, in that more than being a stated hope, it is a *narrated* hope. It is, to use the language of 1 Peter 1:3, a "living hope."

Once the full context and assumptions of Peter's invitation to give an account of hope have been made explicit, its far-reaching implications for a discussion of hope in Africa begin to emerge. For in many ways, African Christians live in a situation not very much different from the Christians to whom Peter addressed his first letter: at the margins of global economic and political developments, under intense forms of suffering such as those witnessed in Congo. But what the first letter of Peter also makes clear is that an account of hope in Africa requires and points to the church as God's new people in Africa. The church herself is the story of hope, constituted through the death and resurrection of Christ.

Seeing Hope in the Midst of Tribulations

The second dimension of Peter's exhortation is epistemological. The Christian tradition regarded the apostle Peter as the author of 1 Peter and believed that he wrote the letter from Rome, probably from prison, and did so shortly before his death during the persecution of Nero (between 64 and 67 CE).[18] That Peter wrote this exhortation in the context of his own suffering and impending death reveals that he had come to trace in his own suffering the pattern and logic of Christ's suffering and death—as well as his resurrection. This is the reason for Peter's own hope in the midst of his tribulations. Thus Peter's letter in general, and his exhortation to Christians who find themselves in similar situations in particular, is not mere theoretical platitude but bears an autobiographical imprint. Behind his exhortation is his own story.

18. The similarity in both thought and expression between 1 Peter and the Pauline literature has led a number of modern scholars to suggest that 1 Peter may not have been written by the apostle Peter, but by a later writer who was very much familiar with Paul's work. Other scholars, on the basis of a number of features that they consider incompatible with Petrine authenticity, conclude that the letter was probably the work of a later Christian writer. Such features include the cultivated Greek in which it is written (difficult to attribute to a Galilean fisherman), together with its use of the Greek Septuagint translation when citing the Old Testament; the similarity in both thought and expression to the Pauline literature; and the allusions to widespread persecution of Christians, which did not occur until at least the reign of Domitian (81–96 CE). In this view, the letter would date from the end of the first century or even the beginning of the second, when there is evidence for persecution of Christians in Asia Minor (the letter of Pliny the Younger to Trajan, 111–12 CE) (see United States Conferences of Bishops, "1 Peter—Introduction": http://www.usccb.org/bible/1peter/0 [accessed Feb. 2, 2015]).

Paul offers a similar account and example of hope, a hope that does not surrender in times of trouble, but instead is nurtured and strengthened. Indeed, this is true of Paul's own experience in general, but particularly true in his letter to the Ephesians, which in its buoyancy is a kind of rhapsody to God's gift of reconciliation. Here Paul celebrates the breaking down of the "dividing wall" by Christ, who has "destroyed the enmity between us." Paul repeatedly refers to this plan and purpose of God as a mystery (*en mysterio*) (Eph. 3:3-6, 9; 6:19), and the "mystery" has to do with the utter "non-logic," with the "scandal" (1 Cor. 1:23) that an all-powerful God, who could easily vanquish his enemies through a total victory of force (through a kind of "redemptive violence"), would rather absorb the violence of the world, thus revealing the lie of principalities and powers.[19] But for Paul, the goal—the *telos*—of Jesus's cross is not simply to make a mockery of the powers and principalities; it is consistent with God's determination to "restore" creation by redeeming both victim and offender, and drawing them both into the restorative embrace of God's new creation. This is the "gift" of God's reconciliation, given to us "while we were still sinners" (Rom. 5:8). It is this counterintuitive truth that Paul has come to see more clearly, which has been "revealed" (Eph. 3:5) to him in prison.

Thus, Paul writes this rhapsody to reconciliation from a dungeon as a "prisoner of Christ Jesus" (Eph. 3:1; 4:1; 6:20).[20] For it is here in the dungeon that he is able to "see" clearly God's will and purpose: "In all wisdom and insight [God made] known to us the mystery of his will, according to his purpose, which he set forth in Christ as a plan for the fullness of time, to unite all things in him, things in heaven and things on earth" (Eph. 1:8-10). The repeated reference to Paul's being in "prison" is not simply a biographical detail; it is an epistemological claim. The "mystery" is at the same time an epistemology, which is to say, it involves a way of seeing, a "revelation" made possible through Paul's dungeon experience.

The overall conclusion to be drawn from both Peter's and Paul's personal

19. Ched Myers and Elaine Enns, *Ambassadors of Reconciliation*, vol. 1 (Maryknoll, NY: Orbis, 2009), 100-101.

20. On the conditions of jail in Paul's time (which might provide very significant parallels with Eastern Congo)—so horrible that the Roman dungeons were often identified with the horror of perpetual darkness and synonymous with Hades—see Craig Wansink, *Chained in Christ: The Experience and Rhetoric of Paul's Imprisonments* (Sheffield: Sheffield Academic Press, 1996). Quoting the Roman historian Sallust (86-34 BCE), Ched Myers observes: "Some have been crucified, others thrown to wild beasts; a few whose lives were spared, in gloomy dungeons amid sorrow and lamentation drag out an existence worse than death" (*Ambassadors of Reconciliation*, vol. 1, 100-101).

examples is not only a claim that it is possible to see hope in the midst of tribulations. Their examples also suggest a stronger theological claim, namely that there is something about Christian hope that is revealed only through tribulation. It is this claim that Archbishop Christophe Munzihirwa (see Chapter 8 below) is pointing to when he notes, during his own time of hardships in Bukavu, that "there are things that can be seen only with eyes that have cried."[21] Therefore, an account of hope in Africa will have to inquire into the "mystery" and seek to name and display those gifts that strangely only become available through suffering.

Telling Hope

The other key implication of Peter's exhortation to give an account of hope is methodological. I have already noted that the exhortation calls for a display of the concrete, practical, and lived reality of the hope, which points to the key role that stories and storytelling play in a theology of hope. We must note, however, that it is not just any kind of story, not any form of storytelling, that is consistent with Peter's exhortation. In urging his audience to always be prepared to give the reason for the "hope that is in you," he adds, "yet do it with gentleness and respect" (1 Pet. 3:16). I take this recommendation as pointing to the unique *tonality* of Christian hope, which must avoid any traits of triumphalism, but must preserve the elements of gift, gratitude, and surprise at the heart of a Christian experience of hope. But I also take Peter's recommendation for "gentleness and humility" to be calling for a certain *style* of storytelling, one that is able to capture the simplicity and elegance, the goodness and beauty, the ethics and aesthetics, and the ordinary and extraordinary nature of Christian hope.

Theological Portraiture: Narrating Hope in Africa

Recently I discovered the work of Sara Lawrence-Lightfoot and Jessica Hoffman Davis and their "portraiture" methodology.[22] They describe portraiture as

21. See John Allen, *The Global War on Christians: Dispatches from the Front Lines of Anti-Christian Persecution* (New York: Image, 2013), 49.

22. Sara Lawrence-Lightfoot and Jessica Hoffman Davis, *The Art and Science of Portraiture* (San Francisco: John Wiley, 1997). Hereafter, page references to this work appear in parentheses within the text. I am grateful to Curtiss Paul DeYoung, who first drew my attention

a unique method of inquiry that shares some of the features of other qualitative research methods, such as ethnography, case study, and narrative; but it is distinctive in its "blending of aesthetics and empiricism in an effort to capture the complexity, dynamics, and subtlety of human experience and organizational life" (xv). Portraiture has a number of defining attributes, which make it an appropriate methodology for a theology of hope in Africa. First, in its effort to combine empirical research and aesthetic description, and in an attempt to move beyond the narrow focus of social-science research, which tends to focus on problems rather than solutions, on parts rather than the whole, and on "pathology and disease rather than health and resistance," portraiture actively seeks "goodness"—though with the understanding that goodness will always be laced with imperfection (8). This means that the portraits seek to see the whole, to capture something of the essence—qualities of character and particulars of history—some of which the subject might not be explicitly aware of, some of which she might resist, and some of which might feel familiar. For this reason Lawrence-Lightfoot and Davis describe the portraitist as a kind of "boundary sitter" who serves as a "witness" by giving expression through creation of a scene, the selection of a story, and the development of "language and narrative style" (8).

Second, the portraitist is a storyteller. The telling of stories, Lawrence-Lightfoot and Davis note, "'can be a profound form of scholarship moving serious study close to the frontiers of art in the capacity to express complex truth and moral content in intelligible ways'" (11).[23] What makes the portraitist a unique kind of storyteller is that she is interested "not only in producing complex, subtle description in context but also in searching for the central story, developing a convincing and authentic narrative" (12). But what this also means is that, in the way of discerning voices, the portraitist is not simply listening to stories, she is "listening *for* a story."[24] This latter action implies a much more active role for the researcher, because it means that the

---

to Lawrence-Lightfoot and her method of portraiture, which DeYoung himself appropriates in his *Living Faith: How Faith Inspires Social Justice* (Minneapolis: Fortress, 2007), 5. My debt to DeYoung and my connection with what he does in telling the stories of the "faith mystics" in general, and the stories of Bonhoeffer, Malcolm X, and Aung San Suu Kyi in particular, and the affinity to what I am doing here, should be obvious throughout.

23. Lawrence-Lightfoot and Davis here citing Joseph Featherstone, "To Make the Wounded Whole," *Harvard Educational Review* 59 (1989): 367–78, at 377.

24. Fenwick D. English, "A Critical Appraisal of Sara Lawrence-Lightfoot's *Portraiture* as a Method of Educational Research," 22: http://edr.sagepub.com/content/29/7/21.full.pdf (accessed Dec. 2, 2015).

portraitist is creating and molding a story instead of merely searching for one. Portraiture is thus a constructive activity involving intervention instead of a passive observation of life in context.[25]

Finally, the portraitist seeks to speak to a broad and diverse audience and is driven by an explicit activist impulse for intervention and community-building. Whereas standard social science research seeks primarily to inform, portraitists seek to inform *and* inspire.

> With its focus on narrative, with its use of metaphors and symbol, portraiture intends to address wider, more eclectic audiences. The attempt is to move beyond the academy's inner circle, to speak in a language that is not coded or exclusive, and to develop texts that will seduce the readers into thinking more deeply about issues that concern them. Portraitists write to inform and inspire readers. (10)

When I discovered the work of Lawrence-Lightfoot and Davis, I immediately recognized that the method of portraiture was similar to what I was attempting in my work. I argued, in *The Sacrifice of Africa*, against the "prescriptive haste" that characterizes much of the work in Christian social ethics, especially with respect to Africa. The effect of that methodological shortcoming is to obscure much of the creative, dynamic, often unplanned and ad hoc improvisations that constitute a reinvention of a new future. In the last section of that book I profiled three Christian activists in an attempt to display some of that dynamic process connected to the practice of Christianity in Africa. My commitment there to story and storytelling was also an attempt to respond to John Milbank's invitation to rediscover Christian theology as a form of sociology whose task is "to tell again the Christian *mythos*, pronounce again the Christian *logos* and call again for Christian *praxis* in a manner that restores again their freshness and originality."[26]

But even as I worked with the narratives of the faith activists, the methodological approach remained for the most part only implicit. One way I tried to articulate what I was trying to do was to point to my approach as a unique genre of "practical systematic theology"; but that did not make my methodological assumptions any more explicit. In fact, in one graduate seminar, a student wanted to know what I was *doing* in the "blend of narrative, ethnog-

---

25. English, "Critical Appraisal," 22.

26. John Milbank, *Theology as Social Theory: Beyond Secular Reason* (Oxford: Blackwell, 2006), 383.

raphy and theology" that I had used in *The Sacrifice*. In another seminar, one of my colleagues pressed me for clarity concerning my methodology: "Is what you're attempting descriptive, elicitive, or prescriptive: that is, descriptive—describing the agency of these folks; elicitive—arguing that this is how the agents should understand their work; or prescriptive—that they should do A, B, and C because of . . . ? What is it that you are trying to do?"

I replied that I was trying to do all of the above and much more, but I was no more satisfied with that answer than she was. As I was working on *Born from Lament*, I was constantly nagged by the need for greater clarity about my use of stories. Therefore, I was relieved when I discovered the "portraiture" methodology, which in many ways both confirmed and clarified what I was trying to do with stories and which, in light of Peter's recommendation to "make a defense to anyone who asks you for a reason for the hope that is in you; yet do it with gentleness and respect" (1 Pet. 3:15), became an urgent and explicit mandate. For it became clear that an account of hope in Africa would have to be shaped around narratives or portraits of hope on that continent. This is what I wanted and needed to do. As Lawrence-Lightfoot says:

> I wanted to create a narrative that bridged the realms of science and art, merging the systematic and careful description of good ethnography with the evocative resonance of fine literature. I wanted the written piece to convey the authority, wisdom, and perspective of the subjects, but I wanted them to feel—as I had felt—that the portrait did not look like them, but somehow managed to reveal their essence, so that in reading them they would be introduced to a perspective that they had not considered before. . . . And finally I wanted the subjects to feel seen . . . fully attended to, recognized, appreciated, respected, scrutinized. . . . Inevitably, I knew these would be documents of inquiry *and* intervention, and hopefully, leading toward new understandings and insights, as well as instigating change. (4–5)

If the method of portraiture seems to offer the tonality and style necessary to respond to Peter's invitation for an account of hope, it also presents itself as a fresh methodology that can advance theological inquiry in a way that bridges the gap between theology and other disciplines, most notably the nascent field of peace studies. For, if I could through some compelling portraits give an account of hope in Africa, I would be able to trace, at the same time, the inner logic of Christian peacebuilding by locating the agency of Christian peace activists within the matrix of visions, symbols, and stories that constitute their *theological* imagination. But doing so would not only make the activists' agency intelligible, but it would illuminate broader insights regarding the nature of hope in general, nonviolent agency, and the mission and unique role of the church in the search for peace. For one of the unique benefits of portraiture is its ability to capture specific details as well as universal themes and patterns:

> Not only is the portraitist interested in developing a narrative that is both convincing and authentic, she is also interested in recording the subtle details of human experience. She wants to capture the specifics, the nuance, the detailed description of a thing, a gesture, a voice, an attitude as a way of illuminating more universal patterns. (14)[27]

Perhaps the one key difference between Lawrence-Lightfoot and Davis's method of portraiture and the portraits of hope I offer in *Born from Lament* is the explicit theological interest that drives my work. I have noted that, in producing complex, subtle descriptions in context, the portraitist is not only searching for a central story. She not only listens *to* the story; she listens *for* a story. Whereas for Lawrence-Lightfoot and Davis that story can take any number of forms, the story I am listening for has a definite theological shape. As I have noted, in 1 Peter, the reason for hope is located at the intersection of Christ's suffering and death and the gift of his resurrection. That is the story within which Christians have been baptized and within which they are to recognize their own lives—even as they find themselves under persecution. This is the story in its ecclesiological, theological, and practical dimensions that I am listening for. I wish to trace and confirm whether and how the story of hope—of death transformed into new birth, suffering turned into hope, crucifixion into resurrection—is true in the lives and work of the faith activists that I study, and confirms the hope for Africa that they represent.[28]

---

27. According to Lawrence-Lightfoot, the main difference between portraiture and a statistical model is that portraiture involves a different way of thinking about generalization. Whereas in the statistical model of the social science, there is little interest in the characteristics of the single case except insofar as it confirms a generalized model; by contrast, "the portraitist seeks to document and illuminate the complexity and detail of the unique experience of place, hoping that the audience will see themselves reflected in it. . . . The portraitist is very interested in the single case because she believes that embedded in it the reader will discover resonant universal themes" (Lawrence-Lightfoot and Davis, *Art and Science of Portraiture*, 14).

28. Robert Krieg, in *Story-Shaped Christology: The Role of Narratives in Identifying Jesus Christ* (New York: Paulist, 1988), provides the kind of Christological framework that is assumed in *Born from Lament*. Krieg identifies three types of narratives: historical, biblical, and biography. I particularly find the dynamic connection that Krieg makes between biblical narrative and biography illuminating. The lives of exemplary Christians (he uses the story of Dorothy

However, whereas the story of Jesus's death and resurrection is the more immediate story I am listening for, that story is itself located within a broader story of God's journey with humanity and creation, which we have come to know through the biblical witness. The biblical story is thus the broader canvas on which the different portraits of hope that I paint in this study appear. This explains why I introduce each section of the book with a chapter reflection on a biblical text. The overall significance of this structure is that *Born from Lament* moves back and forth between biblical and personal portraits; the effect of these parallel portraits is to locate not only the discussion of hope in Africa within a biblical framework but also the examination of the agency of the faith activists I study within a more explicitly theological framework.

But the biblical framework also explains why a reflection on the book of Lamentations is at the heart of this study, and partly explains the title of this book. I have always been drawn to the book of Lamentations, about which surprisingly little is known (outside the circle of Bible scholars). Nor does it find much use in the church's liturgical calendar (other than in the Liturgy of the Hours during Holy Week). In listening to the various laments of the people in *Dancing in the Glory of Monsters*, I heard echoes of Daughter Zion's laments in the book of Lamentations. And as I thought about writing a book about hope in Africa, I thought Lamentations might not only be a good place to start, but that it might provide an overarching framework for locating the kinds of gifts and resources that might be ironically discovered in the midst of such devastation as exists in Congo and elsewhere in Africa. And so we now turn to a discussion of the book of Lamentations as a way to explore how the claim that "for people who begin from a place of suffering, Lamentations is a book of comfort" might be the case in Africa.[29]

Day) both reflect and offer fresh perspectives into the identity of Christ. The reason, Krieg notes, is that, "while biography refers primarily to the subject, that is, to the man or woman whose life is recounted, it can secondarily refer to another person—the person who served as the subject's role model. It can therefore shed light on the second person known through the eyes of the primary subject. . . . A Christian's life points beyond itself to the risen Lord" (157). Coming from a different angle, James McClendon Jr. makes a similar argument for the need for theology to attend to the lives of witnesses as the lens through which Christian doctrines are revealed. "Unless theology can hear her witnesses," McClendon writes, "unless she can take death in deadly earnest, take its grim enmity into her counsels and be shaped thereby, she ceases to be a serious discipline" (*Biography as Theology: How Life Stories Can Remake Today's Theology* [Eugene, OR: Wipf and Stock, 2002], 84).

29. Kathleen M. O'Connor, *Lamentations and the Tears of the World* (Maryknoll, NY: Orbis, 2002), 3.

PART TWO

Soundscapes of Lament

CHAPTER 3

The Strange Gift of the Discipline of Lament

There is no one to comfort her.

Lamentations 1:17

A woman walks down the paths of her village, which has been destroyed by the militias. She looks from house to house, hoping to find her children, but she cannot find them. She cries out, first for her children, then to anyone who will hear.

This scene, which could have been drawn from Nayankunde (Eastern Congo) following one of the deadliest attacks by militias in 2002, is echoed in the biblical book of Lamentations, which, as the title suggests, is a book of mourning. Thus, attending to Lamentations might not only heighten the depth of pain and suffering in places like Eastern Congo, but it might also point to the theological practice of lament as a way of wrestling and arguing with God in the midst of ruins. A few preliminary remarks are necessary to highlight the historical, literary, and practical dimensions of this extended epitaph following the destruction of the city of Jerusalem.[1]

---

1. Even as I draw from other scholars, my discussion of the book of Lamentations draws largely from—and closely follows—Kathleen M. O'Connor, *Lamentations and the Tears of the World* (Maryknoll, NY: Orbis, 2002). (Hereafter, page references to this work appear in parentheses within the text.) One reason I find this and O'Connor's other work helpful is that she is able to provide theological commentary on Scripture that brings technical scholarship into a theological and pastoral view.

The Book of Lamentations

Historical Context

After the death of King Josiah (609/610 BCE), the Kingdom of Judah entered a period of increasing instability. An initial revolt against its Babylonian over-lords in 597 led to the first siege of Jerusalem. The city fell, and its elite were deported to Babylon. A second revolt (in 589) provoked a second siege, and further pillaging and destruction of the city. The temple was burned down (2 Kings 25; 2 Chron. 36:11–21), many of Jerusalem's inhabitants were killed, and most of the survivors were taken into captivity. Lamentations was in all likelihood composed soon after 587 and is probably the product of the community of Judeans who survived the destruction. Both the tone and imagery of devastation suggest that the author still has strong memories of the atrocities he witnessed.[2] This historical context explains why, in the Jewish liturgical calendar, Lamentations is read on Tisha B'Av (the ninth of Av [July or August]), the annual day of mourning when the Jews commemorate the destructions of the temple (both in 586 BCE and then 70 CE).

Poetry

Another important characteristic is that Lamentations is a collection of poetic laments. That Lamentations takes the form of poetry is significant, since the attack and devastation of the city have left the survivors speechless. Pain, as O'Connor (following Scarry) notes, destroys the victims' capacity for speech. "It renders victims numb and wordless" (5). Poetry is the attempt to give words to what is too deep for words, to speak the unspeakable. Literal speech will no longer do, for along with the destruction of buildings, families, and communal life has come the painful collapse of the very foundations of the people's

---

2. Lamentations is traditionally ascribed to Jeremiah, and a number of things suggest Jeremiah's authorship: the Greek Septuagint (LXX) ascribes the book to the prophet; Jewish tradition also ascribes the book to Jeremiah, as does the Latin Vulgate (*Id est Lamentationes Jeremiae Prophetae*). The early church fathers Origen and Jerome understood without question that Jeremiah was the author of Lamentations. However, Jeremiah's authorship is being increasingly called into question by biblical scholars. Some argue that since its poetic style is different from that of Jeremiah it should be assigned to an unknown eyewitness of the fall of Jerusalem. See Dianne Bergant, *Lamentations*, Abingdon Old Testament Commentaries (Nashville: Abingdon, 2003).

physical, spiritual, and moral universe: survivors now find themselves, like the survivors in the Congo, within a "narrative wreckage" (7). However, Lamentations is a unique poetic form: it conforms to the literary genre of "lament" from Hebrew Scripture and other Ancient Near East documents. In the Ancient Near East there were many lament forms that developed over time to give people a form in which to express the unbearable in various circumstances. These included the funeral dirge, mourning the death of an individual;[3] the city lament, which mourned the destruction of a city;[4] and the lament proper (which took either individual or communal forms). When the poet or poets of Lamentations sought to give expressions to the unspeakable pain that their community was enduring, they drew largely on the form, imagery, and metaphors of these lament forms, which are found in Lamentations in various combinations.

Daughter Zion

One of the distinctive features of Lamentations is the identification of the city as a woman—"Daughter Zion." As Dianne Bergant notes, the female personification of cities was common in the Ancient Near East, which is explained by the fact that "[t]he history of cities is often told through the use of sexual metaphors. Cities are established and defended by men; their land is fertile and productive or barren and worthless; when their walls are penetrated, they are said to have been violated."[5] By depicting Jerusalem as a woman, the poetry of Lamentations sometimes focuses on Daughter Zion's female roles (widow, mother, lover, and rape victim) and sometimes on her city features (walls,

3. Bergant says: "Characteristics of the dirge include: an opening cry of desolation (eka, how!); the summons to mourn, a declaration that death has occurred accompanied by the eulogizing of the deceased; a description of reversal of fortune, an expression of the mourner's grief, a reference to the effect that this death is having on the passerby, and an expression of bewilderment at what has happened" (*Lamentations*, 16–17).

4. F. W. Dobbs-Allsopp, in *Lamentations*, Interpretation Commentary series (Louisville: John Knox, 2002), says that the city lament genre is best known from ancient Mesopotamia, where it originated. The purpose of the city lament was that "these compositions were performed as a part of the cultic ceremonies in which the foundations of the old sanctuaries were razed, just prior to the initiation of any restorative work" (7). Dobbs-Allsopp identifies at least nine features of the city lament genre: subject and mood; structure and poetic technique; divine abandonment; assignment of responsibility; divine agent of destruction; weeping goddess; lamentation; restoration of the city; and return of the gods (9).

5. Bergant, *Lamentations*, 15–16.

buildings, gates, temple, and streets). Moreover, the personification of Jerusalem as a woman not only evokes Israel's covenant relationship as Yahweh's bride (see, e.g., Isa. 54:5; Jer. 31:32; Ezek. 16:60; Hos. 2:7), but, more specifically, results in a focus on the shame and humiliation that befalls Daughter Zion due to her infidelity. In this context Daughter Zion is depicted as an adulterous woman who now has been abandoned by her lovers, has become "filthy," and those who honored her now despise her, "for they have seen her nakedness . . . her uncleanness was in her skirts" (Lam. 1:8–9).

Literary Structure

Lamentations consists of five distinct poems, corresponding to its five chapters. The poems use the literary structure known as "acrostic," a pattern based on the twenty-two letters of the Hebrew alphabet. Chapters 1, 2, and 4 are true alphabetical acrostics: there are twenty-two verses, and each verse begins with a successive letter of the alphabet. Chapter 3, which has sixty-six verses, still follows the acrostic structure, with every third verse corresponding to a letter of the alphabet. Only the last chapter deviates from this structure, though it is still "alphabetical" in that it has twenty-two verses. The question, of course, is why does the writer (or the writers) of Lamentations—in the midst of the destruction, desolation, and trauma that surround them—take the trouble to structure the laments using the acrostic and alphabetical forms? There may be a number of reasons for this, all of which shed light not only on the particular book of Lamentations but on the nature of lament in general. The first possible explanation is that the acrostic and alphabetical forms were intended to be an aid for memorization. As I have noted, the Jews read Lamentations on the annual commemoration of the destruction of Jerusalem; given that the commemoration of the Tisha B'Av reaches as far back as tradition goes (cf. Zech. 7:3, 5; 8:19), it may be that the book was composed as a liturgical text to be recited during the commemoration.

But the acrostic and alphabetical devices of Lamentations are also deeply symbolic. They embody the struggle of survivors to contain and control the chaos of unstructured pain. The alphabet gives both order and shape to suffering that is otherwise inherently chaotic, formless, and out of control; at the same time, it signifies the enormity of suffering as a vast universe of pain, extending from A to Z, to which nothing more can be added (O'Connor, 12). Furthermore, the alphabetical and acrostic devices point to a total destruction—the unmaking of creation. According to the Talmud, in the original act of creation God used the twenty-two letters of the alphabet for each of the seven days of creation. The 154 (22 × 7) verses of the book of Lamentation symbolize that the seven days of creation have found their nemesis in seven days of *anti*-creation.[6]

The Many Voices of Lamentations

At least five distinct voices can be identified in Lamentations.[7] The first voice is that of a narrator who relates what has befallen the city (1:1–11, 15, 17; 2:1–19). The second voice is that of Daughter Zion, the city personified as a weeping mother who recounts her own destruction and cries out in grief (1:9, 11–22; 2:20–22). A third identifiable voice is found in chapter 3; it is the voice of a *geber*—a "strong man,"[8] or veteran[9]—who provides his own experience of the devastation. Next, in the fourth chapter, is the voice of a "poet," who describes the total collapse of both domestic and civic life in the destroyed city.[10] Finally, the fifth voice is the choral voice of Jerusalem, composed of the people as a community.

The one voice that is never heard, the voice that would explain the purpose of the devastation and the accompanying desolation, the voice that would bring comfort, is the voice of God. Throughout the misery and anguish, the accusations and entreaty, God is silent. The combined effect of the multiple voices, the anguished cry of Daughter Zion, the powerful images of the destruction and its effects, and the conspicuous silence of God in the text is a gripping expression of suffering and desolation in the wake of Jerusalem's destruction. A quick overview of the content of the book helps to capture the sense of desolation but also confirms lament as a theological practice: a way to name what is going on, to stand, to hope, and to engage God in the midst of ruins.[11]

---

6. "Lamentations: The Prayer of the Desperate," in *The African Bible* (Nairobi: Pauline Publications, 1999), 1397.

7. See William F. Lanahan, "The Speaking Voice in the Book of Lamentations," *Journal of Biblical Literature* 93, no. 1 (1974): 41–49.

8. Traditionally, this man has been identified as the prophet Jeremiah. The personal anguish the man describes in this chapter corresponds to the sufferings of Jeremiah (Jer. 9:1; 15:10–18; 20:7–8). Bergant, *Lamentations*, 16.

9. Lanahan, "Speaking Voice," 45.

10. Bergant, *Lamentations*, 16.

11. The reconstruction owes in no small measure to O'Connor, whose reading I follow closely.

"There Is No One to Comfort Her"

In the opening chapter of Lamentations, two speakers—the personified city and an unidentified narrator—draw the reader into a world of pain, loss, and abandonment. The narrator speaks first and describes the state to which the once beautiful city, Daughter Zion, has been reduced. Describing the city as a woman, he points to her tears, humiliation, and devastations. Enemies attack her; lovers betray, expose, and humiliate her; and her people have gone into exile. "There is no one to comfort her" (1:2). When Daughter Zion speaks in the second part of the poem, she does not address the narrator, but addresses God directly: she invites Yahweh to look (*ra'ha*), and pay attention (*nabat*), "for I have become worthless" (v. 11). When Yahweh does not respond, she turns to the passersby and invites them to see and consider her suffering: "Is it nothing to you who pass by on the way? Pay attention and look! Is there any pain like my pain, which was severely dealt upon me?" (v. 12); "Give heed to my groaning; there is no one to console me" (v. 21).

In chapter 2, the interaction between the narrator and Daughter Zion continues at a higher pitch. The focus of the poem shifts away from the weeping woman toward God, who is now depicted as her enemy and assaulter. The narrator does most of the speaking, but now he no longer speaks as a distant observer. He stands with her and speaks on her behalf, accusing God, whose beloved she once was, of betrayal and abuse, even of excessive and calculated rage. And though he still addresses us and not God, it is God's actions that he is obsessed with as he lays Daughter Zion's tragedies at the feet of God. Daughter Zion equally lays her tragedies at God's feet: "Look, Lord, and consider: Whom have you ever treated like this?" (2:20a).

Chapter 3 is different from the other chapters structurally: it has sixty-six verses, and the acrostic intensifies (the verses are shorter, but each strophe—a division of the poem—has three verses, and each of these verses begins with the same initial letter). This change in the structure itself seems to signify a deepening of the lament and its intensity. An anonymous new figure—the strong man (O'Connor, 44), or defeated veteran (Lanahan, 45)—is the chapter's principal speaker. The poem refers to him as a *geber* (3:1, 35, 36, 39), that is, "a male charged with the defense of women, children and other non-combatants" (O'Connor, 44). But instead of defending others, the speaker himself is a captive who is unable to fulfill his protective role. His inability to defend even himself magnifies his powerlessness: "I have become a laughingstock for all nations. . . . He has sated me with bitter food, made me drink my fill of wormwood; he has broken my teeth with gravel, pressed my face in the dust"

(vv. 14–16). The community also speaks in this poem, joining the strong man in corporate words of confession and lament (vv. 40–47) as they acknowledge that "terror and the pit have been our lot; desolation and destruction" (v. 47).

By the time we come to chapter 4, the speakers (an unidentified narrator and the people) appear exhausted and hopeless. Everything about the poem—its tone, structures, and even length—grows smaller and less intense, even though the scenes are as vividly horrifying as anything in the book so far. The first sixteen verses, spoken by an unnamed narrator, are uttered in a monotone, as if the tragedy has left him stunned and depleted. He takes the reader on a tour of the city after the invasion, alternating his attention between domestic and public scenes; in this way he shows that the invasion destroyed *every* aspect of life, as well as the foundations of civic life. The second speaker (4:17–22) is the people, their plural voice providing a dramatic, first-person testimony of the invasion that has reduced everything to rubble, and survival is shown to be bitter: that is, it would be better to be dead.

The last chapter is a petition, spoken in the first-person voice of the people and demanding God's attention. Like much of the book, the people's prayer is bleak, bitter, and without hope (5:2–18). It is the shortest poem, and the only one that is not an acrostic (even though it is alphabetical), as if the "desolation previous poems sought to contain by poetic structures breaks loose here" (O'Connor, 71). The poem recounts the atrocities in the occupied land, and the destruction is total: "Everything that constitutes common life has come undone. Physical necessities, personal safety, honor, and human dignity—all have buckled and collapsed, along with the city's buildings and walls" (O'Connor, 71). The people's energy for living has been extinguished: "Joy is gone from our hearts; our dancing has turned to mourning" (v. 15). Since the beginning of the poem, the people have been asking God to "remember," "look" at, and "see" their misery. In a final plea, they ask God to "restore" them, but it is not clear that the people have any hope that God will respond: "Give us anew such days as we had of old. Unless you have indeed rejected us, and in full measure turned your wrath against us" (v. 22).

The sobriety of this conclusion leaves Daughter Zion and her children in the unyielding grip of suffering, with no immediate visible help from God, no consolation, and not much hope for the future. Lamentations is thus a very difficult book. But, as O'Connor claims, for people "who begin from a place of suffering, Lamentations is a book of comfort" (3). The question therefore is, in what ways is Lamentations a comfort for people who live in the ruins of destroyed cities and villages? What hope does Lamentations offer for those whose society is dominated by genocide, civil wars, and massacres—as is true in the Congo? Part of the answer might lie in the realization that the kind of lament that is depicted in Lamentations is not a simple sentiment; rather, it is a complex set of emotions and actions that constitute a form of prayer—that is, a way of turning to God in the midst of ruins. As O'Connor suggests, "Laments are prayers that erupt from wounds, burst out of unbearable pain, and bring it into language. Laments complain, shout, and protest; they take anger and despair before God and the community. They grieve. They argue. They find fault . . . [even] as they cling obstinately to God and demand for God to see, hear, and act" (9). Lament thus becomes a way of naming what is going on, of standing and of hoping in the midst of ruins.

Disciplines of Lament

Seeing and Naming What Is Going On

As I have observed above, what the reader meets in Lamentations is not one but many voices. This is significant in that the various voices offer different perspectives of what is going on. F. W. Dobbs-Allsopp notes:

> [E]ach perspective views the reality of pain and hurt but in different em-
> bodiments and using different language. If the great multiplicity of images
> of suffering in Lamentations foregrounds the depth and breadth of these
> horrific events, the extended encounter with these specific personae focuses
> most sharply the personal and individual embodiments of the victimization,
> as the hurt and humiliation of particular and identifiable figures are shown
> repeatedly.[12]

In the end, what emerges from the different voices is a layered topography of pain and suffering. Take, for instance, the two voices of Lamentations 1. The poem opens with the narrator describing the state to which the once beautiful city has been reduced. His is an outsider's perspective. From the *outside*, the narrator focuses repeatedly on her losses and reversals of circumstance, on her fall from princess to slave, from fully inhabited city to a lonely widow on a hill. He sees her loss of power, wealth, honor, status, and security. He tells of her betrayal by lovers, the penetration of her temple by the foe, and the devastation of her inhabitants. He blames her for her suffering and remarks

12. Dobbs-Allsopp, *Lamentations*, 42.

on her lack of a comforter. Daughter Zion speaks from *within* the trauma. She is immersed in emotions, overwhelmed by horror; she grieves over her dying inhabitants and is desperate because of her children's plight; she weeps endlessly. She agrees with the narrator that her destruction is an act of God, the God who batters and brutalizes her, and she agrees that she must accept blame for her rebellion and infidelity. And yet, she desperately calls on God to "look," see, and pay attention. Yahweh is her only comforter; but even Yahweh has turned away from her: "[M]y comforter is far from me, the one who would turn my spirit" (1:16b). If her situation is desperate, it is not because there is "no one to comfort her"; rather, it is because her only would-be comforter, the one who would turn her spirit, has himself turned away from her.

If the various voices help to create a topography of pain and suffering, the various images and metaphors reveal the depth of anguish, shame, and desolation. In the second chapter, Daughter Zion speaks of herself as *trapped* in a net, given over to her enemies; in her midst lies a heap of dead warriors who have been crushed in the winepress; her eyes run with tears, and she is filled with pain; her bowels are churning and her heart is turning over; she is groaning and heartsick. For the veteran in the third chapter, "the dominant image . . . has been that of encirclement: the speaker has been imprisoned, trapped in the drowning pit, surrounded by his enemies."[13] The enemy has sated him with bitter food, made him drink his fill of wormwood; he has broken his teeth with gravel, pressed his face in the dust. Similarly, the poet's tour of the devastated city offers chilling images of a place where everything has been turned upside down: where gold has become "worthless pottery"; where the starving children are worse off than jackals' cubs; the rich are eating garbage (3:3–50); the aristocrats, once so fair to behold, are now reduced to skeletons; and mothers cook and eat their children (4:7–10).

If the various perspectives, images, and metaphors name the depth and effects of the destruction, they also point to various levels of responsibility for the city's destruction. In the opening chapter, the narrator blames Daughter Zion. However, as he enters her space of horror (Lam. 2), he no longer accuses Zion of bringing her tragedies upon herself; now he spreads the blame around. The religious leadership let her down. The prophets failed Daughter Zion by not pointing out her iniquity; instead, they lied to her and preached falsely (seeing "empty and vain visions" [2:14]). The passersby failed her too: they offered neither help nor comfort, and they mocked her (v. 15); Zion's enemies engulf, chew, and greedily swallow the city (v. 16). And Yahweh did what he

13. Lanahan, "Speaking Voice," 46.

planned (v. 17). The overall conclusion is that Zion's suffering is a tragedy whose cause was multiple failures, not Zion's sin alone.

Peace scholars remind us that the suffering wrought by human violence is never simple or of one cause; rather, it emerges from complex networks of direct, structural, and cultural violence.[14] In the endless turning of Lamentations' anguished cries, the complexity and immensity of Jerusalem's destruction is grasped and named. It is a complexity and immensity that Pastor Philippe of Kisangani comes to grasp and name as he cries for his three dead children, killed in the brutal fighting in the Congo. There were too many people to blame: "Mobutu for ruining our country. Rwanda and Uganda for invading it. Ourselves for letting them do so. None of that will help bring my children back."[15]

Standing within Ruins

The title of the book of Lamentations in Hebrew is *hkya* (*'ekah*)—variously translated in English as "how," "alas," or "oh," which is the first word in the Hebrew text in 1:1, 2:1, and 4:1. *'Ekah* is not a word as such; it is a cry of mourning that the Israelites used in funeral dirges, similar to the wailing cry (*wooowe* in Luganda) that announces death in many African communities. In *The Body in Pain*, Elaine Scarry points out that pain does not simply resist language; it actively destroys it, "bringing about an immediate reversion to a state anterior to language, to the sounds and cries a human being makes before language is learnt."[16] *'Ekah* is such a cry, and thus it represents the first and most primordial attempt to give voice to the experience of suffering. Thus the opening cry of *'ekah* signals that Lamentations originally "was meant to serve the survivors of the catastrophe simply as

14. I am grateful here to Kyle Lambelet's "'How Long O Lord?': Practices of Lamentation and the Restoration of Political Agency," unpublished article, Duke Graduate Conference in Theology, Fall 2014; Johan Galtung, "Cultural Violence," *Journal of Peace Research* 27, no. 3 (1990): 291–305; Peter Uvin, "Global Dreams and Local Anger: From Structural to Acute Violence in a Globalizing World," in *Rethinking Global Political Economy: Emerging Issues, Unfolding Odysseys*, Routledge/RIPE Series in Global Political Economy 11, ed. Mary Ann Tétreault, Robert A. Denemark, Kenneth P. Thomas, and Kurt Burch (London: Routledge, 1990); Kathleen M. Weigert, "Structural Violence," in *Stress of War, Conflict and Disaster*, ed. George Fink (Amsterdam: Elsevier/Academic Press, 2010).

15. Jason K. Stearns, *Dancing in the Glory of Monsters: The Collapse of the Congo and the Great War of Africa* (New York: PublicAffairs, 2012), 248.

16. Elaine Scarry, *The Body in Pain: The Making and Unmaking of the World* (New York: Oxford University Press, 1985), 4, cited in Dobbs-Allsopp, *Lamentations*, 33.

an *expression* of the horror and grief they felt" at the destruction of Jerusalem.[17] A number of features of this cry of lament are worth noting.

First, a whole range of emotions—grief, guilt, anger, compassion, forgiveness, hope, despair, shame—are evoked, contemplated, voiced, and sifted through the cry of *'ekah*. Second, the cry of anguish might have a cathartic effect on Daughter Zion, but it is also an invitation to the audience to see and hear Zion's anguish and to stand with her. In this connection, the narrator's "conversion" in the second poem is quite telling. As I noted above, in the first poem the narrator stands as a detached and objective observer to Daughter Zion's fall, which he describes in cool terms. In the second poem, something has happened to the narrator. He no longer speaks as a distant observer but as an overwrought participant in Zion's unbearable suffering. He stands with her and speaks on her behalf. He no longer blames her; instead, he accuses God of the violent abuse of daughter Zion. How can God treat his special "footrest" in such a way? God has become an enemy: he has swallowed up Israel (2:5). In the second part of the poem (2:11–19), Zion's pain affects him so deeply that it becomes his as well. His eyes "waste with tears"; his gut wrenches, and he appears to vomit (his "bile is poured out on the ground," v. 11). The horrors of her life break in on him, as he witnesses the breaking of the daughter of "my" people (v. 11). The narrator has entered Zion's space, her world, her horror. He sees. And as he does see, he is moved with rage, but also with helplessness: "What can I say for you? What can I compare to you . . . who can heal you?" (v. 13).

Standing in Daughter Zion's space is what brings the narrator to the breaking point as he is "overcome with his own fury" and "anger pours from him . . . as he tries to understand the devastation he sees" (O'Connor, 33). It is this breaking point that leads him into action. He speaks to Daughter Zion for the first time, as though finally recognizing her humanity (2:13). Until now, he has only spoken about her, described her, and been numbed by her condition. Now he addresses her with dignity. He calls her tenderly and addresses her as "Daughter of Jerusalem" and then "Virgin Daughter Zion." The previously disengaged narrator now becomes the passionate advocate. He uses a series of imperative verbs that urge, beg, and command her to take action, to move from a passive and accepting victim of assault to an active and expressive agent for her own life. "Cry out with your heart to Adonai, oh wall of Daughter Zion; let tears run down like a torrent day and night; do not let yourself stop; do not let your eyes be still" (v. 18).

---

17. Dobbs-Allsopp, *Lamentations,* 37. Hereafter, page references to this work appear in parentheses within the text.

With these emotion-saturated urgings, the narrator may be trying to push the city woman out of her numbness and call her to take action: "Arise, cry out in the night" (2:19). She is to cause a scene, create a fuss, cry out in the night at the beginning of the watches, when guards come to take up the watch at the walls. She is to pour her heart out like water, as if her heart had become tears; she is to do this before the face of God. She is to stand before Yahweh, encounter God, reveal her sobbing world to God, beg God, lift up her hands (O'Connor, 41).

The narrator's attempt to arouse Daughter Zion to action actually works. She appeals directly to God: "'Look, YHWH, pay attention.' She uses the same Hebrew verbs (*rā'āh* and *nābaṭ*), the first meaning 'to see' and the second 'to see with attentiveness' or 'to consider'" (O'Connor, 42). "Should women eat their offspring, the children they have borne? Should priest and prophet be killed in the sanctuary of God?" (2:20). Even God should realize that this is too much! Daughter Zion's unbridled anger at God is unmistakable as she, like the once detached narrator, reaches the breaking point. It is the same breaking point that one senses in the other poems, as the defeated veteran (Lam. 3), the poet (Lam. 4), and the community (Lam. 5) as they cry out to God and ask—in fact, insist—that God "look," "see," and "be attentive."

What the foregoing observations confirm is that the cry of lament (*'ekah*) is not only emotionally, psychologically, and physiologically important; it is every bit as crucial and theologically significant in the context of suffering as anything we can physically do (Dobbs-Allsopp, 36). Moreover, what the observations confirm is that the cry of lament is a dynamic and generative cry whose potential is to create a community of solidarity and compassionate advocacy. Thus, the invitation for God to see is an insistence that God stand within the same space of lament, fully aware that doing so cannot but bring God to the breaking point of compassionate advocacy on behalf of those who are suffering. It is a call for God's action on behalf of God's suffering people.

Hoping in the Midst of Ruins

It should be clear from the foregoing discussion that the ability to name pain and voice grief is in itself a form of hope. As Dobbs-Allsopp notes, "in naming grief, grief itself becomes owned, valorized, and thus ultimately consolable and healable" (37). Accordingly, the hurt of Daughter Zion, who is able to articulate that pain (1:20–22) and even rage at her God (2:20–22); of the veteran, his suffering unabated, summoning God's help (3:55–63) and inveighing against his enemies (3:64–66); and of the community, able to address God, if only with hard questions and unhappy avowals (5:19–22)—all these are forms of registering, resisting, and defying suffering and thus holding in check the despair and silence of shattered lives, and thus can be considered "hopeful" (Dobbs-Allsopp, 46). However, as an explicit theme, there seems to be hardly any hope in the book of Lamentations, except in the middle of the third chapter, when hope makes a surprising appearance in the middle of the veteran's lament:

> Yet this I call to mind
> and therefore I have hope:
> Because of the Lord's great love we are not consumed,
> for his compassions never fail.
> They are new every morning;
> great is your faithfulness.
> I say to myself, "The Lord is my portion;
> therefore I will wait for him."
> The Lord is good to those whose hope is in him,
> to the one who seeks him. (3:21–25)

Given its more or less central location within the central chapter of Lamentations, it might be tempting to look at this as the theological center of the book (indeed, for many congregations, these are the only verses from Lamentations that make it into worship). But this would be misleading and it would be to distort and simplify the overall complexity of the poetry, which actively resists explanations or justifications of human suffering (Dobbs-Allsopp, 48). It is thus important to lay out the full context of this expression of hope in the midst of lament so as to highlight its possibility as well as its unique character.

The first thing to note is that this sentiment of hope in the middle of the third chapter of Lamentations is both abrupt and unexpected. The veteran narrates his experience of captivity in first-person speech: "I am the man who has seen affliction" (3:1); his enemy drives him into darkness and turns his hand against him every day (vv. 2–3). The attacks are daily and physical, as the enemy wastes his flesh and breaks his bones (v. 4), as if the strong man were an animal being slaughtered for a meal. The enemy traps him, hems him in, chains him, and silences him. From the pit into which he has been thrown, there is no escape. "Even when I cry out for help, he shuts out my prayer. . . . A lurking bear he has become for me; a lion in ambush" (vv. 9–10). The result is total desolation and despair: "My soul is deprived of peace, I have forgotten what happiness is. . . . My splendor is gone" and with it "and all that I had hoped from the Lord" (vv. 17–18). The very act of remembering his affliction is "wormwood and gall" (v. 19). Given the desolation, it is all the more surprising when the strong man notes, "This I remember and therefore I hope" (v. 21). It is as though the veteran changes his mind in the middle of a stanza, weaving hope and despair together in shocking abruptness.

Moreover, the basis of the strong man's hope is a God remembered rather than encountered. "This I call to mind, therefore I hope." Three later verses that express hope are also memories:

> I called on your name, Lord,
> from the depths of the pit.
> You heard my plea: "Do not close your ears
> to my cry for relief."
> You came near when I called you,
> and you said, "Do not fear." (3:55–57)

But the strong man's hope is also fragmentary, uncertain and even contradictory. Numerous times in this poem of chapter 3, the veteran flip-flops between doubt and hope, between the memory of God's faithfulness (in the past) and his own present despair. Soon after the veteran's testimony of hope in 3:22–25, he hurls accusations at God:

> You have covered yourself with anger and pursued us;
> you have slain without pity.
> You have covered yourself with a cloud
> so that no prayer can get through.
> You have made us scum and refuse. (3:43–45)

Even as he admits that the taproot, the unseen source, of his confidence is God's own faithful character (Yahweh's love is not finished; Yahweh's mercies never end, they are new every morning [3:23]), he hesitates: "Perhaps there is still hope" (v. 29). Even as he remembers that "the Lord's rejection does not last forever" (v. 31), he complains: "You have not forgiven us" (v. 42). He goes back and forth. Given these observations, it would be wrong to conclude that 3:22–25 is the theological center of Lamentations. What the observations point to, however, is the unique character of hope that emerges in the midst of ruins. Three aspects need to be highlighted about the kind of hope found in Lamentations.

First, it is a fragile hope. The strong man's hope appears in the thick of despair, not apart from it. It is unsteady: it comes, goes, and comes again—repeatedly. It is not only a remembered hope; it is surrounded by uncertainty, doubt, and hopelessness. When he finds himself at the bottom of the pit, when all is lost, the strong man surprisingly remembers God's mercy and thus finds hope. As O'Connor notes, the strong man finds hope "only after hope has vanished. Then hope appears unbidden in the thick of despair, not apart from it. Unresolved tensions, enormous doubt, and intellectual confusion coexist with hope. Hope comes, fades, eludes, disappearing as if God has come into the room and left again" (114).

Second, hope's appearance in the "thick of despair, not apart" from it confirms that hope cannot be plotted on a linear trajectory as the ultimate result of a process of grieving or mourning. There is no clear manual, no neat progression of steps, on how to move from lament to hope; no clear promise of going through lament and then living happily thereafter. In Lamentations 3, lament and hope are inexorably bound together like twin daughters. As Clifton Black has noted, "the spine of lament is hope."[18] The inverse is equally true: the spine of hope is lament.

Finally, the gift of hope. That the veteran's hope is unsteady is also connected to its surprising appearance. Hope appears in the strong man even though his circumstances have not changed. It shows up when it is least expected—at the bottom of the pit, of all places—when all is lost! But this also includes the possibility that it may not show up when it is expected. Nowhere is this more evident than at the end of Lamentations. Even as the people pray, in the final poem, to "restore us to yourself," there is a hesitation and submission: it might not happen because Yahweh may have "utterly rejected us" (5:22). Thus the book ends, leaving the Daughter Zion in ruins, her prayer for restoration apparently unheeded. All this points to hope as sheer gratuity, as grace, as gift. O'Connor says:

> Biblical hope does not emerge from proper reasoning or new information. It is not optimism or wishful thinking. It is not a simple act of the will, a decision under human control, or a willful determination. It emerges without clear cause like *grace*, without explanation, in the midst of despair and at the point of least hope. It comes from elsewhere, unbidden, illusive, uncontrollable, and surprising, given the pit, the place of no hope. (57; emphasis added)

18. C. Clifton Black, "The Persistence of Wounds," in *Lament: Reclaiming Practices in Pulpit, Pew, and Public Square*, ed. Sally A. Brown and Patrick D. Miller (Louisville: Westminster John Knox, 2005), 54.

If lament is a way of hoping in the midst of ruins, that hope is always vague, unsteady, unexpected, and a faint memory. It is also a hope surrounded by silence, not an empty silence, but a dynamic silence that is at the same time a form of waiting, longing, and groping for restoration and healing.

Groping for Restoration in the Midst of Ruins

Pain, I have noted above, has the ability to destroy language, to reduce the victim to silence. This silence is a form of powerlessness, a paralyzing form of despair. Therefore, the ability to voice grief, to find words to speak the unspeakable and to name pain, is a form of resistance to the paralyzing silence. This is actually what the various voices in Lamentations have realized. But it is instructive that the strong man, in the midst of his barrage of words, as soon as he remembers God's promises as the reason for hope, counsels and urges his audience to silence (3:26–28):

> It is good to wait quietly
> for the salvation of the Lord.
> It is good for a man to bear the yoke
> while he is young.
> Let him sit alone in silence,
> for the Lord has laid it on him.

This silence is different from the silence of voicelessness. This silence is dynamic, a form of agency, within which a number of things are happening. So it is important to explore the significance of this silence—what it does and what disciplines are nurtured within it. Doing so will confirm that, like lament, hope is not a simple sentiment but a set of practices that are connected with the longing for restoration.

In the first place it is worth noting that it is in the context of the silence that the strong man remembers God's faithfulness: "This I recall, therefore I hope" (3:21). But if the strong man's silence evokes the memory of the past, it anticipates the future. It is in silence that one waits patiently for God's intervention, as the strong man counsels: "It is good to wait quietly for the salvation of the Lord" (v. 26). At the same time, the silence cultivates the courage and resilience required to "wait" for the Lord: "It is good for a man to bear the yoke while he is young. Let him sit alone in silence, for the Lord has laid it on him" (vv. 27–28).

Another equally important aspect of the silence counseled by the strong man is that it is out of it that a recognition of the need for repentance issues. I have already noted that in the second poem the narrator no longer accuses Zion of bringing her tragedies upon herself; rather, the narrator spreads the blame around to her religious and political leaders, her enemies, the passersby, and even God. Important as this acknowledgment is of multiple and complex responsibilities, Jerusalem needs to see, recognize, and repent of her own responsibility. In the first poem, Daughter Zion recognizes her rebelliousness (1:18) and her many sins, which have become a yoke around her neck. But here in the third chapter, the strong man issues a clear invitation to repentance in the context of his silent and unsteady hope: "Let us examine our ways and test them, and let us return to the Lord. Let us lift up our hearts and our hands to God in heaven, and say, 'We have sinned and rebelled'" (3:40–42). The confession and penance open him up to imagine, long for, and earnestly pray for a world beyond his current plight: "My eyes will flow unceasingly, without relief, until the Lord looks down from heaven and sees" (3:49–50). This was Daughter Zion's persistent cry for God to "look down and see." It is the same cry that the communal voices raise in the fifth chapter. Behind this plea for God to "look, see, and remember" (5:1–18) is the hope for the restoration of Daughter Zion and her children: "Restore us to yourself, Lord, that we may return; renew our days as of old" (5:21).

The overall conclusion from these observations is that the various practices engendered in silence—memory, patience, courage, penance, and prayer for restoration—are part of the package for the strong man's rationale for "why I hope." Silence is both the dynamic ground within which these practices take shape and the form through which the unsteady hope of lament is expressed in the ruins of shattered existence.

Turning toward and around God

Lamentations offers not one but many images of God, and there are also many—and at times even contradictory—ways of relating to God. When Daughter Zion first speaks, she invites God to "look" and "see" her distress (1:20). The Lord does not look, which leads to her desolation: "There is no one to comfort me, no one to restore my spirit" (1:16). In the second chapter the Lord has become like an enemy, since he has not only allowed Daughter Zion's destruction (1:17) but has "rejected" Daughter Zion—in fact, poured out his wrath on her. He has "trampled," "hurled down," "swallowed up," "torn down," "cast to the ground," and "withdrawn his hand" from Zion, and has burned her down. We encounter the same image of God as an enemy in the strong man's description of his own assault, where, like a raging bull, God has "broken my teeth with gravel and he has trampled me in the dust" (3:16). However, as we noted in the previous section, in the midst of the lament, the strong man remembers God's faithfulness (3:21), which does not end, and his mercies, which are renewed each day. Therefore, he will cry out to the Lord without relief "until the Lord looks down from heaven and sees" (3:49-50).

Contradictory images of God thus emerge from Lamentations: God is invited to see, but he does not look; God and only God can comfort Daughter Zion, but he does not; God rejects, but not forever (3:31); God causes grief, but he takes pity in the abundance of his mercies; he has no joy in afflicting; yet nothing happens unless the Lord ordains it. All these images are here in the book of Lamentations, with no attempt to resolve them—resulting in a kind of "theological confusion" (O'Connor, 52).

What are we to make of this theological confusion? There are at least three possible insights related to the confusion. First, the theological confusion reflects an honest and truthful engagement with God, without theological escapism. Because the speakers confront God directly with the reality of unbearable suffering, the relationship of humans to God in Lamentations is complex, even contradictory. But this in many ways reflects the human experience of God in the context of suffering. The God encountered in lament is at once liberating, abusing, silent, and indifferent.

Second, the various (even contradictory) images of God in Lamentations reflect an engagement with God on a very "deep," "primal," and "personal" level, the level of a covenant relationship, in which God is not an abstract category, nor simply a benevolent benefactor, not simply the God that one has come to know through a community's experience—but a God that one has personally encountered in a covenantal relationship as "my God." Given this personal encounter, Daughter Zion can risk turning to God in ways that may seem shockingly unorthodox.

Third, what the various postures reflect is that what is at stake in Daughter Zion's (and her children's) turning around God in the grief and anguish of their devastation is the covenant relationship with God that seems threatened by the trauma of destruction, where everything they knew and believed about God seems to be lost. In the end, this is the reason that Daughter Zion weeps, not so much because of what she has lost and endured (painful as that might be), but because God refuses to "look," to "see," and to pay attention to her in her plight. This is what obsesses her as she realizes that her comforter, her only comforter, has turned away and there is no one to comfort her, no one to restore her spirit (1:16). In fact, her comforter, her lover has become like an enemy. It is the same covenantal relationship that has been rendered uncertain through the experience of devastation that the communal voices of chapter 5 desperately long for in their final prayer. Thus do they cry out to God: "You, and only you (*'atah*) . . ." (5:19–22).[19] No one and nothing else can help them bear the wreckage in which they find themselves. And so, in a final plea, they ask: "Restore us to yourself, Lord, that we may return; renew our days as of old" (5:21). With a verb of turning, the people demand the restoration of the covenant relationship and renewal of life. Like Daughter Zion, they omit requests for the return of past glories—the good old days. O'Connor notes:

> They want something far deeper, something primal. They ask for a turning around of God, for a conversion of God's heart back to them. They want God to turn from abandoning and rejecting them. And they themselves want to return to God. They want their relationship restored. But God's turning is what matters, for they have been turning to God throughout the book. (78)

This conclusion, valid though it is, still leaves many questions about the fact that, despite the insistent plea for God to "look, see, and remember," God does not answer; God does not comfort; in fact, throughout the book of Lamentations, God does not speak. What kind of God is this, a God who remains silent at the moment when his voice is especially needed? Of course, it may be that the fact that God remains silent in Lamentations simply reflects the harsh truth that, in the middle of their shattered lives and livelihoods, people are often not able to hear or feel the assuring voice or touch of God. It may also be that God's refusal to speak has the purely pragmatic effect of creating the necessary space for human speech and thus creates space for human healing. As O'Connor notes, "God's silence in Lamentations leaves wounds festering, open to the air and possibly to healing. The benefit of exposed wounds is that they become visible and unavoidable. Left exposed, they require us to see, acknowledge, and attend to them" (88).

19. Lamentations 5:19–20 reads: "You, Lord, reign forever; your throne endures from generation to generation. Why do you always forget us? Why do you forsake us so long?" O'Connor notes that the address uses the independent personal pronoun "you" (*'atah*). The pronoun is an attention-getting device, an emphatic appeal to awaken God's notice and to make a personal connection with God, as if to say, "You, YHWH, no one else, only you, the one who rules from generation to generation" (77).

But that analysis leaves matters on a purely psychological and pragmatic level and does not enter the rich theological matrix of Lamentations, which emerges from within a deep religious context of a covenant relationship with God. Might it be that, within that covenant context, the silence of God points to a fresh dimension of God? Might the silence of God in Lamentations be a theological key that presses beyond the standard picture of an omnipotent and omnipresent God, who punishes wrongdoing and rewards good conduct, to suggest a mysterious God—a God who might in some ways be "powerless" in the face of human evil and who might grieve and suffer violence? The possibility of a vulnerable God behind the silence of God suggests that Daughter Zion's lamentations may, in fact, reflect Yahweh's own lamentations. But contemplating such a possibility is already moving the discussion of the question of God in the midst of suffering beyond theodicy ("Where was God . . . ?") and into the realm of ecclesiology and ethics, to questions about the kind of community that is formed and the actions that are generated in the face of a suffering God and a suffering humanity.[20] This is a discussion that I will explore more thoroughly in the following chapter.

My intention in this chapter has been to explore O'Connor's observation that, for a people who begin from a place of suffering, Lamentations is a book of comfort. I have wanted to explore the ways that Lamentations can be a resource—and even a gift—for communities and individuals in the midst of ruins. My exploration has confirmed that lament, at least the kind of lament captured in the poetry of this biblical book, is not simply a sentiment; it is a complex performance, a discipline, that involves many actions: crying out, exercising memory, maintaining silence, repenting, and earnest praying. In the end, our exploration has confirmed that the public practice of lament is at once a way of naming what is going on, a way of standing and engaging God in the midst of ruins. In other words, it is a way of hoping in the shattered ruins of life.

But what seems to emerge from our discussion up to this point is that, if Lamentations is able to evoke and express all these forms of agency in the wake of Jerusalem's destruction, it is partly—and in a great measure—due to the unique genre of poetic lament. For, as I have noted, one of the unique gifts of poetry and artistic expression is their ability to supply words for what is too deep for words. Our exploration of poetry thus leaves us with both a desire and a curiosity to discover whether any similar poetic and artistic expressions

---

20. See, e.g., David Bentley Hart, *The Doors of the Sea: Where Was God in the Tsunami?* (Grand Rapids: Eerdmans, 2005).

have emerged in the context of Africa's experience of devastation and many communal and individual displacements in the wake of violence. Are there any such expressions in Africa that may bear similarity to Lamentations' poetic genre, and that may reflect similar resources and ways of defining what is going on, standing and engaging God, and even hoping in the midst of ruins?

Already in Stearns's *Dancing in the Glory of Monsters* we encounter glimpses of lament expressed in the stories of survivors of Congo's massacres. In the wake of the rich insights from Lamentations, it becomes obvious that a more elaborate exploration of poetry, music, and other artistic expressions of lament from East Africa will be necessary, and that such an exploration could shed light on the cultural moorings of hope in the midst of Africa's civil wars and cycles of violence. To an examination of such poetry, music, and art from East Africa's landscape of lament we now turn.

CHAPTER 4

The Threefold Gift of Cultural Expressions of Lament

war has destroyed our home
. . . war has destroyed our home
. . . our home is already quiet
. . . our home is already dead

Jeff Korondo

Toward the end of our reflection on Jason Stearns's *Dancing in the Glory of Monsters*, I examined some vignettes of lament from survivors in the wake of Congo's violence and devastation. I noted that the more one looks at the images and metaphors that are used to express the inexpressible losses of the survivors, the more one realizes that what has been lost (through the violence) and what is grieved is not just the loss of loved ones. The sentiments point to a loss that is far deeper: the loss of an anchor for the future, the loss of community, and eventually the loss of humanity. This conclusion is confirmed by John Lederach and Angela Lederach in *When Blood and Bones Cry Out*.[1] Drawing attention to the metaphorical structure of social healing, the Lederachs note that war and violence displace people on many levels: at the basic physical level, violence leads to a loss of place (displacement); loss of safety (insecurity); and loss of voice (voicelessness). The loss on the physical level penetrates far and beyond, and it points to a much deeper loss on the metaphorical level: the loss of personhood, of identity, and of humanity. What the Lederachs confirm is that naming (and healing from) such violation—which destroys the essence

---

1. John Paul Lederach and Angela Jill Lederach, *When Blood and Bones Cry Out: Journeys through the Soundscape of Healing and Reconciliation* (Oxford: Oxford University Press, 2010).

of innocence, decency, and life, and thus "penetrates beyond comprehension and words"—takes more than ordinary language.[2] It requires the metaphorical language of poetry. Accordingly, in *When Blood and Bones Cry Out*, the Lederachs explore the metaphors of sound, music, poetry, and mothering to point to the dynamic and continuous reality of social healing in the midst of violence.

My exploration of the book of Lamentations has highlighted this unique gift of metaphor and poetry, a gift well captured by Scott Ellington, a biblical scholar and professor in the School of Christian Ministries at Emmanuel College, in his discussion of the psalms of lament:

> Ordinary language seems wholly inadequate to articulate such a horrific bereavement, so it is not surprising that such prayers resort to the language of poetry and metaphor. Poetry describes novelty through the free play of images. It allows for ambiguity and openness, both putting experience into words and leaving space for those words to take on altered meanings in new situations. Metaphors, by combining familiar images in novel ways, reach toward an expression of that which is surprising, other, and to a certain extent, indescribable.[3]

Here I wish to explore representations of music, poetry, and other forms of artistic expression that have emerged from Northern Uganda and the Congo in the context of war and violence. The exploration here is not comprehensive, but I hope that this preliminary treatment will highlight an area for further theological attention and research that is much needed. My immediate aim is to explore the threefold power of these cultural expressions of lament to (1) give voice to the grief of the community; (2) name what is going on; and (3) express the longing for restoration and social healing. To the extent that the poetic laments are able to do so, they become a unique register of hope in the midst of the violent devastation of Northern Uganda and Eastern Congo.

2. Lederach and Lederach, *Blood and Bones*, 2.

3. Scott A. Ellington, *Risking Truth: Reshaping the World through Prayers of Lament* (Eugene, OR: Pickwick, 2008), 27.

Finding a Voice in Northern Uganda's Displacement

Gang Otyeko Ling

For over twenty-five years (from 1986 until around 2010, when Joseph Kony's forces withdrew to the Congo and Chad), Northern Uganda was engaged in a bloody conflict that pitted the Ugandan army against Kony's Lord's Resistance Army (LRA). The conflict left thousands of civilians tortured, raped, or dead, tens of thousands of children abducted and forcefully recruited into the rebel forces, and millions of people displaced from their homes. According to a study released in 2008, Northern Uganda had some of the highest levels of posttraumatic stress disorder (PTSD) recorded anywhere, with an estimated 54 percent of the population suffering from the condition.[4] In the midst of this protracted context of social trauma, contemporary and indigenous expressions of music and poetry emerged, created by local artists and shared widely among communities.[5] Perhaps none captures the depth of lament as profoundly as does "Gang Otyeko Ling" ("Our Home Is Already Dead") by Jeffrey Opiyo, who goes by the stage name Korondo.

Opiyo was eighteen and still a high school student when he produced "Gang Otyeko Ling," his first recorded song. The fighting between Kony's LRA and the Ugandan Army was devastating, with the result that the majority of the Ugandan population was forced into camps for internally displaced persons (IDP). Opiyo

4. Bayard Roberts et al., "Factors Associated with Post-traumatic Stress Disorder and Depression amongst Internally Displaced Persons in Northern Uganda," *BMC Psychiatry* 8, no. 38 (2008): 4: http://www.biomedcentral.com/1471-244X/8/38 (accessed Dec. 16, 2015). See also Lindsay McClain Opiyo, "Community Peacebuilding through the Arts: Addressing the Past in Post-Conflict Northern Uganda," paper presented at "Engaging the Other" Conference, University of Free State, Bloemfontein, South Africa, December 2012.

5. Lindsay McClain Opiyo, "Artistic Suggestions for Peaceful Transition in Northern Uganda: What Youth Are Saying," *African Conflict and Peacebuilding Review* 2, no. 1 (April 2012): 152–63. On the role of art in general, and music in particular, in peacebuilding in Northern Uganda, see Linday McClain Opiyo, *Bed Ki Gen: Northern Uganda's Creative Approaches to Peace and Healing* (Knoxville, TN: Self-published, 2009). Bed Ki Gen is Luo for "'Have Hope.'" It is shaped around the three metaphors of voice, vision, and community. Opiyo depicts how, through art, the people of Northern Uganda discover their voices and tell their stories, express their visions for the future and strengthen their communities. I am grateful to Lindsay, who first introduced me to Music for Peace (MFP), which she cofounded in 2009 with Jeffrey Opiyo (now her husband) and Jahria Okwera. MFP is "an initiative of performing artists in northern Uganda that was created to promote the power of music for peacebuilding and social change, and to build solidarity among artists from conflict and post-conflict zones in Africa" (see http://www.mfpuganda.org/about/).

had heard an announcement over the radio about a community youth music competition, so he and a neighbor friend skipped school and went to audition.

"By then I had not realized the power of music for peacebuilding," Opiyo said. "I did not know things like activism or lament. I just wanted to sing and express what I felt as a youth."[6] It turned out that "Gang Otyeko Ling" not only expressed Opiyo's sentiments; his feelings also found a great deal of resonance and "sonic echo" within the community.[7] As "Gang Otyeko Ling" became popular (and was regularly played on FM radio), it also became the collective voice of lament of Northern Uganda.[8]

"Gang Otyeko Ling" is a mourning song, a wailing for "our home," which is dead:

Wululululu, wululululu, I am yelling and I am pleading!
Wululululu wululilile, it pains my heart, let's talk instead.

Lelelilile lelelelele, we cry with our hands over our head.
Where do we turn to? Our home is quiet.

Even though you try to stop me, my brother, let me say this,
Because even for food we have to line up, but Acholi were farmers.

6. Interview, Bethany House, Entebbe, Jan. 10, 2015 (hereafter cited as Bethany House Interview). Jeff Korondo's music became more explicitly "activist" when he was introduced to a peacebuilding perspective through Lindsay McClain Opiyo and the visit of Rosalind Hackett (from the University of Tennessee). While Dr. Hackett would go on to form (in 2006) the Jazz for Justice Project (to raise funds, awareness, and support for music and the arts as tools for postconflict reconstruction and peacebuilding in Northern Uganda), McClain would cofound MFP (see preceding footnote).

7. See John Paul Lederach and Angela Lederach on "sonic voice" as a "sensation of feeling sound rise from within and take the form of words that enter a shared space and are received by and touch others. In return, a response comes back and touches the one who spoke. In this process, people participate in creating resonance" (*Blood and Bones,* 67).

8. For this first recording, Opiyo won first prize in the competition; what is more, he got a calling. The ability to give voice to the mourning and thus create sonic echo in the community kept him going. He was soon commissioned by Save the Children (2005) to do a song on Children's rights—"Wan Otieno"—which also became very popular. In 2006, Save the Children took him to Bundibujo (Western Uganda) for a day of the African Child. Save the Children commissioned another song (2007), which he wrote against defilement, and in 2008 the World Health Organization commissioned Opiyo to compose a song about malaria. In 2009 he cofounded Music for Peace, and that same year he organized a community-wide competition leading up to a cultural exchange in Sierra Leone. Opiyo's music was finding a "sonic echo" beyond Northern Uganda.

The earth has squeezed descendants of Luo.
Darkness everywhere.[9]

It is an elegy for the home that was destroyed by war—and is no more.
Thus the refrain:

war has destroyed our home
. . . war has destroyed our home
. . . our home is already quiet
. . . our home is already dead

This song revolves around the rich metaphor of "our home," which operates on a number of levels. On one level, "Gang Otyeko Ling" is about the loss of the physical homes (which were either burned down by the rebels or abandoned due to the government policy of settling civilians into camps for IDP). On another level, it is the whole way of life of the descendants of Luo, their sense of belonging, their dignity—in a word, their *culture*. The loss of home also signifies humiliation (lining up for food) and loss of identity. Everything people knew is dead! The home is quiet. On the deepest—perhaps most complex—level, the Lederachs point out that the absence of any voices from the home signifies a loss of humanity:

[V]oicelessness creates the experience of being numb, without a capacity to feel, to touch or to be in touch. This is in fact the impact of violence. It deadens, numbs and silences life. Those who experience it close at hand experience a loss that reaches below and beyond words. Here we enter the terrain of the unspeakable, the search for finding ways to name experiences and events that are beyond words and comprehension. The search in such an uncharted geography represents a groping journey to touch and feel again, to find ways to feel the meaning of experiences that defy—and are never adequately expressed by—rational explanation.[10]

"Gang Otyeko Ling" also mourns the death that is everywhere. Here, too, death operates on a number of metaphorical levels: from the actual physical death, to the devastation of the land, to the maiming by land mines, to life in

9. Unless otherwise specified, all translations of the laments in this chapter are mine.
10. Lederach and Lederach, *Blood and Bones,* 66.

the IDP campus, to HIV—all in the wake of the war. Death is everywhere, so everyone is weeping:

> Fighting for this entire time has brought disasters to our home
> No more cattle because of this struggle!
> Even orphans, even widows, others limbless—all over our land
> Living in camps, with no food
> Sexually transmitted diseases, AIDS also around there
>
>
> People are dying, some are rotting, some are eaten by dogs—war has
>   destroyed our home!
> Very great homes have been burnt to ashes
> Our kinsmen have become refugees
> Our culture is dying because war has destroyed our homes
> Women weeping, children also cry, men mourning
> Korondo also cry, Jammie also cries
> Lelelilile lelelelele, we cry with our hands over our head
> Where do we turn to? Our home is quiet
> We have left our homes, it pains my heart
> Sleeping in hideouts to save our generation.

As he wails for the home that is dead, Korondo comes to a breaking point, to a point of "enough is enough," and thus turns to the audience with a sorrowful plea to various groups—elders, fighters, youth—to bring an end to the war. Why can't we realize that war is bad? he asks:

> Elders of Acholi, leaders of Acholi, let's sit down and discuss peace
>
> Let's join hands and bring peace to our home
> Hey my brothers still in the bush
> Let's come back home and start developing our land
> It is our time now, for us to get peace
>
> Even if you were a fighter—there is forgiveness for you
> Even though you were an opposition—there is forgiveness for you
>
> If you are still fighting in the bush, please, let's talk!
> We need peace.

The theme of displacement features prominently in Korondo's music. The Lederachs are right to note that perhaps no metaphor captures this sense of displacement more than the IDP does, and this operates on a number of metaphorical levels. On the literal level, the IDP signifies a loss of place—of being forced out of their homes and off the land. On another level, displacement points to the experience of "being lost," of being "uprooted."[11] They have lost a sense of belonging. On yet another level, losing a sense of place is losing a sense of purpose. "In this sense, displaced people search for significance, often in pursuit of finding direction in what is essentially a quest for identity: 'Who' are we in this unknown social landscape? Accordingly, the question of 'where' we are is always intimately tied up with 'who' we are."[12] That is why displacement is a feeling of being lost within oneself.

All of these metaphorical levels are at play in "Gang Otyeko Ling," as Korondo mourns the fact that "our kinsmen have become refugees . . . living in camps with no food." However, it is Korondo's "Okwera Nono" ("You Reject Me for Nothing") that captures the displacement at these multiple levels with painful poignancy, as he sings of the plight of the child soldier. On one level the song is autobiographical: Korondo himself had been abducted by the rebels when he was a child, but he managed to escape. In his experience he again finds resonance and "sonic echo" with other formerly abducted children. In "Okwera Nono," the child soldier who returns home is rejected. This was the experience of many child soldiers who either escaped from the war or returned home as a result of government amnesty. Because many had been forced to kill their parents, burn down their family homes, terrorize their own communities, and the females among them had become "wives" to rebels and bore rebels' children, they were neither welcomed nor accepted back into their own communities.[13] "Okwera Nono" captures the stigma of such a child soldier who finds that he is displaced from both home and the bush—with nowhere to go. "What if it were you, what would you have done?" the child soldier poignantly asks the community:

> My people, you reject me for nothing
> Where do I go?
> Maybe it was meant to be like that

11. Lederach and Lederach, *Blood and Bones,* 59.
12. Lederach and Lederach, *Blood and Bones,* 60.
13. One of the effects of the conflict in Northern Uganda (as in Congo) has been to blur the distinction between victim and perpetrators, since many of the fighters were the so-called child soldiers who were either abducted or forcefully recruited into the rebel forces.

What if it were you? What would you do?
Maybe it was meant to be like that
What if it were you? Where would you go?[14]

The power of this song is in naming not only the double identity of the children who are caught between innocence and guilt, between being victims and perpetrators, between the bush and the home, but it is also the burden that "our little ones" are carrying. These are the "heavy loads" of guilt and trauma that the children carry as witnesses and perpetrators of unspeakable havoc.

Our little children are returning from the bush with different kinds of
    problems
Look! They are returning from the bush after an immense suffering
Carrying heavy loads, witnessing horrific murders and trekking long
    distances!
Most painful is that they are forcing them to murder against their wish.
If it were you, what would you do?

But what makes these heavy loads even heavier is not only that the little ones are not welcomed back home, but that there is no home to return to. Just as their innocence has been irreparably shattered, their once beautiful homes have become a jungle of enmity. The formerly abducted kids are caught between a rock and hard place, and their lament represents the lament and displacement of the community.

There is this issue of returning home, even so, it has its problems.
Go to the villages, there is enmity, there are quarrels, there are land
    wrangles;
There are murders and there is bloodshed;
There are land mines and even deaths.

The Lamentations of Lamalo

Korondo's song about the plight of the abducted children ends up naming the social displacement under way, a theme that is particularly pronounced

14. Translation by the artist.

in Abim's *The Spill of Blood and the Lamentations of Lamalo*.[15] A Catholic priest from the Archdiocese of Gulu, Father Abim describes himself as a "no-nonsense Acholi who loves to love and hates to hate."[16] *The Spill of Blood* is an "elegy,"[17] from one "who has grown up and lived in a war situation for over twenty-six years,"[18] one who, like the strong man of Lamentations, has experienced the devastation of the war firsthand. Born in 1977, Abim lost his father when he was nine years old, leaving Abim's mother to care for Abim and his six siblings by herself, as well as four other children who came to live with them. In 1993, at the peak of the LRA war, Abim joined Lacor Junior Seminary. During that time he lost many classmates as a result of abductions, and some were even killed on their way to the seminary. His brother and his only uncle were also killed, and he very narrowly survived abduction himself. He would lie on his bed at the junior seminary, unable to sleep because he was over-whelmed with emotions of pain, anger, fear, and uncontrollable sadness. His mind would be filled with voices and images of abductions and dead bodies. A priest at the school encouraged him to write down what he felt and saw, and that is how he started writing poems at the age of fifteen.

At the heart of *The Spill of Blood* is the figure of Lamalo, a grieving mother, a figure who operates as a metaphor on at least two levels. On the one hand, Lamalo is Abim's own grieving mother. After the disappearance of her hus-band, Abim's mother was not only inconsolable, but she was also left alone with twelve children to look after. She would sit at the grinding mill and sing painful songs of lament, beginning in a low hum, followed by words as her laments grew louder. She did not want the children to hear her laments, but "we would sneak in behind her and hear her mournful songs, which would leave us all crying," says Fr. Abim.[19] But Lamalo is also a metaphor for Northern Uganda: like Daughter Zion in Lamentations, Lamalo is Northern Uganda personified, grieving for all her children and the destruction of her people. Her grief is like a spear thrust deep in her heart:

> Mama, why do you cry?
> My son, my son, come and I tell you

---

15. Paul Peter Rom Abim, *The Spill of Blood and the Lamentations of Lamalo* (Rossendale: Rossendale Books, 2011).

16. Interview with Fr. Abim at Bethany House, Entebbe, Uganda (Jan. 10, 2015); hereafter cited as Bethany House interview.

17. Abim, *Spill of Blood,* 10.

18. Abim, *Spill of Blood,* 16.

19. Bethany House interview.

> Sit at my feet and listen to me
> I have been pierced in the heart
> The center of my life
> The noise of battle kills me
> My son, see how your kindred have fallen . . .

The poem runs down a catalogue of the realities that have been visited on Lamalo's children: the noise of battle, children fallen and abducted, life in the IDP camps, and so on:

> Oh son, a spear in my heart
> But I struggle to live
> The big-eyed elephant has entrapped us in the camps . . .

> My son, my son
> I am pierced to the heart
> I depend on donated food
> Measured in kilograms . . .

> My son, I am dying
> And my tear glands run dry of tears.
> Your sister is defiled
> When her breasts are still emerging . . .
> With small hips and bumps . . .
> She is like the green mango fruit
> thrown down by the wind;
> She is destroyed at the beginning of her life . . .

The painful descriptions pile up till they reach unimaginable proportions, pointing to the inhuman level to which the community has been reduced:

> They [the rats, rebels] carry away our children
> They kill your father
> They boil your teacher in a saucepan
> Like eggs, the head of your teacher swims
> In the dry gin pot [*agulu Kongo*] of your mother
> We gather not for a funeral
> But to feast on the teacher's head.
> When did we become cannibals?

Who has ever eaten his father?[20]

This is the inhuman situation in which Lamalo struggles to live: she has nowhere to turn for help, nowhere to find hope.

No hope, no life is possible.
What can I do, my son?
Where can I turn?
To whom should I cry?
It is a spear in my heart.

Even though Abim's poems are occasional, inspired by moments of great excitement or extreme sorrow, the particular events and stories become metaphors that reflect a deeper sense of communal dislocation. "My Compound Is a Graveyard," for example, was inspired by the tragic story of a man whose wife and six children were all killed by rebels in one day. He took his blanket and went inside his hut to grieve. The following day, another group of rebels found him and asked why he had not fled, and where the children were. He took them outside and showed them the fresh graves that he had dug to bury his family in. When the rebels threatened to burn his hut and kill him, the man said that that would be all right—after all, he was already dead.

That man became a metaphor for Northern Uganda: in "My Compound Is a Graveyard," the image of the graveyard symbolizes the liminal space—of the living dead—a space just like what is described in *Dancing in the Glory of Monsters*, where the people are now "living on top of [their] dead." Thus, even though the poem refers to specific challenges the community is facing—living in refugee camps, no place to cultivate food, and no plot to build a house on— it draws attention to a far deeper form of displacement: the strange, ghostlike community where "children are smashed on trees"; young girls are raped; and "the teacher's head [is] boiled in a saucepan." The graveyard names the unspeakable, the transformation of a once beautiful community into a community of zombies:

Look, my son
Where can you cultivate food?
Where can you build a house?
My compound is a graveyard

20. At times the rebels would boil people and force the family to eat the flesh.

Of children smashed on trees,
Children who die of famine,
Those who are abandoned,
The ones who die of AIDS.

Oh, a true graveyard of men young and old;
Your father beheaded just yesterday
Your brother buried without his head,
And your sister still young
With her breast just emerging
And ready for a man to elope
Was raped and murdered in cold blood.

The rats carry out pillages all over the land,
Carrying the young and murdering the old.
You burnt away the grass,
What shall your shelter be?

Nothing more but seven feet
Into the heart of the soil
Just in my compound—a graveyard.

My son, I am pierced to the heart;
The poison exhausts my blood.
The gods have forgotten us,
Our ancestors are asleep,
Maybe they have gone for a journey.
Turn, Lord, and answer the plea of your people
Tormented with all sorts of horrors.

Abim's poems, therefore, are a sonic echo of the many stories of unspeakable events the community has endured. In an interview, Abim noted that there were many stories like that of the man whose family had been killed and who told the rebels that he was already dead. For instance, there is the story of two mothers who were forced by the rebels to kill their children. One mother did so, but the other mother refused, saying that, whether or not she killed her child, the rebels would end up killing her anyway. The rebels left them. The mother who killed her son went mad. There were also many stories of rebels coming from the bush to rape their sisters, kill their parents, burn the homes of the community. What all these stories reveal is the state of nihilistic desolation that the community was reduced to.[21] The sense of despair was brought into sharp focus for Abim when President Museveni visited Gulu town. The day before his visit, an ambush on the road to Atiak had killed many people, including children. In his speech the president did not even mention the incident. Instead, he offered the usual promises of security and development. That is when Abim wrote "When Nothing Really Matters," reflecting the state of nihilistic desolation that had descended on the community as a result of the war.

> But when nothing begins to matter,
> What do I have to mind about?
> Life becomes meaningless,
> Rules are no longer binding,
> Every demand of life is a burden.
> Life can never be good,
> But no sin [crime] do I see,
> For nothing matters.

> But when nothing matters, there is nothing good,
> Neither is there anything bad, for nothing matters.
> I am unconcerned and I give up life,
> I have neither won, nor have I lost;
> All these are illusions.
> The state of helplessness
> Covers Northern Uganda,
> No hope is seen in the barrel of the gun,
> No prayers are heard by the gods,
> And no sign of peace is visible.
> No man, no woman is happy
> So, does anything really matter?

> Oval faces cover me up
> The smell of blood is heavy in the air
> A stream of blood runs through the land
> No one is there to stop it; for it doesn't matter.
> We swim in the blood of our fathers,

21. Bethany House interview.

Our sons too young to swim are drowned.
Oh, war is when others see nothing that matters
Yet everything does matter more than ever . . .

Naming the Unspeakable in Eastern Congo

One encounters a similar sense of desolation as that captured by Opiyo and Abim in Northern Uganda in a number of poems and popular songs from Eastern Congo. These poems and songs reflect a sense of "inexpressibility": what has happened to the community and the country is too deep for words! It lies below and beyond words. The pillage, rape, and massacres that occurred during the years of fighting in the Congo—what have come to be known as the "Congo Wars"—have brought the community to a place of total silence. Words are "useless" to express the grief and anger of the community. Joêl Baraka, a young poet from Bukavu, captures this "end of words" rather poignantly in *Ceci ne peut s'exprimer* ("This Is Inexpressible"):

> *Des paroles et des idées sont impuissantes*
> *Ceci ne peut s'exprimer . . .*

> Words and ideas are powerless
> This cannot be expressed . . .

> Horror mixed with despair and anger dwell in me
> The instant I hear them and the cries of those women
> Assaulted at Kamanyola, at Bunyakiri, at Shabunda, at Masisi
> By those monstrous creatures hosted yesterday.
> Oh, the price of hospitality!

> Words and ideas are powerless
> This cannot be expressed . . .[22]

His anger and grief are connected to specific places and the memory of what happened at Kamanyola, Bunyakiri, Shabunda, and Masisi. Here refugees from the 1994 Rwanda genocide were welcomed. But the refugees soon turned

22. Joêl Baraka AM, extract from *My Loves My Sorrows*, youth poetry (2012).

into looters, and in the end their presence also became the occasion for the invasion and destruction of communities by Rwandan forces.[23] The memory of the hospitality betrayed and cries of so many massacred and raped overwhelms Baraka with anger and tears. It forces him into a convulsion as he hears politicians give their speeches with complete disregard for the grief around them:

> I tremble as under a painful thorn
> The moment I hear the misleading and hypocritical speeches
> Of those Machiavellians coming from nowhere,
> Those insensitive, those unconscientious, those careless ones.
> Do they know the grief of the martyrs felled by their blow?
> Words and ideas are powerless,
> This cannot be expressed . . .

Like Korondo, whose wailing is unrestrained, Baraka's anger and grief led to a breaking point. In another poem, *Ma vengeance invincible* ("My Invincible Revenge"), Baraka pours out the raw emotion of desire and determination for revenge. And here, to the names of Kamanyola, Bunyakiri, Shabunda, and Masisi are added memories of what happened at places like Kasika, Makobola, Dongo-Aru-Ariwara, places where massacres of unimaginable magnitude took place. His hatred for those who committed these massacres is undisguised.

> Neither lightning nor exponential thunder
> Could ever appease my hatred,
> Facing the wicked, facing the dreadful ones,
> Taking shots at my brothers in Kasika-Makobola.

> Neither hurricane Katrina, nor a cyclone of any kind
> Will ever annihilate my invincible revenge
> Against all those criminals, against all those blood-thirsty ones
> Who have pillaged, burned and sabotaged Dongo-Aru-Ariwara.

"My Invincible Revenge" alludes to the invasion by "those impious armies guided by the destructive flame / Those who have destroyed and cruelly sabotaged the cities of my country" (a thinly veiled reference to the Rwandan invasion). These have not only destroyed the villages and cities of "my country,"

---

23. Many of the refugees were suspected of being Interahamwe militias who had perpetrated the Rwanda Genocide in 1994.

they have pillaged, raped, and murdered with impunity. Nothing can console the unspeakable grief in his soul: he cannot bring himself to forget or forgive what they have done:

> Neither sweet songs, nor lyrical poetry
> Could soften the anger inspired in my soul.
> In view of cruel violence endured by my honorable mothers,
> In the knowledge of sexual slavery suffered by my poor sisters,
>
> Neither Apostle Paul, nor Muhammad the prophet, nor the virgin Mary
> Could ever convince me to forgive
> For all those impious armies guided by the destructive flame
> Those who have destroyed and cruelly sabotaged the cities of my
>   country . . .

He can hardly wait for the day of revenge to come, when these armies would be pushed out of Congo. He anticipates the jubilation on "the day of my victory. . . . I will hold shaky palms." While Baraka's two poems above voice the overwhelming emotions of anger, hatred, and revenge, a number of other poems and songs, such as the popular Swahili song *Dunia Ime Chafuka* ("The World Is Tarnished"), testify to the fear that overwhelms the community. *Dunia Ime Chafuka* was composed by the director of a Catholic church choir in Nizi, twenty miles outside Bunia, following a clash between the Gegere and Lendu tribes in which many people were killed. The song became popular in the Catholic church and throughout the village.[24]

In talking about the loss of safety, the Lederachs note that violence destroys what was understood and known. What was assumed, taken for granted as "normal" on a daily basis, has disappeared, and as a result people suspend or completely lose the capacity to feel at home: "Violence destroys this feeling and the capacity to be oneself without mistrust or pretension; it destroys a sense of at-homeness."[25] Rather than feeling surrounded by love, acceptance, and protection (as one expects in a home), "they are enveloped by threat, fear, and animosity, and worse, the constant presence of complete unpredictability in the living of daily life."[26]

24. The song was recorded in Matembo, sung by a young choir member who previously sang in the choir in Nizi, where she learned the song (interviewed by Mumbere Nzoera Eleazr, Mar. 17, 2015).
25. Lederach and Lederach, *Blood and Bones,* 63.
26. Lederach and Lederach, *Blood and Bones,* 64.

One can get a glimpse of the loss of safety on various levels in *Dunia Ime Chafuka*, which is a cry to God about the suffering in Congo. The song's refrain, "Father, Father, we suffer a lot here in the Congo," is like Daughter Zion's cries in Lamentations: it is a mournful plea, as it were, an invitation to God to see the community's suffering. The suffering has to do not only with what they have lost—"homes [that] have been burnt" and "goods left behind"—but also with the fear that has wrapped itself around the community like an envelope and plagues every moment of their day: "We fear at all times; we are afraid." The song evokes a sense of being "surrounded by enemies" and by "many rebel groups"; of life on the run ("we are refugees"); and of being pursued and hunted down like animals, with "no place to hide" and "no place to feel safe."

> The world, the world, the world is tarnished.
> So is everything it contains.
> We the Congolese are surrounded by enemies, and they destroy us.
> They make us suffer, and life is heavy for us to bear.
> There are many names of rebel groups
> And they make us afraid.
> We don't know where to hide,
> We are refugees.
> We suffer from hunger; where are we going to hide?
> We fear at all times; going to school and in our farms, we are afraid.
> Father, father, we suffer a lot here in Congo,
> Congo has been disrupted.
> Some [of us] have left their goods at Kamango,
> Their homes have been burnt.
> Father, father, we suffer a lot here in Congo.

The effect of living a life that is perpetually on the run, pursued by enemies and with no place to hide, has left the community with no hope and has deflated their energy for living. They are enervated, not only in these lyrics but in the slow, monotonous melody of another popular local church song that is sung both in Lingala and French:

> Listen to the voice of our beseeching
> Listen to the voice of our beseeching
> We are praying to you, Lord. [repeat]
> Listen to the voice of our beseeching

We are praying to you, Lord. [repeat]
We are tired from the war
We are tired from the war
We are praying to you, Lord. [repeat]

Listen to the voice of our beseeching
As we pray to you, God. [repeat]
We Congolese are tired [repeat]
We pray to you, God. [repeat]

A number of poems and songs also name the contradictions of war and the irony and futility of fighting in order to secure peace. This is seen in the popular song *Une Minute de Silence*, from Uvira:

Oh, for peace, many have died
Oh, for peace, relatives have disappeared
Oh, for peace, a minute of silence.
Wars we have seen of all kinds, exported, of course
But surprisingly they have rewarded with ranks and positions
those who yesterday raped our mothers, mutilated our little sisters,
Stabbed our grandmothers—up to the point of burying them alive at
      Mwenga/Kasika.

Whereas Baraka focused his hatred on the invaders, *Une Minute de Silence* turns to "my fellow Congolese" as it names not only the contradictions, the absence of logic in the war, but also its madness. Making reference to war as a spell that has been cast, the song compares war to a powerful drug under whose influence the Congolese have visited the unimaginable on their own country and people.

Who drugged the Congolese?
Who bewitched them?
Who deceived the Congolese?
What kind of narcotic did you take, Congolese,
To the point you ended up eating the flesh of our compatriots,
To the point you burn food markets and sabotage the economy,
To the point you sell land where they just buried our dead,
To the point you burn the national park of Kahuzi Byega?
      Scourge!!!

Nearly cursed Soldiers,
Oh! Misfortune, scourge, bad luck
To rape a little girl in the sight of her dad, to make a father or a mother
     walk around naked in the yard,
To force a mother to have sex with her son.

Rape and sexual violence are constant themes in the songs and poems
from Congo. The last line in the song above refers to the unfathomable act
of forcing a mother to have sex with her son. A number of other songs and
poems express similar sentiments of inhumanity: they embody the cries of
these women and name the unfathomable reality of sexual violence. One such
poem is *Les Femmes s'interrogent*:

Hear the tears and cries of daughters and sons of Congo.
You leave us with tears and scars in our hearts. Oh, barbarians!
You have raped our mothers who have given birth to us.

Have pity, have pity . . .
Our mothers are raped, our sisters are raped, and our grandmothers are
     raped,
Truly have pity.
Our mothers raped in the sight of their children,
Children raped in the sight of their parents; truly have pity.
Truly have pity.
And this in the field,
At the market,
At school,
In the open air, at night as well as by day.

Les Femmes s'interrogent ends by drawing attention to the plight of the
children:

Who now will raise those children born from rape?
What will be the identity of those unwanted innocents?

Just as the deepest lament of Daughter Zion and the community in the
book of Lamentations was for the children, "her precious gold," the songs from
Congo lament the war's atrocities committed against the children. In a moving
poem, entitled *Malheur* ("Misfortune"), Baraka captures their plight: the child

has witnessed so many unimaginable horrors that "Malheur" has become her proper name! She not only lives in unfortunate circumstances; she *is* Misfortune, which in the cultural context of the Congo is the same as "Curse." The poem captures so many powerful dimensions that it warrants quoting it in its entirety:

> See the ashes of your father
> Burned alive this morning at 6:00 am
> As the sun rises
> Lighting up the village in the sight of everyone.
>
> Look at the entrails of your mother
> Cut into pieces by machete
> After being raped by the war lords
> At 12:00 noon, when the sun reached its zenith.
>
> Behold the debris of your little brother,
> Poor baby crushed with force by his sister at 3:00 pm
> As the sun rays were burning
> In the extremity of the village horrified by these demons!
>
> Here the clothes of your suicidal brother whom they forced
> To watch the rape of his mother at 4:30 pm
> At the time when the sunlight was still shining.
> On all our villages terrorized in the sight of all.
> Look at the path traversed by your sisters
> Under the deathly threat of the cursed ones
> At 6:00 pm when the distant sun rays
> Still shine on the baggage they carried by force.
>
> Understand that in the next nine months
> Your sisters will come back to the village, all pregnant
> To give birth to children who will not know their fathers
> And yet, who will be our future leaders
> Oh, Misfortune![27]

When war broke out in Bunia (in the Hema/Lendu conflict) in 2000, a number of people were displaced and were forced to seek refuge in Beni.

27. Joël Baraka AM, Extract from *My Loves My Sorrows,* Youth Poetry (2012).

The sight of important and respectable people in the community reduced to living in camps or on the street was deeply moving. Nothing, however, was as touching as the sight of the many orphans in the camps and streets of Bunia. Mbwaghara Vahwere David is currently a fourth-year student in theology at the Université Chrétienne Bilingue du Congo (UCBC) and was then serving as a children's pastor at La Grace Church. He composed a song for the children's choir of his church, *Cauchemar d'un Enfant Congolais* ("Nightmare of a Congolese Child"). The metaphor of a never-ending nightmare turned reality captures the plight of the Congolese child. Sung in French, the song found immediate sonic echo in the community, bringing many people to tears. It is still a popular song in Beni and Bunia. Because it captures so many dimensions of the child's unspeakable suffering, I will quote it in its entirety.

> Incredible but true
> Why pour my tears out?
> No one can explain it.
> At evening the gang came;
> Without explanation
> The shot was fired;
> When my mother ran to save herself
> They split her head in two.
> We were saved but we don't understand
> Why this atrocity? Why?
> My brother, shot through the head from afar;
> My sister, kidnapped and wounded;
> My aunt, pregnant, her baby torn apart from her;
> My uncle in his home, burned alive;
> My cousins made to enroll in war.
> Who is left? My grandmother, thrown into a ravine.
> Why? Why?
> Now I am alone, no defense, no help,
> Hunger and begging my companions at day
> Mosquitoes and dew my blanket at night
> Loneliness my bosom friend.
> I call upon the conscience of the atrocity initiators
> The collaborators from near and far
> The malefactors, to lighten our pain,
> For we are the victims, the innocent.
> Dear friends, come to Jesus,

He is our only shelter.
It is your power that fills me,
In you I want to live, I love to live.
You are the rock where I shelter,
The Lord of my life.

In this particular song the children are described as "victims" and as "innocent." But one key effect of the Congo Wars, just as with the war in Northern Uganda, has been the blurring of the distinction between victims and perpetrators, since many of the fighters are the so-called child soldiers. "Cauchemar d'un Enfant Congolais" has only a veiled reference to the children who have been forcibly recruited into fighting: "cousins made to enroll in war."

As I have noted with respect to Korondo's "Okworo Nono," the naming of the plight of the abducted children ends up naming the social displacement that is under way. It is this theme of displacement in the foundations of community life that Joêl Baraka poignantly captures in "La Pire d'Ignominie" ("The Worst Ignominy"), where he contemplates the unthinkable viciousness that occurred in places like Kasika, where the priest was taken from the altar and shot in the head, nuns were raped and strangled, and the consecrated hosts were scattered around the church.[28] The massacres in Kasika and other places (Makobola, Kitshanga, and Dongo, Aru-Ariwara) reflected the descent to a new low, where "nothing really matters," where nothing is sacred, and where human beings (those who carried out these atrocities) have descended to a level below that of animals, and the nation has become a stronghold of all evil.[29] This is what Baraka defines as *la pire d'ignominie*:

The nation fissured by violence
Harbored the bastion of all evil.
At Kasika, at Makobola, at Kitshanga and elsewhere,
Living humans' lives were seen and buried
By those vile ones, inspiring me to disgust.

They spoiled, burned, killed all on their way
Sabotaging up to the sacred places of the Church,
Profaning the host and sanctified objects,

---

28. See Jason K. Stearns's account in *Dancing in the Glory of Monsters: The Collapse of the Congo and the Great War of Africa* (New York: PublicAffairs, 2012), 155–56.

29. Abim, *Spill of Blood*, 83.

Violating and covering the sacred one with shame.
Oh my Congo! Oh my Congo!

In the same way, specific stories and events in Abim's *The Spill of Blood* signal underlying shifts and displacements in society's values and self-identity. The memory of massacres and violence that took place in specific places—Kasika, Masisi, Uvira in Congo—points to a deeper unraveling of the nation and thus calls for lament for "my Congo" ("my beloved Congo")—and, beyond that, a lament for "mama Africa." This is what the popular Swahili song "Nakitikita" ("I Am Dismayed") from Uvira (Shabani Yabin) conveys:

I sit down thinking about my country Congo,
its shame is so huge. . . .
A rich country with many resources,
A rich country with our forests, but people are dying of hunger . . .
I am dismayed, I cry for my country Congo . . .

A similar sentiment of being overcome with dismay is conveyed by another popular Swahili lament for "Congo, my country."

Kimokyo ni tena nikuona sisi wa congomani kuishi kaka hali ya
*   kutapanisha ndani ya inchi yetu.*
Eh! Mola je kuwa siku moja tutaishi ndani ya amani katika inchi yetu?
Ah! tunalia Hu ! Huu ! Congo! We are suffering. [repeat]
Kwetu Congo, sisi watoto hatuna tena tumaini la maisha. Unaweza lala,
*   una wazazi lakini uta amka kesho na wewe ni ya tima. Unaweza lala*
*   na wewe utajiri lakini uta amka na wewe umkini*
Uh! Uh! Congo! We are suffering.

What is making me suffer is seeing that we Congolese are living in a
    complicated situation in our country.
Eh! God, is there a day when we will live in peace in our country?
Ah! We are crying, Hu! Hu! Congo! We are suffering. [repeat]
In our home, Congo, we the youth don't have the hope of living anymore.
You can sleep when you have parents, but you can wake up tomorrow and
    find yourself an orphan.
You can sleep when you are rich, but you can wake up when you are poor.
Uh! Uh! Congo! We are suffering.

Other songs locate the displacement of Congo within a wider African context, and lament the politics of greed, war, and tribalism within Africa. "Africa Weanda Wapi?" ("Where Are You Going, Africa?") composed by Mbwaghara Vahwere (whose "Cauchemar d'un enfant Congolais" I have already discussed), is one such song.

> *Africa waenda wapi?*
> *Katika mambo yako ya vita . . .*

> Where are you going, Africa?
> Going through your war affairs.
> Affairs of bloodshed
> In a rude system of politics.
> People are killed like wild animals,
> The cause all but unknown.
> Orphans and widows are growing in number;
> We all groan for peace.

> Those who sow beans cannot reap maize;
> Neither will the Congolese who sow war harvest peace.
> As children of one father, let us sit together, love one another.
> Let's rid ourselves of war. [repeat]
> War kills, war makes suffering, war must not be.

> Tribalism will not solve our problems,
> Nor killing others.
> Shedding blood will not solve our problems.
> The problems of Africa concern us now;
> It is for us to sit and agree.
> As children of one father, let us sit together, love one another.

Longing for a New Day

If the effect of the endless cycles of war and violence has been the displacement of individuals and communities on multiple levels, the songs and poems from the region offer a glimpse into the pain, anguish, and helplessness of the displacement. In this connection, a key aspect of the poems and songs is the brutal honesty with which they use various metaphors and descriptions to define that displacement. Their once beautiful lives and communities have now been reduced to a life on the run, a form of "graveyard" existence, characterized as "madness," misfortune (curse), "spell" (nightmare), shame, and nihilism. The songs and poems are piercingly sad. However, for all their honesty and sadness, they do not reflect a sense of despair, but "a longing for an end to the nightmare" and the recovery of a sense of place, safety, and voice, even within the ongoing realities of war and violence. "Cauchemar d'un Enfant Congolais" expresses the longing for a "shelter" as a prayer and invitation to come to Jesus the Rock:

> Dear friends, come to Jesus;
> He is our only shelter.
> It is your power that fills me;
> In you I want to live, I love to live.
> You are the rock where I shelter,
> The Lord of my life.

In Korondo's "Gang Otyeko Ling," the longing happens at the breaking point, just when he contemplates the total devastation of the war: everything is dead. That is when the lament turns into an invitation to end the war. The poem "Une Minute de Silence" brings Baraka to the same breaking point of resistance and to an "enough is enough" moment. The title itself, "Une Minute de Silence," is symbolic on a number of levels: on one level, it is a longing for a pause—a moment of silence—thus an interruption of the economy of war by way of a different experience—even if briefly. But "une minute de silence" is also a pause for memory: to remember that another world is possible, and thus to remember the martyrs of peace, who lived by this stubborn conviction and thus gave their lives in the struggle for peace. The song "Une Minute de Silence" is an invitation to join the company of these witnesses; at the same time, it is a reminder of the cost of peace and thus the mobilization of courage:

> Enough.
> May the state or the Congolese government give us back our dignity,
> May the Congolese authorities take urgent measures
> For peace.
> Monsignor Kataliko died,
> Archbishop Munzihirwa died,
> Governor Magabe died,

the traditional chief Francois Mubeza died,
in Kisangani and Ituri they died, in Walungu, Kabare, Shabunda, they
    died
in Kasika, Makobola, Mwenga, they died. Four million Congolese died
For peace, it seems. A minute of silence.

The women's song from Uvira, "Les Femmes s'Interrogent," is also very
clear in its longing for an end to the war and a return to peace. This song
is also very explicit in expressing that this peace ("lasting peace in the
Congo") will be established only if the rapists and rebels come "home." As
John and Angela Lederach suggest, the metaphor of bringing the rebels
and rapists "home" plays on many levels. First, it suggests the return of
the rebels to the community, to a physical home. But it also suggests a
sense of returning them to normality, getting them back from the state of
animal-like existence (in the bush) to civilization and civility. Therefore,
returning the rebels "home" is about rehumanizing them; bringing them
back to their senses. But home also signifies a place of rest. For people who
have been on the run, hunted down, who have run out of breath, and who
have been suffocated by the pillage, violence, and rape—bringing the rebels
and rapists home means that the community can now "breathe." Thus the
women sing:

> If I had power, I would go into the deep forest to track you,
> Then bring you back to your homes
> So that we breathe,
> And so that lasting peace may be established in Congo.

The deep longing for lasting peace is also reflected in Stephen Ndeykosi's
English poem "A Cry for Life" (2005, from Ituri), which appeals to different audiences—"the international mafia," the European Union, the warring
armies—to "let us live."[30]

Let Us Live

Uranium ! What is it?
We don't know . . .

30. From Stephen Ndeykosi, *A Cry for Life: Ituri Drama* (Bunia: Peace House, 2005),
18–20.

Oil, Where is it?
We have no idea . . .

Coltan, Where is it?
We don't know . . .

Oil, coltan, uranium, gold,
Mafia come and take them.
Trust, business, cattle, farms,
Friends come and take them. But
Let us live. Let us live.
We are the human race,
Legal Congolese children,
We want to live. We ask to live.
We ask to live.

What also comes through in this and a number of other poems and songs is the brutal honesty of how the songs define what is happening, often moving from a sense of victimhood to an acknowledgment of the community's own complicity in the suffering. I have already referred to "Une Minute de Silence" and its focus on the Congolese who are responsible for visiting unimaginable atrocities on their own people. Abim's "Let Us Repent, My People" is by far the most honest in its call to "let us examine our ways."[31] Even as Abim acknowledges the complex factors that fuel the conflict in Northern Uganda, he calls the community to remember and thus take responsibility for their past violent behavior in the Luweero War.

Let us repent, my people,
I am calling on you at the top of my voice.
The sons of my mother,
Listen, the daughter of my chief,
Attend to me, you defeated generals.
Put on your mounting garment,
Clean your ears for this.

Listen, you who made other people
Sing funeral songs in times of joy,

31. Abim, *Spill of Blood,* 75–79.

You who forced them to dance without music,
Your sins are haunting your offspring.

You bisected women open
As if you were bisecting chickens,
Oh crazy bastards
And senseless sons of my mother . . .
Do not hide your face, my bull.
Listen here, toothless lion:
Was it not you who fed dogs
With human flesh at Luwero,
You who rubbed your bloody hands
In the mouth of those
Who did not share in your crime?

You pounded babies in a mortar
As you do with sorghum . . .
Were you not the ones who burnt men,
Women and children alive in huts?
The blade of the axe has turned on you . . .

Are we not paying for our sins?
Must we not bear some responsibilities
For our actions?

Turn, my people,
The blood of the innocent cries out.
Repent for what you have done,
Call the elders and carry out your pagan cleansing,
For a bad omen has caught the soul of the country
And an evil spirit has invaded the shrine of life.

In this call for repentance, as in the book of Lamentations, there is a groping for restoration, a longing for a new day, a different future that can only emerge from an honest, repentant, and humble posture. Furthermore, the new day can come only as a gift from "above." "In writing the poems," Abim notes, "there is always an experience of being torn apart. . . . There is a mixture of defeat (despair) and a longing that something will change, a hope that what is going on . . . will soon end. This negative force would become positive. Deep in my heart, I want all of my lament to turn into a song of joy."[32] One perceives a clear sense of that longing turned into expectant anticipation in Abim's "Who Will Lift Me Up?"

> My eyes are weary looking up for help,
> There is none that seems to come.
> Who will lift me up?
> I am thrown in a pit,
> I see no hope,
> I am waiting
> For the one who can lift me up . . .
>
> But who will hold my hand and lead me to peace?
> Who will see my miseries?
> Do I have to expect others to do it for me? Nevertheless, what do they do?
> They want to bury me alive,
> They throw big stones at me,
>
> But who will lift me up?
> I have to lift myself up
> Like a drunkard seeking his way home . . .
> Sitting to cry like a child
> Deprived of his or her meat,
> By a chicken who will not help.
> Yes, no one will wipe away tears!
> Blood continues to flow.

The anticipation of a new day is even more explicit in "The Sun Will Rise," the last poem in *The Spill of Blood*.

> The sun will rise,
> A new day will break,
> It may delay, but it will rise to
> A new day of peace and prosperity.
>
> Our land will be cultivated again,
> Our cattle will increase in number,

32. Bethany House interview.

Our women will be fruitful again,
And a great and holy generation will be born.

The lamentations of my mother will end,
Her grief will cease,
Her sorrows will be ended forever,
Her tears will be tears of joy . . .

La Femme Profanée

Even though we have treated separately the capacity to voice grief, to name the unspeakable, and to express a groping for restoration in the songs and poems from East Africa, these do not exist as separate functions. The three are simply dimensions that are often present together in the same song or poem. In isolating them, my goal has been to highlight the multiple—but obviously complementary—dimensions of the music and poetry that have emerged in the context of war and displacement in Eastern Africa. However, the expression of lament is not limited to music and poetry; it includes other artistic productions, such as sculpture. In a powerful piece of art, *La femme profanée*, Eugene Sanyambo has captured the different dimensions of lament in a way that both illuminates and encapsulates the various aspects of lament that we have been exploring in this chapter.

La femme profanée ("Abused Woman") was erected by the artist in March 2008 at Metanoia High School, run by the Protestant Free University of the Great Lakes (Université libre des pays des grands Lacs [ULPGL]), near Goma.[33]

The woman is naked, which reflects her vulnerability, and is painted white, a reflection of her innocence. Black military boots step on her breasts, arms, and legs, representing the brute force of militarized violence. But the boots

---

33. Eugene Sanyambo was born in Bukavu in 1964. He has explained his interest in art as innate, that it manifested itself at an early age, when he was fascinated by drawing and reading comics. After graduation from secondary school, he moved to Kinshasa to attend the Academy de Beaux Arts. He then began to work in Kinshasa organizations where he would have an opportunity to teach art to others. When he came to Goma, his friend Busange Jean (the other artist who worked on the sculpture with him) helped him get work (particularly sculpting statues) around the city until he secured a job with ULPGL, where he has been working since that time, teaching children aesthetics and drawing (interview by Rebecca Camp, Goma, July 25, 2015; hereafter cited as Goma interview).

La femme profanée. Photo by Sylvestre Kimbese, February 2014.

are empty, signifying the anonymous yet ubiquitous violence of the rebels and other armed gangs. The boots are also torn (with gaping holes where the toes are visible), which, according to Sanyambo, reflects that even the people who perpetrate violence on others are themselves victims.[34] The image of the torn boot is thus a metaphor for the paradoxical "strong-weak," "victim-perpetrator" identity of the child soldiers that Jeff Korondo captured in his song "Okwera Nono."

The position of the woman is also highly symbolic. She is half sitting, half lying down, reflecting the strange "graveyard" existence of the "living dead." The boots hold her feet, arms and chest down, and thus make it impossible for her to breathe, to sit upright, or to stand up. The boot on her breasts not only humiliates her; it also destroys her potential for nurturing care and thus her identity as "mother." She will never be able to feed her children.

On the most obvious level, *La femme profanée* is a lament for the many raped girls and women during the Congo Wars. On a broader level, the woman

34. Goma interview.

La femme profanée. Photo by Rebecca Camp, August 2015.

(weak, exposed) represents all Congolese children, women, and men—all the victims of brutality and violence.[35] On yet another level, *La femme profanée* is the Congo itself. It is significant that the base on which the sculpture rests is the map of the Congo, for it is the Congo, Mother Congo, who has been violated, raped, and brutalized through the endless cycles of war.

Another very powerful symbol of the sculpture is the lamb in the background. According to Sanyambo, "the sheep represents the symbol of Christ. The woman is leaning on Christ, who remains her last refuge. There is no solution for this woman except to take refuge in Jesus, which is our belief as Christians."[36] Therefore, the presence of the lamb provides a Christian interpretative framework, and actually makes the sculpture a kind of *Pietà*—an inverted *Pietà*. For, whereas the mother holds her lifeless son in Michelangelo's *Pietà*, here it is the lamb (son) who holds the lifeless mother!

35. "I saw that women were suffering, but I also saw that men were suffering. I took an enlarged view of the situation. The woman is symbolic. In our culture women are often represented as the more 'feeble,' so I used the figure of the woman to represent weakness—not the weakness of women, specifically, but of all people" (Goma interview).

36. Goma interview.

Left: The base of the sculpture is in the shape of the Democratic Republic of Congo. Right: The artist, Eugene Sanyambo, with his sculpture. Photos by Sylvestre Kimbese.

The Strange Gift of Lament

The aim of this chapter has been to provide a glimpse into the laments that have emerged from Eastern Africa in the context of war. I have presented some of the music and poetry that was written in Northern Uganda during the Lord's Resistance Army War (1986–2006) and in Eastern Congo during the Congo Wars. My aim has not been to offer a thorough analysis of the laments (a task that calls for a full-fledged study on its own). Instead, I have largely let the laments speak for themselves in order to give the reader an opportunity to feel the full range of the writers' emotional pull as they invite us to hear and see the suffering they have witnessed. Allowing the laments to speak lays bare the narrative wreckage of abiding in the ruins. By way of conclusion, I wish to emphasize four points.

Lament as Public

At the end of the preceding chapter on the book of Lamentations, we examined lament as not a simple sentiment but a complex set of sentiments and responses, ways of crying out, seeing, standing, hoping, and groping for restoration in the midst of ruins. We noted the unique gift of lament poetry, that is, its ability to make possible this multilayered agency at a time when the very possibility of agency seems to be threatened by the violence that has shattered the foundations of human existence. The lament songs and poems from Eastern Africa have proven to be such a gift. In their ability to give voice to the grief of the community, to name the ineffable, and to express the deep longing for restoration, they are not only a rich field of agency, but they reveal how and what agency looks like in the context of violence: "If the foundations are destroyed, what can the righteous do?" (Ps. 11:3). In the poetry and songs of lament, one begins to trace an answer to the psalmist's question, namely: "She cries out." Thus, the painful expression of grief is in itself a gift—an odd gift, to be sure—but part of the gift has to do with the fact that this crying out is *public*. In this connection, one cannot help being struck by the fact that a number of lament songs and poems from Eastern Africa became "popular."

What I have noted above with regard to the sonic echo Jeff Korondo's "Gang Otyeko Ling" produced in the community is true in general. His loud and public "wululululu" is similar to the *'ekah* of Lamentations: the cry of mourning for the entire community, the cry that mourns "our home," "our land," "our people," "our culture," "our country." I highlight this public dimension because, especially in the modern and individualistic culture of the West, discussions of lament tend to focus on the individual and on private expressions of grief. Yet the brief exploration of laments in this chapter confirms that a unique gift of the African cultural context is to allow—and even encourage—the public expression of grief, which is able to point to the communal and cosmic bonds of human existence that are threatened by violence.

An Invitation to "See"

As we examine the various songs and poems of lament from Eastern Africa, we cannot but be struck by their brutal honesty. This confirms that behind the ability to find words to express the inexpressible and to name the unnamable is the ability to see truthfully the harsh reality of violence and its effects on all dimensions of human existence. But because violence also often destroys our capacity for truth, truthful seeing is particularly hard, or "bitter," in the context of suffering. And yet, as Abim notes, this bitter herb has to be swallowed.

> For I know truth is bitter,
> As bitter as the calabash seed—keno,
> As bitter as death that kills the chief,
> Like the death of a first-born son.
> Yet it should be swallowed.[37]

37. Abim, *Spill of Blood*, 54–55.

Abim understands his lament poetry as a way of "swallowing" the bitter truth. Other poems invoke the image of "hearing," while others refer to this engagement as a form of "seeing." Thus Baraka's titling his poem "Malheur" is the result of a disciplined gaze on the misfortunes visited on the Congolese child as the result of the senseless fighting. He invites his audience not to "turn away," or overlook, or gloss over the suffering, but to honestly look and see. Hence he introduces each stanza of the poem with a deepening invitation to *voici* ("see"), to *voilà* ("look"), to *regarde* ("behold"), to *tiens* ("grasp"), to *sache* ("understand"). With each invitation he wants the audience to sustain the gaze—and not to turn away from the bitter truth. The hope, of course, is that with the seeing comes understanding, and with understanding comes the assuming of responsibility. The anticipation is thus that seeing truly will bring us to a breaking point, to a moment of "enough is enough," which is the starting point for transformative agency and liberating struggle. Herein lies the power of poetic lament: it forces us to "see"—and thus to assume responsibility and take action.

This is also what makes poetic lament a discipline. For not all poetry or music can bring us to the kind of truthful seeing that Baraka invites the reader into. In fact, music, poetry, and art can also be a form of consolation in that they can provide an escapist route into otherworldliness, a way of turning away and avoiding the bitter truth. This explains Jeff Korondo's critical assessment of the contemporary music scene in Northern Uganda. "Back then, during the troubles," he recently observed, "we sang meaningful songs. Now the young people are singing nonsense, not constructive. . . . The youth simply copy American rap music and Nigerian lewd songs."[38] Implicit in Korondo's critique is the perception that truthful laments, ones that find sonic resonance and echo in the community, the kinds of laments we have been examining here, require attentiveness and disciplined work. Asked how he composed the poems in *The Spill of Blood*, Abim noted:

> At times the poem just overwhelms me, and I cannot sleep until I have written it down. Then I am able to go back to sleep or concentrate on something else. At other times, it keeps at the back of my mind, and I keep working on it, until finally I am able to express it. But that is at times difficult. I do not find the words right away. . . . I keep trying.[39]

38. Bethany House interview (January 2015).

39. Bethany House interview. A similar experience of lament as "working it in" is behind the composition of the Negro spirituals: "I will tell you, it's dis way. My master call me up and

Lament as Theology

One cannot help observing the deep connections between the laments from Eastern Africa and from the book of Lamentations. For just as Daughter Zion and the different voices in Lamentations break into a funeral dirge over the destroyed city—*'ekah*—so Abim notes in the introduction to *The Spill of Blood*, in the context of the war in Northern Uganda: "I cannot but burst into an elegy. I lament and weep as I see the adversaries in the war closing their eyes to the plight of the innocent."[40] As the *'ekah* ("how?") is a voice of protest, the laments we have explored in this chapter reveal a similar protest in the *wululuuu* cries, but also in the implicit—and often not so implicit—"enough is enough." And just as different voices use different metaphors and descriptions in the book of Lamentations to name the destruction, the songs, poems, and artwork from Eastern Africa offer various rich images to name the displacement. Given these and a number of other similarities, it is surprising that Lamentations (or the laments in the book of Psalms) has not played a more explicit role in the church's liturgical and pastoral life in Eastern Africa.[41] For not only would an explicit connection between Lamentations and the social context of Africa provide a rich context and starting point for African theological exploration, the absence of this explicit connection leaves African theology, whether pursued under the dominant aegis of enculturation, liberation, or reconstruction, as an exercise in theological speculation, which fails to connect with the memory and lived experiences of the African peoples.

If theology is about the truth of our lives and how this is connected to our experience of God, then the lament songs, poems, and art represent a crucial theological moment and nexus. These songs and poems do not have a pre-theological content; they are the very content and form of the people's encounter and engagement with God. They are not merely background ma-

---

order me a short peek of corn and a hundred lashes. My friends see it, and it is sorry for me. When dey come to de praise meeting dat night dey sing about it. Some's very good singers and know how; and dey work it in—work it in, you know, till dey get it right, and dat's de way" (see Peter Paris, "When Feeling like a Motherless Child," in *Lament: Reclaiming Practices in the Pulpit, Pew, and Public Square*, ed. Sally A. Brown and Patrick D. Miller (Louisville: Westminster John Knox, 2005), 116.

40. Abim, *Spill of Blood*, 10.

41. In a workshop on Lament, where I read Lamentations with several church leaders, many regretted the fact that this book is not known at all, even though "this is our situation" (Bethany House interview [January 2015]).

terial to our theology; they are the very locus within which the theological experience and expectations of our people are expressed.

Lament as Hope: Beyond Resilience

The notion of resilience has become increasingly popular in the field of trauma healing, where it describes the mechanism by which individuals and communities that have been "hard hit by violence find an innovative way to survive," and even, "against the odds . . . to flourish."[42] In fact, for the Lederachs, resilience is the key to social healing: "Several of these metaphors create an organizing concept—social healing is resilient—that seems particularly important to and for communities living in contexts with sustained patterns of direct and structural violence" (72). The conclusion places resilience within the broad context of one's life journey, where "resiliency suggests that no matter the difficulty of the terrains faced by the traveler, they stay in touch with a core defining essence of being and purpose, and display a tenacity to find a way back as a way forward that artistically stays true to their well-being" (70).

It should be obvious from the overall drift of this chapter that I have benefited greatly from the Lederachs' analysis of the metaphors of place, safety, and voice in *When Blood and Bones Cry Out*. But I am skeptical about their conclusion that resilience is the key to social healing. I am particularly unconvinced about the notion of resilience as something internally generated, an "inner quality" that is "needed to survive extreme conditions yet retains the capacity to find a way back to experience the defining quality of being and the essence of purpose" (68). For what the poems and songs from East Africa display is a sense of utter helplessness; and in that desperation the voices and pleas are directed beyond themselves—and beyond their communities—to an invisible and, at the moment, silent power, to God or Allah. Jeff Korondo's "Gang Otyeko Ling," as well as a number of other poems and songs, express the plea quite explicitly:

> Where do we turn to? Our home is quiet,
> We have left our homes, it pains my heart.
> Sleeping in hideouts to save our generation.

42. Lederach and Lederach, *Blood and Bones*, 69. Hereafter, page references to this work appear in parentheses within the text.

Oh! Our North, full of problems!
God in heaven, please save us today! Allah, you are great, save us!

This turning to a power beyond, to a "God heaven" or to "Allah," may, of course, reflect the deep religiosity of African communities and peoples. But even those songs and psalms that do not appeal to God directly are still very "psalmic" in the sense that they involve an implicit cry ("hear me, O God"). Dorothée Sölle is correct when she notes that the first language out of suffering is psalmic. By this she means that the first agency within suffering is "finding a language that leads out of the uncomprehended suffering that makes one mute, a language of lament, crying, of pain, a language that at least says what the situation is." Such language, according to Sölle, does not simply reflect a similar genre and structure as the psalms of lament, but more specifically the fact that behind the anguished cry and lament is a "hear me, O God."[43]

This observation is definitely true with respect to the laments from East Africa. But what this means is that what we are witnessing in these songs, psalms and works of art is not resilience, "the capacity by which communities hard hit by violence find an innovative way to survive." What we are encountering in the songs and poems is not simply "adaptability, resourcefulness, and a capacity to face and creatively negotiate risky situations" (Lederachs, 69). What we are witnessing is an anguished turning to God as captured by the popular lament of the women from Uvira:

Wamama wanaliliya eee [repeat]
Twende mbele eee [repeat]
Vita inasimama aa
Turudi nyuma aa [repeat]
Umaskini unatusongaa
Ngambo na ngambo [repeat]
ubakaji una simama

Women are crying.
When we go forward, war;
When we turn back, famine;
When we go on the side,
the rapists are waiting.

43. Dorothée Sölle, *Suffering*, trans. Everett R. Kalin (Philadelphia: Fortress, 1975), 70–72.

> Stretch a tent over us, oh Lord, so that we may not be blown away by the
> wind. [repeat]
> During the time of hardship, Father, so that we may not be blown away by
> the wind,
> During the time of war, Father, so that we may not be blown away by the
> wind,
> During the time of threat we may stand firm.
> Place the cover upon us, Lord, so that we may not be blown away by the
> wind. [repeat]
> Because of poverty we may not be blown away by the wind. [repeat]

In this song the women express their feelings about having nowhere to turn. Their only refuge is God, whom they entreat to provide shelter (a tent). The God envisioned in this lament is a powerful and protective God who is able to stretch a tent over the frightened, crying, and battered women. But in other instances, the God they turn to is, ironically, ineffective and weak, unable to offer shelter from the violence. In fact, this God is herself a fellow sufferer, the victim of violence, like the lamb on which Sanyambo's *La femme profanée* is leaning. And when Sanyambo claims that this (slain) lamb is "the last refuge that will take *la femme profanée* out of her misery," he is offering a profound theological commentary, namely, that whenever people suffer, God suffers with them. In the words of Sölle, "Where no help is possible [Christ] appears not as the superior helper but only as the one who walks with those beyond help."[44]

The reflection on the laments from East Africa thus brings us to the same conclusion and to the doorstep of a profound theological mystery in the same way as the book of Lamentations does: namely, what we encounter in lament is not simply a silent God but a suffering and vulnerable God. In the following pages we need to explore in greater depth the reality of the God of lament in order to uncover the possibility and form of agency that might be generated in the anguished turning to God in lament. We do so by focusing on the psalms of lament.

44. Sölle, *Suffering*, 177.

PART THREE

The God of Lament

CHAPTER 5

The Psalms of Lament and the Silence of God

How long, O God, will you hide your face?

Psalm 13:1

I have suggested earlier that there were many lament forms in the Ancient Near East that developed over time as a way for people to express the unbearable suffering they had experienced or were experiencing. When the Israelites sought to give expression to the unspeakable pain they endured, they drew largely on the repertoire of lament forms, images, and metaphors that were available to them. Perhaps it should not be surprising to note that Israel's laments are not limited to the book of Psalms. Laments pervade the entire Hebrew Scripture and are an essential part of what the Bible says happened between God and the people. The psalms of lament in the psalter constitute only a portion of the laments contained in the Old Testament.[1]

At the heart of Israel's social, political, and religious life is the central conviction and experience of Yahweh as a saving God. Yahweh is not only the creator of the world and sovereign ruler of nations; Israel is God's chosen nation, which, through a covenant relationship, enjoys God's special favor and protection. For biblical Israel, therefore, safety and security are found not in military strength or wealth or technological advantage, but in the covenant relationship with Yahweh. Thus in the moment of crisis, because they believed

---

1. Claus Westermann identifies three stages in the history of the lament: the short laments of the early period (e.g., Gen. 25:22; 27:46; Judg. 15:18; 21:2–3); the rhythmically structured laments of the psalms; and the laments of the prose prayers of the later period (Ezra 9; Neh. 9) (*Praise and Lament in the Psalms* [Atlanta: John Knox, 1981], 23).

that God can, should—and indeed, would—do something to save them, they complained, mourned, wept, chanted dirges, and cursed. They praised God, but they also assailed the ears of God, protesting God's continued silence and pressing God for deliverance.

However, the fact that laments pervade the Old Testament, and that they are an essential part of what the Bible says about what happened between humans and God, points to a similarity between the African and biblical contexts; and it points to another possible reason why many African Christians relate quite readily to the Old Testament. This observation pushes us to probe the biblical experience of lament more deeply by raising a number of questions that are relevant for Christians in Africa today. How did Old Testament communities and individuals relate to God in the midst of storms, upheavals, and moments of suffering? How did they express their lament? What form did these cries to God take? How did they live with God when things did not get better? What did they discover about God and God's love, promises, and covenant through the experience of suffering? These and similar questions invite a close investigation of the concept of lament and its presence in the Old Testament, especially in the book of Psalms. This is especially necessary if we are to more fully appreciate how the cry of lament is not a cry of despair but is a form of hope that involves turning to God. This conclusion itself will bring us to inquire not only into Israel's relationship with God, but the nature of God that is revealed through the cry of lament. A closer look at the psalms of lament offers us a good place to start this conversation.

The Psalms of Lament

A Book of Praises

Glenn Pemberton's *Hurting with God: Learning to Lament with the Psalms* makes a number of observations that can help us understand the central role that the psalms of lament played in Israel's life and worship. The first observation is that the book of Psalms is composed of a total of 150 psalms, representing the different categories of praise, royal psalms, thanksgiving, and laments. Sixty of these are known as psalms of lament (or 40 percent of all psalms). What is remarkable about this observation is that, while psalms of praise constitute almost 30 percent of the total and psalms of thanksgiving about 18 percent, the largest category of psalms is the psalms of lament. This is all the more surprising when one realizes that the book of Psalms is, in fact, a book of *praises*.[2]

Another key characteristic of the psalms of lament is suggested by the English title, the "book of praises." "Psalm" is derived from the Greek *psalmoi*, which means (instrumental) music and the words accompanying the music. This points to both the *musical* characteristics (sung) and the *liturgical* context (for use in public worship). By this observation I mean to point out that the psalms of lament are not simply private prayers but the public and communal voice of the worshiping assembly.

I point to these characteristics to highlight lament as the inner core of Israel's social and religious life. To the extent that the social, religious, and political life of the Israel community centered on God and worship, it is framed and saturated by lament. A closer look at the internal structure of the lament psalms provides further critical insights into the central role of lament in Israel's faith experience.

The Contours of Lament: Their Inner Structure

Scholars generally recognize five elements within the structure of the lament psalms:

(1) Address: It is an invocation of Yahweh confirming lament as a prayer directed to God.
(2) Complaint: The description of the problem, which might range from mild concerns (e.g., Pss. 4, 26, 61, 120) to desperation concerning overwhelming difficulties (Pss. 39, 79) and life-threatening disease (Pss. 6, 38); from complaints about an enemy to accusations against God (Pss. 44, 88, 89).
(3) Request: The laments do not simply complain; they ask for a specific response from God, to whom the cry is directed.
(4) Motivation: This articulates the reason God should help, which might range from an assertion of righteousness to appeals to God's own character and mercy.

---

2. The Hebrew title for the book is *Sepher Tehilim*, the "book of praises." Thus Israel's hymnal, her book of praises, is by and large a book of lament! See Glenn Pemberton, *Hurting with God: Learning to Lament with the Psalms* (Abilene, TX: Abilene Christian University Press, 2012), 27.

(5) Confidence/praise: This is a confession of trust in God's help or assurance of God's assistance.

These elements do not exist in any particular pattern, and certainly not all the elements exist in every lament psalm (e.g., Ps. 88 completely lacks confidence). On the whole, however, the psalms of lament will bring together these elements, which are best exemplified in Psalm 13:

> *Address:*
> "How long, O Lord . . ."
> *Complaint:*
> "Will you forget me forever?"
> "How long will you hide your face from me?
> How long must I take counsel in my soul
> and have sorrow in my heart all the day?
> How long shall my enemy be exalted over me?"
> *Request:*
> "Consider and answer me, O Lord my God;
> light up my eyes."
> Motivation:
> "Light up my eyes, lest I sleep the sleep of death,
> lest my enemy say, 'I have prevailed over him,'
> lest my foes rejoice because I am shaken.
> But I have trusted in your steadfast love;
> my heart shall rejoice in your salvation."
> *Confidence:*
> "I will sing to the Lord,
> because he has dealt bountifully with me."

Turning toward and around God

That the psalms of lament follow a recognizable pattern or structure confirms that biblical lament is not simply a form of unrestrained speech; it is structured prayer. But the presence of a clear structure, with recognizable elements, also points to a series of "internal transitions" within the lament—from cry, to petition, to confession of trust, to praise. And though in Psalm 13 the elements follow one after another, the elements need not and quite often do not exist in any particular pattern. At any rate, the various elements cannot be understood as phases that progress along a linear trajectory. Instead, they are rather like "contours"[3] that reflect a kind of circling around (to use John Lederach and Angela Lederach's metaphor[4]); a movement in and out. The movement is not only a "turning toward God"; it is also a "turning around God," which reflects an underlying intimacy with God. Scott Ellington notes:

> A relationship of trust, intimacy, and love is a necessary precondition for genuine lament. When the biblical writers lament they do so from within the context of a foundational relationship that binds together the individual with members of the community of faith and that community with their God.[5]

Ellington's observation suggests that biblical lament, to use a different image, reflects deep immersion in the covenant relationship with God and with the community of faith. This observation is important because the loss of lament in our time (more on this later) may simply reflect the loss of a deep covenant relationship with God and with a community of faith.

The combined effect of the above observations is to bring us closer to a good definition of biblical lament, identified first by what it is not, and second, by its distinct characteristics. Biblical lament is not unrestrained speech; it is not simply a form of venting or whining; neither is it a phase or necessary step in the healing or grieving process. Biblical lament is a structured and "complex language of complaint, protest and appeal *directed to* God."[6] And the fact that

3. Pemberton, *Hurting with God*, 61–66.

4. John Paul Lederach and Angela Jill Lederach, *When Blood and Bones Cry Out: Journeys through the Soundscape of Healing and Reconciliation* (Oxford: Oxford University Press, 2010).

5. Scott A. Ellington, *Risking Truth: Reshaping the World through the Prayers of Lament* (Eugene, OR: Pickwick, 2008), 7.

6. Pemberton, *Hurting with God*, 30. This is the closest I come to a definition of lament, which points to the relationship with God as the one nonnegotiable characteristic of lament theologically understood. After citing my work on lament in the introduction of their book, Eva Harasta and Brian Brock note that "though there is a resurgence of interest in practical theologies of lament . . . these theologies ignore crucial theoretical problems. In effect, they commend lament to the church without saying what it is." See *Evoking Lament: A Theological Discussion*, ed. Eva Harasta and Brian Brock (New York: T&T Clark, 2009), 1. While I see that this has been the case with my work, I am not sure that the chapters in *Evoking Lament* succeed in offering a definition of lament. But I am not even sure that we need a strict definition of lament, because I think that the experience of lament is better described than defined. For as Bruno Shah notes, "as a practical dynamic of Christian mystery, 'lament' is often better left for the poet's, the mystic's, or the phenomenologist's *description*, not the analyst's or taxonomist's technically absolute *definition*. Theoretical intelligibility surely needs be proffered, even

biblical lament is *directed to God* makes it a distinct *faith* language, with its own vocabulary and grammar for intimate and difficult conversations with the Lord, a way "'to hurt with God' when one is in the midst of a storm."[7]

Lament and Praise

Another important observation connected to the movement, or "circling around," of biblical lament is that lament often moves into praise—a point underscored by the fact that lament constitutes a large part of Israel's "book of praises" (some 40 percent). This observation confirms that, for the worshiping community, no sharp distinction exists between lament and praise. The laments and the thanksgiving songs belong together within Israel's experience and her worship of God. Moreover, the fact that the elements of fear/trust, need/confidence, doubt/faith, sorrow/joy, and death/life are often woven together in one psalm highlights another key feature of biblical faith: the confidence to voice before God the entire gamut of one's experience and emotions. This confidence is born out of the covenant relationship, within which to assume that there could be a relationship with God in which there was only praise and never lamentation would be to fall short not only of filial relationship of the covenant experience but of humanity's creaturely existence.[8]

The shift from lament to praise within the lament psalms also points to another significant feature: that lament and praise are not simply juxtaposed.

---

as it proceeds from praxis, if communities of knowledge and love are to share their wisdom beyond the confines of local contexts, let alone remain rooted in history and tradition. But concomitantly . . . there is a kind of apophasis involved in the praxis of lament. Experientially, the nature of lament is such as to blur basic lines of categorical distinction. 'Lament' bleeds between notions of 'cry' and 'call,' between boundaries of individual and communal, and between relations amongst believers and relations to Jesus. Lament opens a fissure in the sepulchral bedrock of human understanding, over whose dark abyss the Spirit blows, and out of which Jesus rises as the life of final truth. As a result, lament is a place of graced encounter with the one who is coming in judgment (and who is indeed already near), while unveiling the new creation." See Bruno M. Shah, OP, "The Apocalyptic Wound of Lament: The Cry and Call of Hope" (unpublished PhD paper, University of Notre Dame, Fall 2015), 13.

7. Pemberton, *Hurting with God*, 26, 75.

8. Closely connected with this observation is the relationship between lament and thanksgiving. Elaborating on this connection, Pemberton notes: "Thanksgiving and lament not only grow from the same soil of faith but are part of the same organism. The practice of thanksgiving grows out of the prior practice of lament, so that loss of lament actually threatens a second type of faith talk: thanksgiving" (Pemberton, *Hurting with God,* 26).

Often, with rather an unexpected movement, lament turns into praise, and the speaker breaks into song: "I will sing to the Lord, because he has dealt bountifully with me" (Ps. 13:6). Such a transformation generates a "fresh perspective and new language . . . so that the song of praise that follows lament is not the same language as the praise that precedes it. This new song is shaped by the memory of pain and the silence of God, and bears witness to the memory even in the midst of praise." Therefore, the possibility of lament turning into praise "reflects a transformation and innovation, a novelty that is only possible with the articulation of both pain and belief."[9]

Biblical lament, then, has the potential to bring one to a new place, to a new depth, and thus to a new song of praise, which is qualitatively different from the praise before. This new place is also a kind of seeing, not simply in terms of mental insight, but in the sense of a depth of knowing and experience. It is this kind of seeing that Job points to when he notes: "I had heard of you by the hearing of the ear, but now my eye sees you" (Job 42:5). It is as if Job is saying that, through his experience of loss, abiding uncertainty, and unrelieved suffering—and his relentless turning toward and around God—he has come to "see" in a new way. It is this kind of seeing generated by way of anguished turning toward and around God that is the basis of an odd and yet profound song of praise. We will meet this same kind of seeing in Jeremiah, the weeping prophet (see Chapter 7), as a way of knowing: *yada'*, which means a close and intimate relationship with God. It is this kind of seeing that Christopher Munzihirwa (Chapter 8) is hinting at when he claims that "there are things that can be seen only by eyes that have cried."[10]

Finally, the fact that lament would turn into or conclude with a vow of praise (as it does in Psalm 13) suggests the inner connection between lament and hope in the biblical psalms. Far from being a cry of despair, biblical lament brings together lament and hope, and confirms that the two are "twin sisters," or, in the words of C. Clifton Black, that "the spine of lament is hope" and that lament is "the deep and irrepressible conviction, in the teeth of present evidence, that God has not severed the umbilical cord that has always bound us to the Lord."[11]

---

9. Ellington, *Risking Truth*, 28.

10. John Allen, *The Global War on Christians: Dispatches from the Front Lines of Anti-Christian Persecution* (New York: Image, 2013), 49.

11. Pemberton, *Hurting with God*, 73, citing C. Clifton Black, "The Persistence of Wounds," in *Lament: Reclaiming Practices in Pulpit, Pew, and Public Square*, ed. Sally A. Brown and Patrick D. Miller (Louisville: Westminster John Knox, 2005), 54.

Complaint as Both Lifeblood and "Risk" of Covenant

Complaint is a key element within the biblical lament. As already noted, the element of complaint in the lament psalms ranges from an expression of mild concerns (Pss. 4, 26, 61, 120) to desperation due to overwhelming difficulties (Pss. 39, 79) and life-threatening disease (Pss. 6, 38); from complaint about one's enemies to protests of innocence (Pss. 7, 26). The overwhelming presence of the language of complaint, questioning, and protest in the Psalms suggests that Israel understood complaint as an essential dimension of the covenant relationship. It is not those who lack faith who complain, but those recognized for strong faith who bring their most honest and passionate feelings to God. Dobbs-Allsopp observes:

> Complaint reaffirms the radically relational nature of the divine-human relationship that undergirds biblical faith. There is of course no question as to God's ultimate sovereignty in this relationship. But the prominent role of lament and complaint . . . reminds God that God's sovereignty is exercised to the benefit of God's covenant partner, and therefore not only does it tolerate human input, it requires it.[12]

It is within this context that complaint is understood as the lifeblood of the biblical notion of covenant: it ensures that the relationship is alive, dynamic, and open. Here faith is real, contested, actively negotiated. Complaint is "the material base from which power of God is activated to transform, destabilize, and reorder the world.[13]

Once the full implications of this observation are grasped, it becomes obvious that lament not only reflects and affirms the covenant relationship, it also puts it at risk. In *Risking Truth*, Scott Ellington notes that to lament is to embark on a journey of a double risk.[14] The first risk has to do with the complaint of lament as a form of protest, which destroys the conventional, stable language in addressing God. To lament is to refuse to accept things as they are; it is to protest God's continued silence, and to press God for deliverance. One who laments challenges God: "How long, O God?" "Why must I go about mourning?" "Why do you hide your face?" Using these and similar

---

12. F. W. Dobbs-Allsopp, *Lamentations*, Interpretation series (Louisville: John Knox, 2002), 38.

13. Dobbs-Allsopp, *Lamentations*, 38–39, quoting Walter Brueggemann.

14. Ellington, *Risking Truth*, xi.

complaints, the laments proclaim boldly that not everything is all right. God has not delivered; he has hidden his face from the people. No question seems illegitimate, and no expression of doubt off-limits. Thus the complaints about God's inactivity or silence range from nagging questions about God' presence (Pss. 13, 108); to complaints about God's not being faithful to his promises (Pss. 44, 88, 89); to accusations about God's assault. The sentiment of God as an enemy, which we encountered in Lamentations, is expressed in a number of psalms of lament, for example, Psalm 39:9–10: "You are the one who did this. Remove your scourge from me, I am overcome by the blow of your hand" (NIV).

But lament involves another risk. The complaints and accusations of God do not take place in a corner, confined to the heart of the sufferer; they spill out in groans, pleas, and shouts before God and the assembled congregation. This kind of complaint cannot but risk the dismantling of a stable, though dysfunctional, rendering of reality, with no assurance of being able to offer something enduring in its place. Thus Ellington notes:

> To lament is to face loss and to admit openly that things have gone horribly wrong. . . . Lament is to cast into doubt, to challenge, and perhaps even finally to reject the "standing answers" that heretofore had provided a framework in which to understand God. Lament reaches toward the hiddenness of God, rejecting every pious platitude that insists that everything is as it should be and raising fundamental questions about God's faithfulness and justice.[15]

It is for this reason that lament involves the risk of "newness." In refusing to accept things as they are, in protesting the conventional, stable, and safe forms of addressing God, the one who laments abandons the known world and any vestiges of order and refuge that it provides. This requires courage and a leap into the abyss. For what is clear from the foregoing discussion is that the lamenter's complaint puts God on the spot, and in so doing runs the risk that God may neither answer nor move, that his silence will endure. That is why, for Ellington, looming behind many of the biblical laments is the basic question: "Can this God still be trusted? . . . Open lament risks exposing a new reality, that the God who brought his people out of Egypt and into the land of the promise no longer is a God who saves."[16]

15. Ellington, *Risking Truth*, xi–xii.
16. Ellington, *Risking Truth*, 3–4.

I have found Ellington's attention to the double risk in the complaints of lament extremely insightful, even though I do not think that it is God's saving ability that is put at risk by the lamenter's complaint. In this connection, the message of Psalm 39, quoted above, is instructive, though not unique. For even as the psalmist accuses God of acting like an enemy in verses 9–10 ("You are the one who did this. Remove your scourge from me, I am overcome by the blow of your hand"), just two verses before that accusation he had prayed, "And now, Lord, what future do I have? You are my only hope" (v. 7).

But what is at stake, and thus at risk, is the kind of future relationship and experience with God and the uncertainty of what that might look like. In other words, even though the covenant relationship with God is the central resource in the psalms of lament, and their writers frequently draw on memories of God's deliverance in the past as they searched for a fresh experience of God in the present crisis, there is always a risk that the experience of suffering and crisis may reveal a totally new, totally strange, totally unexpected God, not simply one who confirms but also one who destabilizes the past experience of God.

Thus, the fact that God quite often remains silent and hidden in the midst of the people's anguished cries for deliverance raises serious questions, not so much about God's saving power, but about what kind of God would remain silent and unresponsive to the peoples' pleas. Might God's silence point to a God who may be in some ways "powerless" in the face of human evil? Might God's silence point to a mysterious facet of God—not an uncaring and unmoved God, but a God who himself suffers and laments with his people? If we grasp this possibility, then what begins to emerge from the background of biblical lament is the reality of a vulnerable and suffering God. We need to explore, even if briefly, the biblical evidence for this conclusion and to perceive its far-reaching theological, social, and practical implications.

The God of Lament

A comprehensive discussion of the nature and reality of God's pathos within the biblical tradition would take us beyond the scope of this work.[17] So it will suffice here to make a few broad references and observations. I have already noted that biblical lament is grounded in and made possible by the covenant relationship. However, the fact that God binds himself in a love (covenant)

17. See, e.g., Abraham Joseph Heschel, *The Prophets*, 2 vols. (New York: Harper and Row, 1969–71).

relationship with Israel opens God up to the possibility of God's own lament. The biblical tradition bears witness to this fact in a number of ways. Already in Genesis, after the Fall, the Bible presents a God who is searching for his errant creation: "the Lord God called to the man and said to him, 'Where are you?'" (Gen. 3:9). In Exodus, the dramatic story of the liberation from Egypt is set in motion by a God who cannot bear to see Israel suffer ("I have surely seen the affliction of my people who are in Egypt and have heard their cry" [Exod. 3:7]). The prophets, in particular, speak of a God who is compelled by his compassion for his people. Isaiah describes God as a new mother who cannot help but respond to the cries of her baby (Isa. 49:15). Jeremiah, the weeping prophet, so identified with God in the pain concerning the failed covenant that it is hard to tell the prophet's tears from God's (Jer. 8:18–9:11). Hosea, in his own dramatic way, depicts the prophet's identification with God's anguish via the metaphor of a failed marriage. The failed marriage of the prophet mirrors God's failed marriage to Israel, God's adulterous bride. Even then, God can only grieve, because he cannot give her up:

> How can I give you up, O Ephraim,
>> How can I hand you over, O Israel . . . ?
> My heart recoils within me;
>> my compassion grows warm and tender. (Hos. 11:8)

The prophets, particularly Jeremiah and Hosea, are called to announce God's pathos, which they do, both in words and gestures, such that their lives take on the form and shape of God's lament. However, not only do the prophets reflect God's own lament, it is revealing that God's laments also begin to sound increasingly (in structure and form) like the human prayers of lament: "Woe to you, O Jerusalem! How long will it be before you are made clean?" (Jer. 13:27). "Why do you seek further beatings? Why do you continue to rebel?" (Isa. 1:5).

The same God who bound himself in the covenantal relationship with Israel in the Old Testament is the incarnate God, whom we have come to know in the New Testament as Emmanuel ("God with us"), thus bringing the possibility and reality of divine pathos to an unprecedented level. Thus, Jesus not only weeps at the death of Lazarus (John 11:35) and over Jerusalem (which I will also discuss below); but his cry from the cross, using a psalm of lament (Ps. 22:1: "My God, my God, why have you forsaken me?"), brings to full circle God's identification with suffering humanity. Accordingly, in their allegorical interpretation of the Psalms, the early church fathers saw prefigured, not only in Psalm 22 but in other psalms, Christ's—and thus God's—own cry on the cross.[18] But in this interpretation, the church fathers were merely affirming God's total identification with suffering humanity through the incarnation, which finds its ultimate expression on the cross.

This brief overview shows that the silence of God in the psalms of lament cannot be interpreted as that of an uncaring God. On the contrary, God's silence may point to a God who stands with his people in their suffering, and thus suffers and laments with them. This is perhaps why, far from being a source for resignation and despair, the notion of a vulnerable and suffering God yields immense personal, social, and political possibilities, as a number of historical and theological considerations confirm.

Hurting with God

The African-American gospel songs are some of the most powerful expressions of the black slaves' faith, and they can be heard as a testament of faith that God was present with those slaves, even while they were living in the "whirling vortex of Godforsakenness."[19] These songs of lament are saturated with sorrow and agony, and they reflect the harsh conditions of slavery. And yet, for all their inevitable sadness, slave songs are characterized by a spirit of resistance, confidence, and hope. For the slave communities, what made the "confidence" possible was not only the slaves' belief in God's determination to free his people (in this connection, the story of Moses and Israel's liberation from Egypt was a powerful and imaginative model as it was told and retold within the slave quarters); but, more specifically, their identification of their own suffering with Christ's forsakenness on the cross. Therefore, a number of spirituals allude to the crucifixion, thereby conveying that the slaves were confident that Jesus understood them because he knew misery and anguish

18. On the christological interpretation of the Psalms, including all the controversies surrounding such interpretations in the early church, see Richard Price, "The Voice of Christ in the Psalms," in *Meditations of the Heart: The Psalms in the Early Christian Thought and Practice*, ed. Andreas Andreopoulos, Augustine Casiday, and Carol Harrison (Turnhout, Belgium: Brepols, 2011), 1–16. For a full-length study of the evocations of the psalms of lament, with particular reference to Mark's Gospel, see esp. Stephen A. Ahearne-Kroll, *The Psalms of Lament in Mark's Passion: Jesus' Davidic Suffering*, Society for the Study of the New Testament Series (Cambridge, UK: Cambridge University Press, 2007). Both Augustine and Origen are specific in interpreting Psalm 22 as referring to Jesus Christ; see, e.g., Augustine's *Expositions on the Book of Psalms*, vol. 1 (New York: Augustinian Heritage Institute, 2000).

19. David Emmanuel Goatley, *Were You There? Godforsakenness in Slave Religion* (Maryknoll, NY: Orbis, 1996), 72.

from his life and violent death. They resonated with the agony of Jesus's crucifixion in their songs, which were, in turn, the source and reason for their endurance and hope.[20]

It was precisely for this reason that the spirituals played a key role in inspiring, mobilizing, and giving voice to the civil rights movement. The "freedom songs" were essentially new versions of the Negro spirituals, with updated lyrics that reflected the specific needs of the civil rights movement. Commenting on the role of those songs during the Albany Movement, Martin Luther King Jr. observed: "The freedom songs are playing a strong and vital role in our struggle. They give the people new courage and a sense of unity. I think they keep alive a faith, a radiant hope, in the future, particularly in our most trying hours."[21] In the most trying hours, the civil rights activists, just as the slaves before them, found consolation and the determination to overcome their bondage in the fact of God's own bondage and suffering.[22]

Dietrich Bonhoeffer, who was formed by the pathos of the songs of the black congregation of the Abyssinian Baptist Church in Harlem when he was a student at Union Seminary, was to find similar consolation and determination in the "helplessness of God" as he sat in the prison cell in Germany awaiting execution. In a letter to Eberhard Bethge (July 18, 1944), he wrote from his prison cell:

> Before God and with God we live without God. He is weak and powerless in the world, and that is precisely the way, the only way, in which he is with us and helps us. . . . Here is the decisive difference between Christianity and other religions. Man's religiosity makes him look in his distress to the power of God in the world: God is *deus ex machina*. The Bible directs man to God's powerlessness and suffering; only the suffering of God can help. [23]

20. Goatley, *Were You There?* 66. See, e.g., "Crucifixion": "Dey crucified my Lord an' He never said a mumbalin' word" (66–67, citing James Weldon Johnson, *The Book of American Negro Spirituals,* 174–76).

21. See "Songs and the Civil Rights Movements," Martin Luther King Jr. and the Global Freedom Struggle: http://mlk-kppo1.stanford.edu/index.php/encyclopedia/encyclopedia/enc_songs_and_the_civil_rights_movement (accessed Dec. 3, 2015).

22. Thus, in his book *Why We Can't Wait* (New York: Harper and Row, 1964), calling songs "the soul of the movement," King observes that civil rights activists "sing the freedom songs today for the same reason the slaves sang them, because we too are in bondage and the songs add hope to our determination that 'We shall overcome, Black and white together, We shall overcome someday'" (86).

23. Bonhoeffer, "Letter to Eberhard Bethge," July 21, 1944, in *Letters and Papers from Prison* (New York: Macmillan, 1972), 370.

And just as with the black slaves, the "helplessness of God" on the cross, for Bonhoeffer, does not lead to resignation. Instead, it is a motivation for an even deeper commitment to the affairs of life: "By living unreservedly in life's duties, problems, success and failures, experiences and perplexities, we throw ourselves completely into the arms of God, taking seriously, not our own suffering, but those of God in the world. . . . This is how one becomes a man and a Christian."[24]

For Jürgen Moltmann, the fact of the "crucified God" is both the foundation and critical measure of true Christian theology, since the suffering of Christ is not peripheral to the nature of God but essentially defines it. "When the crucified Jesus is called 'the image of the invisible God,' the meaning is that *this* is God, and God is like *this*."[25] But what makes this the central point of a unique Christian soteriology for Moltmann is the fact that the suffering and death of God on the cross is the key point of contact between God and humanity. As Ellington suggests, with respect to Moltmann's theology, "God's ability and decision to love people opened him to the experience of suffering that comes with choosing a faithless love. But it is precisely God's willingness to love and to suffer that gives his presence meaning in the face of profound human suffering."[26]

Even though William Stacy Johnson finds Moltmann's thesis of divine

---

24. Bonhoeffer, *Letters*, 370.

25. Moltmann, *The Crucified God: The Cross of Christ as the Foundation and Criticism of Christian Theology* (New York: Harper and Row, 1974), 177.

26. Ellington, *Risking Truth*, 39. Here is not the place to engage in a full discussion of Moltmann's theology of hope. For other extensive and helpful discussions of it, especially in its popularized form in the United States, see Margaret B. Adam's chapter on "Moltmannian Hope," in *Our Only Hope: More than We Can Ask or Imagine* (Eugene, OR: Pickwick, 2013). While noting that Moltmannian hope does not represent the nuances and more complex argument of Moltmann's work (56), Adam argues that Moltmannian hope may easily slip into a popular, modern version of hope as steady improvement brought about by human determination and effort. To counteract this tendency, Adam proposes a Thomistic understanding of hope, grounded in the practice of love and friendship with God. The latter not only retains an essential eschatological dimension, it mediates the belief of God's unchanging compassion through the formation and practice of virtue, which makes possible creative agency and perseverance in the face of failure, suffering and when there is "no hope" for things to get better. On the whole I find Adam's critique of Moltmannian hope compelling. I find particularly insightful her attention to lament and disability (the other discourses she points to being nihilism and indeterminacy, and feminism) as discourses through which the theological grammar of hope can be articulated. In this connection, it is especially telling that in addition to resources in Hebrew Scripture, she identifies the lives of saints and martyrs (183) as exemplars of "unhopeful hope," which in itself points to the very essence of theological hope (see Chapter 13 below).

abandonment to be based on an isolated and narrow exegesis of Jesus's so-called cry of dereliction in the Gospel of Mark—"My God, My God, why have you forsaken me"—he arrives at a similar christological conclusion and affirmation of the cross as a manifestation of the divine pathos foregrounded in the incarnation.[27] Thus Johnson notes: "If it is true that in Jesus Christ the eternal word became flesh, then in Jesus' cry of death, the God of life is also crying. . . . In being one with Jesus in his agony, the incarnate God cries out from the cross" (86). Indeed, Johnson notes, what is revealed in the life, death, and resurrection of Jesus of Nazareth is this: "God is as Jesus is; God does as Jesus does; God suffers as Jesus suffers. Indeed, God cries as Jesus cries" (88).

Perhaps what is even more striking is that both Moltmann and Johnson draw the same practical and ethical conclusion from Jesus's cry on the cross. Johnson notes: "Jesus' cry is the decisive divine embrace of the fragility, suffering, and despair that mark the human condition. Indeed, God is never more divine than in God's determination to be our God even unto incarnation, humiliation, and death" (86). What both Moltmann and Johnson suggest is that, if we understand God as incarnate, what he "incarnated was the cry of the people. He became the cry."[28] And since God has made our situation God's own, God is urging us to pay heed to the cries of our neighbors. "It is not enough to confront the cry of Jesus Christ with the resources of exegetical and theological wisdom. To heed Jesus' cry is to give ourselves to it in passionate, pastoral, practical response" (Johnson, 91).

It is a similar conclusion that Richard Wall draws from Moltmann's *The Crucified God*. About Moltmann's theology, Wall says:

> [It] is a plea for Christians to enter into the suffering that God has already entered into, and not remain passive or complacent as outside, "objective" (i.e., apathetic) observers of the human condition. If God does not remain

27. William Stacy Johnson, "Jesus' Cry, God's Cry, and Ours," in Brown and Miller, eds., *Lament: Reclaiming Practices*, 80–94. That cry, which is Psalm 22, is not, Johnson notes, a cry of abandonment but a prayer for deliverance. It is not a cry directed against God, but to God (81). Johnson's argument is that, whereas Jesus cries out only the first line of Psalm 22, a full appreciation of this cry must take into account the whole Psalm, which in fact reveals the psalmist, in his anguish, turning toward God. In his turning, the psalmist recalls (as a motivation for God's answer) how the righteous ones in the past have called on God and have been delivered (vv. 4–5); and—again typical of psalms of lament—a final confident declaration that "God did not hide his face from me but heard me when I cried to him" (v. 24b). Hereafter, page references to this work appear in parentheses within the text.

28. Jim Perkinson, "Theology and the City: Learning to Cry, Struggling to See," *Cross Currents* 51, no. 1 (2001): 95–114, at 113.

above the plane of history dispassionately observing the suffering of the Son on the cross, but is radically "in Christ," involved in and affected by that suffering . . . then we too (as followers of God) must enter into the suffering of our world. In this respect, the cross becomes not only the critique of *all* utopian dreams, but the ground for resurrection, and thus for all hope.[29]

In "The Hidden God," David Tracy argues in the same direction and arrives at a similar conclusion.[30] God's revelation, Tracy notes, is principally through hiddenness. However, Tracy notes that the hidden God is not only humble but humiliated: *deus incarnatus, deus absconditus in passionibus.* The hidden God is *deus crucifixus,* a crucified God.[31] Significantly, Tracy draws the same practical conclusion as do Moltmann, Johnson, and Bonhoeffer: God's hiddenness "drives the Christian not to further theological speculation but to the cross" and to the "memory of suffering and the struggle by, for, and with 'others' especially the forgotten and marginal ones in history."[32] Tracy comes back to this conclusion in a number of other places in his "correlation theology." The role of all correlation theology, Tracy writes, "is to help alleviate the suffering with the resources of the Christian gospel. . . . When the cry of suffering is principally political or social, theology . . . will turn into a political and liberation theology correlating the Christian call for liberation with political, social, and cultural liberation."[33] For Tracy, then, all theology is a form of political theology.[34]

The notion of the crucified God is implicit in much of liberation and political theology. For Gustavo Gutiérrez, the cross is the revelation of God in history particularly in the forgotten, the oppressed, and the "disfigured faces

29. Richard Wall, "Entering into the Passion of this World," a review of Moltmann's *The Crucified God,* found at: http://www.amazon.com/The-Crucified-God-Foundation-Criticism /dp/0800628225 (accessed Dec. 4, 2015).

30. David Tracy, "The Hidden God: The Divine Other of Liberation," *Cross Currents* (Spring 1996): 6-16.

31. Tracy, "Hidden God," 9.

32. Tracy, "Hidden God," 11, 8.

33. David Tracy, "The Role of Theology in Public Life: Some Reflections," *Word & World* 4, no. 3 (1984): 230-39.

34. "The Christian gospel does not hesitate to declare its prejudice, its preference for the suffering—for all the poor, the oppressed, the marginalized, the repressed, the tormented suffering in both social, political and the personal orders. Insofar as Christian theology remains faithful to its call to interpret Christianity for real human beings, it can never avoid its need to become a correlational theology which is also a political theology" (Tracy, "Role of Theology," 238).

of the poor in this world."[35] These are God's "preferred" ones—thus, God's preferential option for the poor.[36] For in these "crucified peoples" is disclosed God's gratuitous and excessive love, which is revealed in weakness, in the cross, in suffering, and in the historical struggle against violence.[37] Thus in Latin American liberation theology, as with Johnson, we come to the same passionate, pastoral, practical response" to God's suffering in the world.[38] As Gutiérrez observes, "Only if we take seriously the suffering of the innocent and live the mystery of the cross amid the suffering, can we prevent our theology from being windy arguments."[39]

My explorations in this chapter lead to a number of significant conclusions. First, both the preponderance of the cries of the lament in the Old Testament and the internal structure of the lament psalms confirm the cry of lament as a turning in and around God. This turning, in its manifold complaints to God in time of need and suffering, is made possible and grounded within the intimate relationship of the covenant.

Second, the prayer of lament, particularly God's silence in the face of Israel's cry for help, points not to an uncaring God but to a God who stands with his people in their cry, and thus laments and suffers with them. In this way, the psalms of lament open up and foreshadow a deep soteriological mystery of the incarnate and crucified God.

Third, the reality of a hidden, powerless, and suffering God, which the cry of lament paradoxically reveals, opens up a huge arena of passionate, pastoral, and practical engagement. For, as Tracy has reminded us, the reality of a hidden or crucified God drives the Christian not to further theological speculation but to the cross and to the "memory of suffering and the struggle by, for, and with 'others,' especially the forgotten and marginal ones in history."[40] The

---

35. Gustavo Gutiérrez, *On Job: God-talk and the Suffering of the Innocent* (Maryknoll, NY: Orbis, 1987), 13.

36. See Gustavo Gutiérrez, *A Theology of Liberation: History, Politics, and Salvation* (Maryknoll, NY: Orbis, 1988).

37. On the notion of the "crucified peoples" within liberation theology, see especially Jon Sobrino, *The Principle of Mercy: Taking the Crucified People from the Cross* (Maryknoll, NY: Orbis, 1994); Sobrino, *Witnesses to the Kingdom: The Martyrs of El Salvador and the Crucified Peoples* (Maryknoll, NY: Orbis, 2003); Leonardo Boff extends the notion of crucifixion to the earth, and thus speaks of a crucified earth. See esp. Boff, *Cry of the Earth, Cry of the Poor* (Maryknoll, NY: Orbis, 1997). For the notion of a crucified people within Asian theology, see Choan-Seng Song, *Jesus, the Crucified People* (Minneapolis: Fortress, 1996).

38. Johnson, "Jesus' Cry," 91.

39. Gutiérrez, *On Job*, 103.

40. Tracy, "Hidden God," 11, 8.

prayer of lament invites and drives the church to the margins, to the crucified ones in history. That is the reason why the eclipse of lament from the contemporary church and social life (which I discuss below) signifies a loss of passion for social justice. For, as Johnson notes, "Knowing that God is *for* us, because God is for the crucified; and knowing that God is *with* us, because God is with Jesus in his cry; so we also know, by the power of the resurrection, that God is always at work among us, calling us to be *for* and *with* one another."[41]

Fourth, given the observations above, the overall conclusion must be to confirm that the cry of lament is not simply a prayer but a social ethic—a passionate, pastoral, and practical engagement on behalf of the crucified of history. Consequently, the notion of a vulnerable/hidden/crucified God needs to play a far more central role in African theological exploration than it has played until now. That it hasn't can be attributed to a number of things, but one suspects that the traditional African religious cosmology makes the idea of a "weak" or "suffering" god impossible to grasp. Within a traditional understanding, Africans do not expect a god to be just another "one of us." They expect their gods to be bigger, stronger, more powerful, and more enduring than humans. A god who does not measure up to this expectation is in serious trouble. Thus, in *Arrow of God*, Chinua Achebe tells the story of the people of Aninta who, when their god failed them, carried him to the boundary between their village and their neighbors' village and set him on fire.[42] But the expectation of gods as "powerful" beings also partly explains why, within the traditional African religious cosmology, the miraculous or extraordinary is really not surprising: it is an everyday expectation. Because the gods are potent forces, the whole cosmos is saturated with miraculous "power." It is thus not difficult to see why, with its emphasis on "miracles" and a "mighty" God who "reigns" supreme, Pentecostalism has become quite appealing to many Africans: from that angle, the idea of a crucified God who continues to suffer with and among his crucified people cannot but seem like foolishness and a stumbling block to many Africans, just as it was to the Jews and Greeks of the first century (1 Cor. 1:23).[43] But "Christ

41. Johnson, "Jesus' Cry," 91.

42. Chinua Achebe, *Arrow of God* (New York: Anchor, 1969), 27.

43. There are, of course, many other reasons for the appeal of Pentecostalism in postcolonial Africa, not the least of which is Pentecostalism's real or perceived image as the conveyor of religious and economic modernity in the continent. See, e.g., Birgit Meyer, "'Make a Complete Break with the Past': Memory and Post-Colonial Modernity in Ghanaian Pentecostalist Discourse," *Journal of Religion in Africa* 28, no. 3 (1998): 316–49; see also David Maxwell, "'Delivered from the Spirit of Poverty?' Pentecostalism, Prosperity and Modernity in Zimbabwe," *Journal of Religion in Africa* 28, no. 3 (1998): 350–73.

crucified" is the most radical, fresh, and hopeful gift that Christianity can offer to the world and to Africa.[44]

This of course is a huge claim that has far-reaching implications—a claim, however, that needs to be substantiated. As we will see in the following chapter, the stories of Archbishop Emmanuel Kataliko and Sr. Rosemary Nyirumbe provide displays of the fruits of this claim and the particular historical, social, and practical dimensions the claim takes in the context of war and suffering in Eastern Congo and Northern Uganda.

44. Accordingly, while the idea of God is not new in Africa, Charles Nyamiti rightly notes that "what is new is the fact that God's power is manifest in weakness: in Christ's humility, meekness, forgiveness of sins, and—most astoundingly—in his suffering, his death on the cross, and its glorious consequences in Christ himself and the whole of creation." See Charles Nyamiti, *African Tradition and the Christian God* (Eldoret, Kenya: Gaba Publications, 1976), 57.

CHAPTER 6

The Saving Power of "Christ Crucified"

The only response to the excess of evil is the excess of love.

Emmanuel Kataliko

There is no other classroom to learn about compassion, love, and mercy than the Sacred Heart of Jesus.

Rosemary Nyirumbe

In concluding my reflections in Chapter 4, I noted that, for all their anguish and poignancy, the laments from East Africa are marked by an unyielding conviction of God's presence in the midst of forsakenness. In this respect, the East Africa laments are not much different from the Negro spirituals. However, while Negro spirituals are very explicit in connecting the slaves' suffering to God's (Jesus's) suffering, the connection between the cries of lament from East Africa and God's own is not as explicit. It is this connection that we need to make explicit in order to bring to the fore the rich theological—but also the immense social, political, and ethical—significance of a crucified God in Africa. For if the notion of a "crucified God" is an implicit political theology (as David Tracy claims, as noted in the preceding chapter), what does that political theology look like in the context of Stearns's *Dancing in the Glory of Monsters*?

If "we discover the features of Christ in the sometimes disfigured faces of the poor in this world" (as Gutiérrez argues), how and where is this discovery located on the African landscape? And if the discovery is not a theoretical discovery but a "passionate, pastoral and practical response" (Johnson), what does such a response look like in Africa? What shape does "the struggle by, for, and with others" (Tracy) take in the context of Africa's crucified peoples? How does knowing the "power of resurrection" (Johnson) play out in the context of the endless or ongoing cycles of violence in Africa? These questions do not press for further theoretical exploration (as Tracy rightly warns) but for concrete displays of passionate and pastoral agency in all its historical and practical dimensions in the African context.

In this chapter I present the stories of the late Archbishop Emmanuel Kataliko of Bukavu and of Sr. Rosemary Nyirumbe of Saint Monica Girls Tailoring School in Gulu as examples of the passionate, pastoral, and practical response to the reality of a suffering God.

Whereas the image of a suffering God was a theme in Kataliko's reflection through the liturgical seasons of Advent and Lent, the adoration and meditation on God's suffering is, for Nyirumbe, integral to her devotional and spiritual disciplines as a sister of the Sacred Heart of Jesus. What they both discovered, however, in the encounter with the reality of God's suffering is a rich theopraxis that reflects the story of a God who responds to evil through an excess of love.

Archbishop Emmanuel Kataliko and the Liturgical Disciplines of the "Excess of Love" in Eastern Congo

Emmanuel Kataliko was installed as Archbishop of Bukavu in May 1997 at a very turbulent time in Congo's political history. His predecessor, Archbishop Christopher Munzihirwa, had been assassinated seven months earlier (see Chapter 8 below). This was two days after Mobutu fled Kinshasa and two days before Laurent-Désiré Kabila took power. A year later, Kabila would fall out with his Rwandan and Ugandan allies, plunging the Congo into the second Congo war.[1] Kataliko's tenure as Archbishop of Bukavu was brief, but its theological, pastoral, and political impact was significant. In fact, for Kataliko, the practical and political concerns were an essential dimension of his pastoral

1. For the general history, see Jason K. Stearns, *Dancing in the Glory of Monsters: The Collapse of the Congo and the Great War of Africa* (New York: PublicAffairs, 2012). For a history that focuses on the region and the Catholic church, see Gérard Prunier, "The Catholic Church and the Kivu Conflict," *Journal of Religion in Africa* 31, no. 2 (May, 2001): 139–62. See also John Kiess, "When War Is Our Daily Bread: Congo, Theology, and the Ethics of Contemporary Conflict" (PhD diss., Duke University, 2011). I am particularly indebted to Kiess, who first drew my attention to the story of Emmanuel Kataliko and whose work provides a compelling account of Christian agency, reasoning, and alternatives during the Congo wars.

ministry, which he viewed through the prism of God's excessive love revealed on the cross.

Soon after becoming archbishop, Kataliko's immediate concern for the beleaguered city of Bukavu was a practical one. In his very first pastoral letter of July 15, 1997, he mobilized the population to repair the city's drainage system: "Our city will soon disappear if we are not careful," he wrote. "We must do something before the next rainy season in September." In order to "save the city," he asked each Christian to contribute at least one Congolese franc toward the rebuilding of the city drainage.[2]

When the second Congo war broke out in July 1998, the Rally for Congolese Democracy (RCD)—a Rwanda-sponsored rebel group—controlled Bukavu and the whole of Southern Kivu. Amid growing anxiety, frustration, and insecurity among the citizens of the city, Kataliko wrote another pastoral letter (September 1998) that encouraged the populace to "stay strong and courageous. The Lord is not abandoning us."

Kataliko's own courage was tested as the country descended further into chaos. By 1999, numerous Maji Maji groups (indigenous militias) had formed and the RCD was exercising heavy taxation on the city. Massacres, such as the one in August 1998 in Kasika (a mere hundred miles from Bukavu) were common, as were reports of pillage and looting. The economic, political, and security situation in and around Bukavu was becoming dire. It was against this background that Kataliko preached his famous 1999 Christmas message, in which he denounced the "empire of greed"—the "insatiable thirst for material things" that had fueled the war and looting. And he called out the RCD and the Rwanda government:

> We are crushed by the oppression of domination. Foreign powers, in collaboration with some of our Congolese brothers, organize wars with the resources of our country. These resources, which should be used for our development, for the education of our children, for healing the sick, in short, so that we may live more humanely, are used to kill us. Moreover, our country and ourselves, we have become objects of exploitation worse than in the colonial era. . . . Everything of value has been looted, wrecked and taken abroad or simply destroyed. Taxes, which would be invested for

2. For Msgr. Kataliko's pastoral letters see *Lettres Pastorales et Messages de Monseigneur Emmanuel Kataliko (18 mai 1997–octobre 2000)* (Editions Archevêché de Bukavu) [translation mine]. In citing Kataliko's pastoral letters, I will not provide page references but will instead make direct reference to the dates or titles of the letters.

common good, are misappropriated. . . . Excessive taxes strangle not only large-scale commerce and industry, but also the mother who lives off her small business. . . . In the city, armed groups, often in military uniforms, burst into our houses, steal the few goods we have left, threaten, kidnap and even kill our brothers. Our brothers and sisters in the countryside are massacred on a large scale. . . . Even the church is not spared. Parishes, presbyteries, convents are sacked. . . . Priests, clergy, and nuns are beaten, tortured, and killed. . . . The moral decline of some of our compatriots has reached such an absurd level that they do not hesitate to betray their brother for a bill of ten or twenty dollars.[3]

Kataliko's sermon struck a chord not only among Catholics in Bukavu, but among Protestants, Muslims, and the entire civil society of the city. A week-long strike was called to protest the high taxes that the RCD had imposed and the continued presence of Rwandan and Ugandan forces in Eastern Congo. The strike closed schools, health clinics, the offices of nongovernmental organizations (NGOs), markets, and transportation—and thus brought the city to a halt. The RCD responded by arresting Kataliko and exiling him to Butembo, his former diocese, accusing him of inciting civil unrest and promoting ethnic divisions. The move backfired: it prompted another round of strikes and inspired a campaign to bring the archbishop back. The exile lasted for seven months until, bowing to local and international pressure, the RCD allowed Kataliko to return to Bukavu, where he was welcomed back by tens of thousands of the city's citizens.

An Excess of Love

But what animated and drove Kataliko's pastoral ministry, both in its practical and political dimensions? From his exile in Butembo, Kataliko wrote letters to the Christians in Bukavu. As one reads these letters, it becomes clear that the heart of Kataliko's passionate, practical, and pastoral engagement as a priest and bishop drew from his understanding and experience of the excessive love of God, which was manifested on the cross. In a Lenten message from Butembo (March 15, 2000), Kataliko wrote:

In these difficult times, let us not doubt the love of God for us. "If God is on our side, who will be against us?" (Rom. 8:31-39). But know the logic of the

3. Emmanuel Kataliko, Christmas message, 1999.

gospel is a logic not of power, but of the cross. "God has chosen the weak of the world to undermine the strong" (1 Cor. 1:27). The only response to the excess of evil is the excess of love.

This excess of love that Kataliko speaks of is the logic of the cross. This is the way God responds to evil, suffering, and violence in the world, by his willingness to become a victim of violence rather than a perpetrator of violence. God conquers the violence of the world through suffering. Kataliko says in his Lenten letter of 1999:

God's suffering servant of Isaiah (50:6–7), although wounded, did not wound others. Although he was subjected to injustice, he did not respond with injustice. Although he was humiliated, he did not humiliate those who were weaker than himself. Although he was suffering, he resisted, keeping in his heart the dream of a society founded on justice, without oppressor or any oppressed (Isa. 42:2–4).

The excess of love, therefore, is a suffering love—God's own suffering—and thus God's crucified love for the world. In the same Lenten message, Kataliko observes:

In this lifelong battle, he knows that in this world justice and love cannot exist unless they are crucified. He thus accepted to be hung on the cross, this instrument of torture reserved for slaves, which the son of God transformed into a means of liberation and redemption. His courage came to him in the certainty that to live with love, to practice justice, and to tell the truth is the only way to have God on your side.

The practical implication that Kataliko drew from this realization was that it is through this "crucified love" that God stands in solidarity with suffering humanity and thus becomes the source and basis of hope for those afflicted. Therefore, in the Christmas message of 1999, Kataliko reminded the beleaguered Christians of Bukavu:

Our Christian message is a message of hope. It is the message of Jesus himself. He, the son of God, showed solidarity with our human condition. Born into poverty, persecuted from the beginning of his existence . . . he died on the cross to make us the love of God the Father. He never avoided the consequences of this solidarity. Thus, facing death, he did not give up.

A Practical Pastoral Ministry

Kataliko's pastoral letters reveal "the excess of love" as the heart of his understanding of God. God's agency in human history, especially God's solidarity with humanity, is revealed in the incarnation and in Jesus's suffering and death on the cross. It is this excess of love manifested on the cross that invites Christians into practical engagement in solidarity with our suffering brothers and sisters. Kataliko understood his own ministry as a priest and bishop to be a response to that invitation.

The son of a carpenter, Emmanuel Kataliko joined a seminary run by the Assumptionist Fathers. Soon after his ordination at the age of twenty-six, he was sent to Rome to study theology. On the completion of his doctorate in theology, he took advantage of the opportunities in Rome and did supplementary studies in sociology. Upon his return to his home diocese of Beni-Butembo, he was appointed chaplain of Catholic movements in the diocese. He formed many associations and encouraged people to join, especially the Coffee Cooperative Society, which was the main cooperative in this coffee-growing area. Appointed bishop at the tender age of thirty-four, he continued to live a practical and simple life.

Numerous stories are told of visitors who would come to see the bishop and find him working in his compound. Mistaking him for a gardener, they would ask him whether the bishop was present and available. He would go to check, and once inside the rectory, he would change into clerical garb and come out to meet the visitor![4] In Butembo, people still speak warmly about his passionate concern for human dignity, and how he was personally involved in the building of roads, bridges, schools, hospitals, and even a university (organized around three practical disciplines: medicine, agronomy, and veterinary sciences). A former priest assistant remembers him as "a humble, soft-spoken but courageous priest. . . . He had not only spiritual but also social/political power in the community."[5] Given this practical dimension of his ministry, it is not surprising that Kataliko's first concern as archbishop of Bukavu was the city's drainage system.

4. Kataliko interview, July 2013.
5. Kataliko interview, July 2013.

A Passionate Pastoral Engagement

But if Kataliko's theology of an excess of love translated into practical engagement in solidarity with the people, it was also a passionate (in the sense of *passio*, i.e., suffering) engagement, which opened him up to suffering in solidarity with his people. Thus in exile he wrote to his fellow Christians in Bukavu:

> When I think about your sufferings, your sacrifice, your prayers of supplication and especially about the population of Kalonge, of Bunyakiri, of Burhale, and of all the regions enflamed in conflict, tears come to my eyes.[6]

Kataliko's solidarity with the oppressed meant that, as a priest and as a bishop, he was to experience the same suffering as his flock. Thus, in the famous Christmas message of 1999, while inviting his Christians to "become aware of the bonds of our servitude" and to "risk the way of liberation," he offered his own commitment to the way of liberation, which involved the possibility of martyrdom, just like his predecessor, Munzihirwa.

> We commit ourselves with courage, with a firm spirit, with unshakable faith, to be on the side of all the oppressed and, if necessary, to the point of shedding blood, as Msgr. Munzihira, Fr. Cluade Buhendwa, the priests and sisters of Kasika, Fr. George Kkuja . . . and many other Christians have done. It is at the price of our suffering and our prayers that we will lead the battle of liberty; that we will also bring our oppressors to reason and to their own inner freedom.

However, if Kataliko invokes the memory of Munzihirwa and others and is willing to stand in solidarity with these innocent victims of the violence around them, what ultimately drove Kataliko and shaped his courage was the memory of God's own suffering. Thus, in a letter from Butembo, he replied to accusations (by the RCD) that he was a major obstacle to peaceful coexistence by inciting interethnic hatred:

> The Christ, the first, paid a high price for his commitment to us. He was crucified because of human perversity that did not support the bright light (John 3:19) projected by his being and his word, onto the heart of man. This can only teach us, especially when he invites us to, like him, put our hands

6. E. Kataliko, Lenten Letter, Butembo, March 15, 2000.

into the wounds of injured humanity. To look for the truth of Christ is, in my current situation, to decide to live, like him, in love, and to fight, like him, against the violence of the sin that divides us, until I give my life, if it is necessary, for the people I love. This is an audacious choice, without a doubt, and its radicalism frightens me and makes me question my capacity to put it into action with my own strength.[7]

What the above words confirm is that, far from being paralyzing, suffering became a form of agency for Kataliko and, ironically, the source of his strength and freedom. Suffering freed him to speak, to act, and to respond to evil with an excess of love, as he reflects:

What a strange call God makes to us: crushed by pain, we are called to announce the end of suffering; prisoners, we become free; plunged in darkness, we become illuminated; sad, we must find joy; murdered, we must proclaim life.[8]

It is into this suffering-transformed-into-agency that he invites the people, noting that the solidarity with the suffering Christ becomes the source of courage:

Courage, my brothers and sisters. Suffering overwhelms us, but we follow Christ, who conquered the world (John 16:33). We are called to pass through our suffering, and in this passage from death to life God gives us a mission, that of Jesus himself, the suffering servant. Despite being oppressed and humiliated today, we are called to remain loyal to God's plan that is love in respect and sharing, in justice and truth, without letting ourselves be contaminated by the mentality of the oppressor, which is to think of oneself, to distrust and to overlook others. People who live thus will become the servants of God.[9]

Kataliko is telling his audience that the suffering they are going through is not a fate they must suffer passively. Their suffering can be transformed into a distinctive form of agency by entering the humanity of the Son of God and Christ's own suffering, "knowing that our sufferings are the suffering of

---

7. E. Kataliko, Reply to Msgr. Fautino Ngabu, Butembo (Mar. 14, 2000).
8. E. Kataliko, Lent, 1999.
9. E. Kataliko, Lent, 1999.

Christ." And "insofar as you have a share in the suffering of Christ, stand firm."[10]

Liturgical Time: The Discipline of "Excess of Love"

Kataliko's ministry as a priest and bishop stands squarely within this "odd" logic of God's excessive love, into which Kataliko invited the Christians through the various seasons of the church's liturgical year. For him, liturgical ceremonies were no mere pious exercises; rather, they are the way by which Christians are introduced and formed into the story of God's excessive love for humanity.

Therefore, liturgical ceremonies are an invitation into a different history and a different epistemology, which allows Christians to see that, for all their pretensions, it is not Kabila, Kagame, Kaguta, or other warlords who control history, but the crucified God. Those familiar with the work of the Mennonite John Howard Yoder will immediately recognize an affinity between the exhortations of Kataliko and Yoder's claim that people who wear the crowns and who claim to foster justice by the sword are not as strong as they think. It is the people who bear crosses that are working with the grain of the universe.[11] What this concretely meant for Kataliko was that, especially in the midst of Congo's wars, he had to remind Christians who the one true master of history is. Thus, at the outbreak of the second Congo war, with Rwandan troops surrounding Bukavu, he reminded the people:

> In the current climate of suffering and in certitude due to this new war, our spirits rise spontaneously to our *Lord, master of history*. Let us ask for his spirit of light and of courage—that he might show us what must be done and that he may give us the strength necessary to accomplish it.[12]

But this also means that the liturgical seasons of Advent, Christmas, Lent, and Easter provide an opportunity to narrate again the fighting christologically, and thus to situate the crisis in Bukavu within the wider drama of the

---

10. E. Kataliko, Lenten letter, Butembo (March 15, 2000).

11. John Howard Yoder, "Armaments and Eschatology," as quoted in Stanley Hauerwas, *With the Grain of the Universe: The Church's Witness and Natural Theology* (Grand Rapids: Brazos, 2001).

12. E. Kataliko, August 13, 1978 (emphasis added).

incarnation.[13] It is this "re-narration" that allows Kataliko to see clearly and name different forms of "servitude" (plunder, violence, greed, oppression) within the current situation. But re-narrating the war within what Kataliko considered a more primary history also reveals concrete options and practical alternatives to resist the various forms of servitude. For as he had noted in the letter of August 1978 quoted above, he (the Lord of history) must "show us what must be done . . . and give us the strength necessary to accomplish it." In his September 1998 pastoral letter, he offered these practical alternatives:

> In the face of violence, let us endeavor to resist with all the strength of our faith, without letting ourselves be taken in by an equal spirit of violence. . . . In the face of poverty that weakens us, react with an effort made in solidarity. In the face of famine that threatens us, let us strive to respond with an even greater engagement in work, without letting ourselves be paralyzed by fear and lassitude. . . . Everyone should work to make sure they meet the needs of their families. . . . Merchants should not succumb to the temptation of profit from the general distress by raising prices of essential goods; farmers should redouble efforts . . . to cultivate the fields and thus produce the necessary food for their subsistence and that of their brothers and sisters in the city.

These concrete alternatives constitute for Kataliko "the work of peace," which does not wait till the end of the war, but goes on as everyday work even in the middle of the war. Liturgical ceremonies are not an extra layer to this everyday work of peace, nor a mere preparation for it; they are at the very core of this daily engagement as they reveal the true nature of peace (as God's gift) and open up the nonviolent alternatives in the pursuit of peace, alternatives that reflect and confirm the logic of "excess of love" revealed in God's suffering on the cross. Thus, in a letter written on March 15, 2000, Kataliko called for an end to the strike and encouraged the people to take up their normal activities, not "forgetting liturgical ceremonies, the source of spiritual strength, of our courage to face the future seriously."

13. As John Kiess notes, Kataliko does not approach the war as a separate sphere of human action with its own time and law, but instead shows how the church's liturgical time of birth, passion, and resurrection remains the determinative lens for Christians throughout rebel occupation ("When War Is Our Daily Bread," 150). "As the season of advent transitions to lent, Katalko moves from the theme of birth which sprung the church into action on the streets of Bukavu to the theme of suffering and the church's entry into the paschal mystery of Christ" (168).

Turning in and toward the God Who Carries Us

I have quoted extensively from Kataliko's pastoral letters to give the reader a feel for the texture of his deeply theological—yet immensely practical—pastoral engagement that is grounded in the reality of a crucified God. In the Lenten letter of March 15, 2000, written from his exile in Butembo, Kataliko invokes the notion of an "excess of love" as an entry point into the mystery of God's humanity and solidarity with suffering humanity.

In the preceding chapter I pointed to the psalms of lament as a turning to God in the moment of pain and suffering. But I also noted that, through the covenant relationship, the sovereign God of Israel has opened Godself to vulnerability. In the words of Scott Ellington: "It is not that Yahweh has removed himself and is far away . . . rather that he is too near and too involved. He has joined himself with his people, indeed married them, and in so doing has lowered his guard and become vulnerable."[14] In the end, Israel's cries of lament are a turning to a vulnerable God—a God who in the New Testament is encountered as a crucified God.

It is this psalmic structure that is revealed in Kataliko's life as a priest and as a bishop, particularly during his time of exile from Bukavu, as the exile letters he wrote from Butembo reveal. In the Lenten message of 2000, Kataliko says: "Recently, as you will well understand, I have been meditating a lot about the life Jesus led before his arrest, fleeing his enemies (John 7:1; 11:54, 57; 12:36). These texts reveal a Christ who truly shared our human condition, in all things except sin." Inviting his audience to turn to the suffering God, he says, "My brothers, during this season of Lent, do not forget to make the way of the cross in the steps of the one who gave completely of himself, to show us the love of the Father."

Kataliko's exile lasted seven months. Bowing to local and international pressure, the RCD allowed Kataliko to return to Bukavu on September 14, 2000, rather coincidentally the feast of the Triumph of the Cross, where the throng of residents chanted: "*Kariibu tena baba*" ("Welcome home, father"). On the following day, the Feast of Our Lady of Sorrows, Kataliko celebrated Mass at the footsteps of the cathedral, an event that was attended by over 40,000 people. In the homily he captured the significance of what he and the people were going through as a "turning" toward a God who "carries us":

14. Scott A. Ellington, *Risking Truth: Reshaping the World through the Prayers of Lament* (Eugene, OR: Pickwick, 2008), 143.

The life of each person is marked by three events: joy, pain, and resurrection. Look at Jesus. . . . In our life we should thank God for everything he has done for us. In our life, there is a time for trial; there is a time where we are no longer; there is a time to remember; a time to take a breath; there is also a time to talk. And in this, *God carries us*. But we should know that our life is all *turned* toward him. (emphasis added)

Even though he did not make specific reference to the psalms of lament, Kataliko's words indicate that he was reading his and his people's experience as a lament psalm. And just as Israel's lament reflected the people's firm conviction in a God who carries them in the midst of their suffering, Kataliko encouraged the people of Bukavu that they, by turning to the humanity of Christ, particularly Christ's suffering and death, would rediscover their own humanity in the face of the inhuman conditions they were facing. Doing so would not only bestow their lives with the courage necessary to stand firm ("Knowing that our sufferings are the suffering of Christ . . ." and "Insofar as you have a share in the suffering of Christ, stand firm") but also would open up for them a number of nonviolent alternatives in the midst of the war. Through these practical alternatives they would, just as the crucified God did, be able to respond to the excess of evil through an excess of love.

In other words, by turning to a crucified God "who carries us," they would be able to discover a new form of transformed agency, a nonviolent alternative in the midst of violence. Another way to put it is this: Kataliko's life and ministry in Bukavu reveal that lament carried him forward as a form of prayer and practical agency. This is what he referred to in his 1999 Christmas message: "risking" the way of liberation. Kataliko's reference to "being carried" by a suffering God did not point to "resilience" or a certain "can-do spirit." Rather, it pointed to the need for Christians to submit to and thus immerse themselves in God's story. It is not only that that story can interrupt the violent history of Bukavu; it is a far more determinative story against which the history of Bukavu, or other political histories, can be read.

The day after celebrating the Mass upon his return to Bukavu, Kataliko left to attend a meeting in Rome, where, on October 4, 2000, he collapsed and died. Though the official postmortem indicated "heart problems," a number of people in Butembo and Bukavu suspected that he was poisoned. An even bigger crowd than the one that had welcomed him upon his return from exile in Butembo (a mere three weeks earlier) attended his funeral in Bukavu. During the liturgical procession of the funeral, as if in a final symbolic show of rebel power, gun shots rang out, scattering the mourners. But that interruption lasted only momentarily: the congregation regathered to resume the procession—and thereby confirmed what Kataliko's life and ministry had been all about: an invitation into the peaceful story of God's excessive love, even if that story is interrupted by war and violence. But the interruption of Kataliko's funeral procession also confirmed a fundamental ontological claim that shaped Kataliko's life and ministry, namely, that it is not liturgical time that interrupts the economy of war and violence; rather, it is war and violence that interrupt the more determinative and peaceful gathering of history that the church's liturgical time marks. Moreover, the interruption by war and violence of the story of God's love, which moves the stars and heavens and directs the history of the world, can only be temporary.

Sr. Rosemary Nyirumbe and the "Sewing" of Hope in Northern Uganda

Sr. Rosemary Nyirumbe, a sister of the Sacred Heart of Jesus, has been the director of Saint Monica's Girls Vocation Training School in Gulu since 2001. The mission statement of the school is: "To offer appropriate, quality and affordable education to vulnerable/disadvantaged girls and women in Northern Uganda." But this statement does not tell even half the story of the school's or Sr. Rosemary's significance, as a result of which she was included in *Time* magazine's 2014 list of the 100 most influential people in the world. For over twenty-five years, the Lord's Resistance Army (LRA) wreaked havoc in towns and villages in Northern Uganda, abducting an estimated 30,000 children from their homes, killing their families and teachers, forcing boys to commit rape and murder, and turning girls (some as young as ten years old) into sex slaves and "wives" of the commanders. Saint Monica's provides a home for the girls, many of them young mothers who escaped from the captivity of the LRA, and offers them practical training in tailoring, catering, and other life-sustaining skills.

However, Saint Monica's offers these girls much more than practical skills and much more than a home. A recent book and documentary—both entitled *Sewing Hope*—provide a good overview of the significance of Saint Monica's and Sr. Rosemary. For example, one of the school's recent projects is making handbags from the pop-tops of soda cans. Most people, of course, consider pop-tops trash, only good to be thrown in the garbage. But pop-tops now provide not only a significant source of income for Saint Monica's; they are also a fitting metaphor for the girls' lives. Once innocent and beautiful, these children came to be considered worthless, discarded as a mere afterthought in the shadow of a terrible war. Kidnapped from their parents at a tender age and forced to serve as sex slaves, they were often shunned by their own communities and called disparaging names. Like the pop-tops, they became rubble for the scrapheap of history.

But just as "what was once rubble is now a beautiful purse, a unique work of functional art and a source of pride for the students who learned to make them," the lives of the girls at Saint Monica's—their image and self-worth—have been stitched back together by Sr. Rosemary and her sisters of the Sacred Heart of Jesus.[15]

"My Eyes Are Always in Pain"

Saint Monica's Girls Vocation School was started in 1983 by a group of Comboni Italian Missionary sisters to provide women in Northern Uganda with practical home-economics skills so that they could be better housewives. When the missionary sisters were forced to leave because of insecure and worsening conditions, they turned the facility over to the Archdiocese of Gulu, which invited the Sisters of the Sacred Heart to run it. When Sr. Rosemary Nyirumbe was appointed the director in 2001, the school was underutilized and running a heavy financial loss. Rebels were terrorizing the region, abducting children; there was an Ebola outbreak; and there were few students enrolled in the school. Nobody knew what to do with Saint Monica's. Neither did Sr. Rosemary, who had no prior training in how to run an educational institution. She had a certificate in midwifery and a degree in development studies.

Jewel was one of the girls at Saint Monica's. Sr. Rosemary soon noticed that Jewel would never look anyone in the eye. She seemed frightened and sad all the time and often flinched when spoken to.[16] One day, Sr. Rosemary called the girl to her office and gently asked her why she never looked at anyone. Jewel avoided her eyes. After much gentle encouragement, Jewel admitted to Sr. Rosemary: "Sister, my eyes are always in pain." Asked why that was the case, Jewel reluctantly and shyly told Sr. Rosemary that she had been with the rebels

---

15. Reggie Whitten and Nancy Henderson, "Introduction," in *Sewing Hope: Joseph Kony Tore These Girls' Lives Apart. Can She Stitch Them Back Together?* (Oklahoma City, OK: Dust Jacket, 2013) [unpaginated].

16. Whitten and Henderson, *Sewing Hope*, 84–87.

for nine years and was a commanding officer, always taking the front line. "I helped them kill many people, and the smoke from the gunshots affected my eye sight."[17]

It had never occurred to Rosemary until then that any of the girls at the school were former abductees of the LRA. Jewel then told Sr. Rosemary the story of her abduction and her experience in the bush. She also confessed: "Sister, I can't keep up in the dress-making class. . . . The rebels kidnapped me while I was still in school, and I never learned how to do the math and other things I am expected to do."[18] Jewel's heart-wrenching story made Sr. Rosemary realize that Jewel and others like her had not lost only their homes, their innocence, and their self-esteem; because they had been deprived of school at an early age, they lacked a basic education. She decided that what the girls needed were practical skills (sewing dresses, e.g., not just studying from books), and even more importantly, an atmosphere of love and forgiveness to help Jewel and girls like her recover something of the dignity and self-esteem that had been shattered as a result of their abduction and years in the bush.

She changed the school's curriculum at once, steering it away from the theoretical, scientific lessons that had previously been taught and focusing instead on the practical skills. She bought ten sewing machines and started teaching girls how to sew dresses and blouses, school uniforms and sweaters. Soon she added cooking lessons, baking classes, and catering. In the meantime, going with Jewel to the market to buy groceries, Sr. Rosemary would give her money to pay for purchases. Jewel seemed puzzled at first that someone would trust her! But as she became more confident in her practical tailoring, with the trust and love from Sr. Rosemary and the other girls, "little by little, she began to look other people in the eye and speak more directly to them."[19]

A Vocation and Mission of "Giving Love"

Sr. Rosemary had found her vocation (her "calling within a calling," as she refers to it), as well as a mission for Saint Monica's, which she now clearly understood as one of helping girls like Jewel experience the restorative love and forgiveness of the Sacred Heart in practical ways.[20] Saint Monica's was now

17. Whitten and Henderson, *Sewing Hope*, 85.
18. Whitten and Henderson, *Sewing Hope*, 86.
19. Whitten and Henderson, *Sewing Hope*, 89.
20. Interview with Sr. Rosemary Nyirumbe, University of Notre Dame, Notre Dame, IN (Mar. 19, 2015). Being a sister of the Sacred Heart was her primary calling; now the unique

going to focus on formerly abducted girls in Northern Uganda. Sr. Rosemary offered an invitation over the radio:

> St. Monica's welcomes all girls who came from captivity, all the child mothers who were forced to serve as soldiers alongside the rebels. Come as you are, with your children, or even if you are pregnant. We'll take you, no matter who you are, and give you the training you need to make a living. Registration starts in three days.[21]

That invitation was radical. As Whitten and Henderson note, openly welcoming pregnant girls, let alone former abductees and their children, into a school, any school, had never happened in Uganda. By the end of the year, Saint Monica's had enrolled over two hundred girls. Like Jewel, the girls were deeply scarred. Some of them had been raped in front of their families before being kidnapped and dragged into the bush; others had been forced to kill their own parents, siblings, and relatives; all were used as sex slaves, "wives" to the rebel commanders. But with an influx of over two hundred girls, Sr. Rosemary and her fellow sisters soon found themselves overwhelmed. They had to improvise on many fronts: baby-sitting (a nursery for the children of formerly abducted girls had to be set up right away), teaching various practical courses, counseling the girls, looking for internships and job placements, and so on. However, by far the most challenging and yet most significant improvisation was the one of love. When the other sisters approached Rosemary because they did not know what to do with the withdrawn and damaged girls, as well as with the children of the rebel soldiers, Sr. Rosemary encouraged them:

> I think what we should do is love and accept these girls and walk with them, in their shoes. Let us accept them as they are and not judge them for what they have done. We must treat them as normal people and not as people who have done terrible things. This is not just about giving them training. It is about giving them love.[22]

---

calling she had found within that vocation had to do with offering God's love and forgiveness to the girls at Saint Monica's. This is what Nyirumbe means by "calling within a calling."

21. Whitten and Henderson, *Sewing Hope*, 94.

22. Whitten and Henderson, *Sewing Hope*, 94–95.

Performing the Sacred Heart of Jesus

While *Sewing Hope* helps to capture the basic outline of Sr. Rosemary's story and her extraordinary work with the abducted girls of Northern Uganda, it does not fully account for the theological logic that drives it—and thus does not give an account of its hope.[23] In order to read Sr. Rosemary as an exemplar of hope, and to display the kind of hope she exemplifies, one has to locate her agency within the same logic as Kataliko's "excess of love." To understand this, one must see her work at Saint Monica's as a performance, an extension of her calling as a sister of the Sacred Heart of Jesus. What Rosemary is trying to do is offer the girls at Saint Monica's the same selfless love that she has found in the Sacred Heart of Jesus.

The youngest of a family of four boys and four girls, Rosemary was adored and doted on by her parents and her siblings. Growing up in such a loving Christian home, she notes, she felt the immense love of God, which partly explains why she decided to join the convent when she was only fifteen years old. The Sisters of the Sacred Heart of Jesus was founded in 1954 in Juba by Bishop Sixtus Mazzoldi, and sisters of this order work in hospitals, run orphanages and schools, and do other forms of social work with youth and children in Uganda, Kenya, South Sudan, and Sudan. Their charism, mission, and everyday spirituality are shaped and centered around devotion to the Sacred Heart of Jesus, which is a symbol and expression of God's infinite love for humanity, made manifest especially in Jesus's suffering and death on the cross. This devotion has a long-standing tradition within the Catholic faith.[24] The image of the Sacred Heart, therefore, evokes not only God's excessive love for humanity but, more specifically, the pierced and bleeding heart of God.

23. In the end, the Rosemary that one encounters in *Sewing Hope* is a "humanitarian" heroine who is motivated by her religious calling. The point I am making is that Rosemary's work with the girls at Saint Monica's is not merely motivated by religious vocation, it is religious work—that is, theological praxis—and accordingly a form of political theology (see notes on David Tracy above). Whereas referring to her work as "humanitarian" is to assume "human" as a primary category to which all other modalities (religious, spiritual, secular) conform, referring to her work as theological praxis is to subsume "human" under the story of God's excess love manifested on the cross, the determinative story that shapes not only God's agency but also human agency in the world.

24. The first feast of the Sacred Heart was celebrated on Aug. 31, 1670, in Rennes, France, through the efforts of Fr. Jean Eudes (1602-1680) and the apparitions of St. Margaret Mary Alacoque (1647-1690) as a tribute to God's love for humanity. In 1856, Pope Pius IX, at the request of the French bishops, extended the feast to the universal church. It is celebrated on the Friday after the octave of Corpus Christi, or nineteen days after Pentecost Sunday.

Not only was the formation program of the Sisters of the Sacred Heart of Jesus permeated by this spirituality of God's excessive and crucified love; every Friday the sisters spent hours in devotion and adoration of the Sacred Heart of Jesus. But the founder of the order, Bishop Mazzoldi, often reminded the novices that this devotion was practical in its orientation. "The work of God starts at the Cross," Mazzoldi often quoted Bishop Comboni, the founder of his order, as saying.[25] In fact, as Comboni wrote in 1877: "The cross has the power to change central Africa into a land of blessing and salvation. The cross releases a virtue that is gentle and does not kill, which renews and descends on souls like restorative dew. The cross releases a great force."[26]

The "gentle virtue" and "great force" that Comboni spoke of is the work of mercy that is born at the foot of the cross. For Comboni, therefore, the work of God is the work of mercy: not our mercy, but God's mercy toward the poor, the suffering, the refugees and those who are needy.[27] This is what Mazzoldi sought to instill in the novices of the Sacred Heart of Jesus through their charism and work with the poor, the sick, refugees, orphaned youth, and the elderly. And as if to bind the Sisters of the Sacred Heart more firmly in solidarity with those they serve, civil war displaced them from their mother house in Juba, and they themselves became refugees in Uganda and Kenya. That is how they ended up with a formation house at Moyo in Northern Uganda. At the age of fifteen, when young Rosemary heard about a refugee congregation of nuns who were themselves living and working with refugees and orphans, she felt drawn to join them.

However, once in the convent, she not only found the daily routines (such as waking up at 5:00 a.m.) challenging; she also found herself resisting the invitation of the cross. Then, one afternoon, she felt the personal call to try out what Comboni had described as the great yet gentle force of the cross:

> I had been avoiding the cross; I did not like the cross. But one day during Friday adoration, in silence I looked at the cross. I saw the cross full of pain and full of suffering. But I also realized that that is what brought salvation to mankind. So, I said to myself, perhaps I can imitate the Sacred Heart, and my little cross will generate love and freedom for my people.[28]

25. Interview with Sr. Rosemary Nyirumbe, University of Notre Dame, Notre Dame, IN (Mar. 19, 2015).

26. "The Cross as Bride," Comboni Missionaries: http://www.comboni.org.uk/combonis _writings.html (accessed Mar. 27, 2015).

27. Interview with Sr. Rosemary (Mar. 19, 2015).

28. Interview with Sr. Rosemary (Mar. 19, 2015).

As she now reflects on her work at Saint Monica's, she notes, "This is what I have been trying to do: my call is to be with the vulnerable; and my call is to make it clear that whatever I am doing is within the charism of the Sacred Heart."[29] In the documentary *Sewing Hope*, we see her hinting at this conclusion: "Whatever I do, I do it with love. If they do not understand it now, I hope they will later come to see that it is love which compels me to do whatever I do."[30]

Soon after Rosemary's religious profession, she was sent to train as a midwife, where, under the supervision of an Italian priest-surgeon, she stitched up patients in the surgical ward. Even though she does not work as a midwife at Saint Monica's, she is stitching together the shattered lives of the girls, using the love, care, support and forgiveness of the Sacred Heart. And just as the risen Christ's body still bore the scars of the crucifixion, Rosemary's hope is that the scars inflicted on the girls will be healed, even if they are not erased.

> Yes, they will always bear scars—emotional, psychological, and physical—of what they have been through. The scars will remain, but they do not have to be so painful, and they do not have to hurt forever. It is not our job to erase them. It is our job to help heal the deep wounds in their hearts.[31]

If Kataliko talked about responding to an excess of evil with an excess of love, Rosemary finds that excess of love in God's forgiving love on the cross. It is this forgiving love that she learned from the Sacred Heart of Jesus and that she now offers to the girls: "God has forgiven you. God loves us. God heals our past. This is why Jesus died on the cross for us."[32]

For her work at Saint Monica's on behalf of the girls in Northern Uganda, Sr. Rosemary has received numerous awards, including the CNN Heroes Award (2007); the UN Women Impact Award (2013); the Uganda Nalubaale Award (2014); and inclusion in *Time* magazine's 100 Most Influential People in the World (2014).[33] These honors confirm Sr. Rosemary's leadership, vision, courage, and innovation on behalf of the girls of Northern Uganda. But none of these awards is as affirming for Rosemary as the realization that her work

29. Interview with Sr. Rosemary (Mar. 19, 2015).
30. *Sewing Hope*, a documentary by Snagfilms (2013), 12.27, 41.35.
31. Whitten and Henderson, *Sewing Hope*, 224.
32. *Sewing Hope* (documentary).
33. She was also awarded honorary doctorates from De Paul University (2014) and Duquesne University (2015). See "The 100 Most Influential People in the World," *Time*, 2014: http://time.com/time100–2014/ (accessed Dec. 4, 2015).

is a true reflection of the Sacred Heart of Jesus: "I do whatever I do because I am a sister of the Sacred Heart. . . . If I weren't religious, I would not be a Sister. That is why I am here."[34] Or, as she put it most recently, "There is no other formula for love, humility and zeal. . . . This formula is not attractive because it is the cross. But there is no other classroom to learn about compassion, love, and mercy than the Sacred Heart of Jesus. . . . This is the highest PhD. We are students every day. We learn from the Sacred Heart of Jesus."[35]

What do Kataliko and Nyirumbe have in common? First, both are impressive in their practical, nonviolent response to war and its effects in Bukavu and Northern Uganda. Their courage and extraordinary leadership are partly borne out by the admiration they have evoked and the awards they have received. While the effect of their work and leadership may be obvious, what may be less obvious is the logic behind their lives and work, and how each of them has reasoned his and her way to the practical conclusions and alternatives each one provides. It is this inner logic that often remains obscured; and to the extent that it does, their agency, while impressive, remains opaque. By taking time to tell their stories and the rich theological matrix in which their lives are grounded, I have hoped to shed light on that inner logic.

Second, our treatment has revealed and confirmed the extent to which the underlying impulse behind their lives and work is a deeper and more personal encounter with the humanity of God and God's solidarity with suffering humanity. In other words, at the basis of their life and work is the christological reality of the crucified God. For Kataliko, Jesus's suffering on the cross manifests the excess of love of God for humanity and the logic of God's response to evil with love. For Sr. Rosemary Nyirumbe, the Sacred Heart of Jesus is the symbol of God's pierced and bleeding heart, which, as Mazzoldi has noted, releases a "virtue that is gentle and does not kill, which renews and restores." In any event, by turning to the crucified love of God, both Kataliko and Nyirumbe are able to discover forms of passionate, pastoral, and practical engagement on behalf of the crucified peoples in Bukavu and Northern Uganda, respectively. And just as Kataliko's life is psalmic, Sr. Rosemary's life is also psalmic, in that it is a turning to the Sacred Heart of Jesus in an anguished cry of "Why, O God?" on behalf of the girls of Northern Uganda. David Tracy has observed

34. Whitten and Henderson, *Sewing Hope*, 214.

35. Interview with Sr. Rosemary (Mar. 19, 2015). She admits: "I am not a very strong spiritual person, who spends a lot of time in quiet adoration. I have learnt over time that all my activities are prayer. The prayer is a form of self-emptying: it is about the acronym SELF: S (surrender); E (I am empty); L (it is your love); F (fill me; make me whole). So, throughout the day, I keep on praying that prayer of SELF."

that the reality of a hidden or crucified God drives the Christian to the cross and to the memory of suffering and the struggle for and with others, especially the forgotten and marginal ones in history. There can be no better evidence for this claim than in the stories of Christian activists like Kataliko and Nyirumbe.

PART FOUR

The Peace of Lament

CHAPTER 7

The Peace-Building Dimensions of Prophetic Lament

And when he drew near and saw the city, he wept over it, saying,
"Would that you, even you, had known on this day the things that
make for peace! But now they are hidden from your eyes."

Luke 19:41–42

Hear this, O foolish and senseless people,
who have eyes, but see not,
who have ears, but hear not.

Jeremiah 5:21

The Gospels report two occasions on which Jesus explicitly wept. The first occurs (recorded in the Gospel of John) at the tomb of Lazarus (11:35), and the second is in Luke (19:41–42). Both events are significant moments in Jesus's life.[1] Here I am particularly interested in the occasion in Luke's Gospel, an incident that the evangelist places at a significant juncture in the story of Jesus's life and ministry. The whole of Luke's Gospel builds up to Jesus's final (in fact

---

1. As Stephen Voorwinde rightly notes, the raising of Lazarus represents the climax of the "book of signs"—as scholars have called chapters 1–12 of the Gospel of John. Toward the close of this section of John's Gospel, the evangelist uses this final sign (the raising of Lazarus) as the crowning piece of evidence to establish the identity of Jesus as the Messiah, the Son of God. See Stephen Voorwinde, "Jesus' Tears—Human or Divine?" *The Reformed Theological Review* 56, no. 2 (May 1997): 68–81, at 68. For a full treatment of the emotional life of Jesus as depicted in the four Gospels, see Stephen Voorwinde, *Jesus' Emotions in the Gospels* (London: T&T Clark, 2011).

only) entrance into Jerusalem: the long journey to Jerusalem (beginning with 9:51), with its forceful suffering motif, is drawing to a close, and Jesus finally has his destination in view—the royal city, where death awaits him.

Earlier in the story, Luke presents Jesus as lamenting over Jerusalem: "O Jerusalem, Jerusalem, the city that kills the prophets. . . . How often would I have gathered your children together as a hen gathers her brood under her wings, and you were not willing" (Luke 13:34).[2] But it is only here, in Luke 19:41, that Jesus actually weeps—in fact, wails: "And when he drew near and saw the city, he wept over it." The Greek word used is *klaiō*, which may be interpreted as audible weeping and particularly "loud expression of pain and sorrow."[3] Jesus's wailing over Jerusalem is all the more pronounced, not just because of the verb used, and not just because, as a man, he is doing something that women typically do, but also because his weeping stands in such stark contrast to the enthusiastic jubilation of the crowds (19:37), who recognize him as the messianic king of Old Testament promise (19:38, citing Ps. 118:26). This juxtaposition—and thus the abrupt shift in Luke's account—of jubilation to lament, of (the people's) shouts of joy to (Jesus's) tears makes Jesus's wailing all the more striking.

A number of scholars suggest that Jesus's impending death fills him with deep dread.[4] (He already knew about it, but now, on seeing Jerusalem, he realizes the inevitable.) Other scholars suggest that it was out of compassion that Jesus wept over the city that was spread out before him because of the

---

2. For an exploration of this connection, see Bruce N. Frisk, "See My Tears: A Lament for Jerusalem (Luke 13:31-35; 19:41-44)," in *The Word Leaps the Gap: Essays on Scripture and Theology in Honor of Richard B. Hays*, ed. J. Ross Wagner, C. Kavin Rowe, and A. Katherine Grieb (Grand Rapids: Eerdmans, 2008).

3. Voorwinde, "Jesus' Tears," 70. In contrast, John uses *dakryō*—a verb that is often translated into English as "weep" and "burst into tears." This word is generally understood as being synonymous with *klaiō*; the only difference is "in the emphasis upon the noise accompanying the weeping in the case of κλαίω [*klaiō*]" (69-70). This would indicate that, while here in Luke Jesus's weeping means a loud demonstrative form of weeping, a wailing, in John "Jesus did not wail loudly, but he was deeply grieved" (Voorwinde, "Jesus' Tears," 70, quoting Leon Morris, *The Gospel According to John*, rev. ed., New International Commentary on the New Testament (Grand Rapids: Eerdmans, 1995), 495.

4. The motif of messianic suffering is the recurrent refrain throughout the travel narrative of Luke's Gospel. The major section opens on an ominous note: "He resolutely set his face to go to Jerusalem" (9:51) (Voorwinde, "Jesus' Tears," 74). From the outset, the goal of Christ's journey is the passion and resurrection. Consequently, Jesus's weeping makes sense when his destination is finally in view. Thus the wailing, according to Voorwinde, is a reflection of Jesus's humanity, that he could be filled with the same emotions and response that any other human approaching death would be. Voorwinde's overall objective is to show that Jesus's weeping is best understood as an expression of human emotion—rather than a divine act.

impending destruction of Jerusalem, which the Jews were unaware of (the city was eventually destroyed in the year 70 CE). There may be some truth in each of these explanations, but they do not take into full account the words that accompany Jesus's wailing, which refer to the people's lack of knowledge about the things that make for peace: "Would that you, even you, had known on this day the things that make for peace!"

The English translation may not convey the odd form of this sentence, which Bible scholars call an aposiopesis (or "broken syntax"), a breaking off of speech due to strong emotions such as anger, fear, pity, and so forth.[5] This construction in Luke's narrative is a juxtaposition of two clashing emotions and realities. On the one hand, there is the jubilant crowd chanting, "Blessed is he who comes . . ." On the other hand, Jesus is wailing. The other set of juxtaposed contradictions contrasts Jesus, being choked up with emotion and obviously knowing the "things that make for peace," and Jerusalem, being unable to grasp these things and instead carrying on as usual. By placing it within this context—telling the story of Jesus's weeping over Jerusalem the way he does—Luke clearly succeeds in establishing Jesus's role within the prophetic tradition of the Old Testament, and specifically with Jeremiah, the weeping prophet.[6] That is why, in order to draw out the theological and practical implications of Jesus's wailing and the interconnections between lament, epistemology, and the conditions for peace, we need to explore Jeremiah's prophecy and weeping over Jerusalem, which anticipates and offers the interpretative context for Jesus's wailing over Jerusalem.

Jeremiah, the Wailing Prophet

Jeremiah lived at a turbulent time in Israel's history, during which the small kingdom of Judah—and with it the Israelite monarchy—came to an end. Becoming a priest at a fairly young age, Jeremiah carried out his prophetic ministry under various kings—before, during, and after the fall of Jerusalem in 587

5. Voorwinde, "Jesus' Tears," 79; see also Luke 22:42: "If you could take this cup from me. . . ."

6. On entering the city, Jesus goes to the temple area, where he finds people in a festive mood, selling and buying. Jesus drives out the money lenders from the temple, and, with a reference to Isaiah and Jeremiah, says, "It is written, 'My house shall be a house of prayer,' but you have made it a den of robbers" (Luke 19:46). See Isaiah 56:7 for the reference to "my father's house" and Jeremiah 7:11 for the "den of thieves." In Matthew's version, the grief over Jerusalem is preceded by a series of woes (Matt. 23:13–33), which establishes a strong parallel with Jeremiah.

BCE. During the forty years of his ministry, he constantly reminded the people of their covenant obligations and warned them that infidelity to the covenant would bring down God's punishment and bring about the destruction of the nation. While the relationship between Jeremiah the prophet and the biblical book that bears his name is complex, a look at the first twenty-eight chapters brings into sharp focus the prophet's warning about the impending destruction of Jerusalem; and it places Jeremiah's mourning at the heart of this warning— and thus of his prophetic ministry.[7]

The first twenty-eight chapters focus on the coming judgment. Jeremiah is called to prophesy to a people who will not heed his message:

> Hear this, O foolish and senseless people,
>> Who have eyes, but see not,
>> Who have ears, but hear not. (5:21)

A number of Jeremiah's oracles in these chapters are about the approaching doom. He sees a vision of a foe from the north pouring destruction over the land like a pot of boiling water being tipped on its side (1:13-15). Even though unnamed, this foe is perhaps none other than the Babylonian army of King Nebuchadnezzar, which is approaching from the north (4:5-7; 6:22-25). But while Jeremiah sees the nation's impending destruction, the people appear to be completely oblivious of this danger:

> For my people are foolish;
>> they know me not;
> they are stupid children;
>> they have no understanding.
> They are "wise"—in doing evil!
>> But how to do good they know not. (4:22)

7. As Kathleen O'Connor notes in *Jeremiah: Pain and Promise* (Minneapolis: Fortress, 2011), scholars must face the problem of the relationship between Jeremiah the prophet and his book, especially given that "the long, complex book resembles a collage constructed of a motley collection of materials like paper, fabric, pain photographs, newspaper clippings, feathers, found objects—all glued together by some not entirely clear connection to the prophet Jeremiah. . . . There are poems uttered by Jeremiah on behalf of God, called 'oracles.' There are prayers, liturgies, and stories about Jeremiah's deeds and his captivities. There are sermons, laments, oracles of hope, proverbs, and many other types of literature. To complicate matters further, the book switches abruptly from speaker to speaker and image to image. Metaphors appear, disappear, and reappear as themes of warning, suffering, and hope circulate across the book and interrupt one another. And perhaps most perplexing of all, the book has little chronological or narrative order" (29).

The problem is not simply that the people are unaware of the impending destruction; "they are all stubbornly rebellious" (6:28) and have thus closed their ears:

> To whom shall I speak and give warning,
>   that they may hear?
> Behold, their ears are uncircumcised,
>   they cannot listen;
> behold, the word of the Lord is to them an object of scorn;
>   they take no pleasure in it. (6:10)[8]

As a result, Jeremiah's wrath cannot be contained as he pronounces God's judgment:

> Pour it out upon the children in the street,
>   and upon the gatherings of young men, also;
> both husband and wife shall be taken,
>   the elderly and the very aged.
> Their houses shall be turned over to others,
>   their fields and wives together. (6:11–12)

The judgment seems so inescapable that three times Jeremiah is ordered by God to stop praying for the people (7:16; 11:14; 14:11). God will no longer listen to the prophet's entreaties or to the people's cry in their time of need: "Though they fast, I will not hear their cry, and though they offer burnt offering and grain offering, I will not accept them. But I will consume them by the sword, by famine, and by pestilence" (14:12). They are past praying for. Instead, God commands Jeremiah to mourn:

> Cut off your hair and cast it away;
>   raise a lamentation on the bare heights,
> for the Lord has rejected and forsaken
>   the generation of his wrath. (7:29)

8. To fully appreciate what Jeremiah is doing, one must read him against the background of the royal consciousness in its tripartite characteristics of affluence; oppressive social reality; and static religion—characteristics that resist interruption, let alone the irruption of an alternative consciousness that reminds people not only of Yahweh's freedom in history, but the covenant obligations of justice for the poor, the oppressed, and the weak. See Walter Brueggemann, *The Prophetic Imagination* (Philadelphia: Fortress, 1978), pp. 26ff.

Jeremiah is to summon the wailing women:

Call for the mourning women to come;
    send for the skillful women to come;
let them make haste and raise a wailing over us,
    that our eyes may run down with tears
and our eyelids flow with water. (9:17–18)[9]

The lament should echo in the entire community as the professional mourners (the women) are instructed:

Teach to your daughters a lament,
    and each to her neighbor a dirge.
For death has come up into our windows;
    it has entered our palaces,
cutting off the children from the streets
    and the young men from the squares.
Speak: "Thus declares the Lord,
    'The dead bodies of men shall fall
like dung upon the open field,
    like sheaves after the reaper,
and none shall gather them.'" (9:20–22)

Again and again the prophet tries to invite his beloved people to mourn: Thus says the Lord:

O daughter of my people, put on sackcloth,
    and roll in ashes;
make mourning as for an only son,
    most bitter lamentation,
for suddenly the destroyer
    will come upon us. (6:26)

Obviously, Jeremiah's invitation was not heeded, and that heightened Jeremiah's own hopelessness as he found himself standing between God (as God's

---

9. See L. Juliana M. Claassens, "Calling the Keeners: The Image of the Wailing Woman as Symbol of Survival in a Traumatized World," *Journal of Feminist Studies in Religion* 26, no. 1 (2010): 63–77.

spokesperson) and the doomed people (whose fate he shared). The whole section of what has come to be known as Jeremiah's "weeping poems" (8:21–9:11) captures the depth of the prophet's lament:

> For the wound of the daughter of my people is my heart wounded;
> I mourn, and dismay has taken hold on me.
> Is there no balm in Gilead?
> Is there no physician there?
> Why then has the health of the daughter of my people
> not been restored?
> Oh that my head were waters,
> and my eyes a fountain of tears,
> that I might weep day and night
> for the slain of the daughter of my people!
> Oh that I had in the desert
> a travelers' lodging place,
> that I might leave my people
> and go away from them!
> For they are all adulterers,
> a company of treacherous men. (8:21–9:2)

What emerges from these poems, indeed from the entire book of Jeremiah, is not only a vision of prophetic ministry grounded in lament, but Jeremiah as the wailing prophet par excellence, a "master of lament."[10]

But what, one might ask, is the point of Jeremiah's lament? Why doesn't he simply announce God's judgment and offer a warning to his people? Why must he lament and wail even *before* Jerusalem is destroyed? And why must he invite the community into mourning "as if for an only child"? What is he *doing* that ordinary prophetic warning would not do? These are the same questions that are raised by Jesus's wailing over Jerusalem (in Luke), and an answer to them might shed light on the conditions "that make for peace," which both Jeremiah and Jesus are able to see, but which the people remain blind to.

A closer look at Jeremiah's lament-saturated ministry reveals that his laments operate on at least four levels: (1) as a social critique; (2) to mourn the covenant; (3) as a reflection of Yahweh's tears; and (4) to announce the newness

---

10. Ellen Davis, "Jeremiah: Master of Lament," sermon delivered at Duke Divinity School Summer Institute, May 29, 2013.

of restoration. These four provide an outline of the conditions or possibilities for peace (*shalom*) as Jeremiah understood it.

Prophetic Wailing: The Things That Make for Peace

Lament as Social Critique: Shallow Peace

In his pronouncements and laments, Jeremiah exposes the rottenness at the heart of Israel's social and political life, where truth disappeared from both institutional life and everyday interaction:

> They bend their tongue like a bow;
>> falsehood and not truth has grown strong in the land;
> for they proceed from evil to evil,
>> and they do not know me, declares the Lord.
> Let everyone beware of his neighbor,
> and put no trust in any brother,
>> for every brother is a deceiver,
> and every neighbor goes about as a slanderer.
> Everyone deceives his neighbor,
>> and no one speaks the truth;
> they have taught their tongue to speak lies;
>> they weary themselves committing iniquity. (9:3–5)

Everyone has abandoned the ways of Yahweh. "They are 'wise'—in doing evil! But how to do good they know not" (4:22). The result is that, while the political leaders "have become great and rich . . . fat and sleek" (5:27–28), this has been realized on the backs of the poor, who are oppressed:

> They know no bounds in deeds of evil;
>> they judge not with justice
> the cause of the fatherless, to make it prosper,
>> and they do not defend the rights of the needy. (5:28)

Jeremiah's harshest criticisms are directed at the religious leaders. These are the ones who should know better and expose the unjust and evil social structures and ills. Instead, "the prophets will become wind; the word is not in them" (5:13).

An appalling and horrible thing
    has happened in the land:
the prophets prophesy falsely,
    and the priests rule at their direction;
my people love to have it so. (5:30–31)

The priests and prophets do not simply participate in the same wicked ways; they offer consoling promises of shallow peace, thus treating "the wound of my people lightly":

For from the least to the greatest of them,
everyone is greedy for unjust gain;
and from prophet to priest,
everyone deals falsely.
They have healed the wound of my people lightly,
saying, "Peace, peace,"
when there is no peace. (6:13–14)

The reference to greed in verse 13 above, just as the reference to the leaders becoming powerful, rich, fat, and sleek, reflects the economic prosperity of unbridled capitalist gain. Walter Brueggemann has observed: "The economics of affluence and the politics of oppression are the most characteristic marks of the Solomonic achievement. But these by themselves could not have prospered and endured, if they had not received theological sanction."[11] In Jeremiah's time, the theological sanction came by way of the reminder by prophets and priests of God's promise, as they pointed to the temple as a confirmation of that reminder, namely, that David's kingdom will last forever.

The theological confidence that the prophets and priests offered was nothing but a consolation whose effect was to prevent a proper awareness of the true condition and the impending destruction of the kingdom. Therefore, Jeremiah warns the people against the priests and prophets:

Do not trust in these deceptive words: "This is the temple of the Lord, the temple of the Lord, the temple of the Lord." . . . Behold, you trust in deceptive words to no avail. Will you steal, murder, commit adultery, swear falsely, make offerings to Baal, and go after other gods that you have not known, and then come and stand before me in this house, which is called

11. Brueggemann, *Prophetic Imagination*, 28.

by my name, and say, "We are delivered!"—only to go on doing all these abominations? Has this house, which is called by my name, become a den of robbers in your eyes? Behold, I myself have seen it, declares the Lord. (7:4, 8–11)

In Luke's account, Jesus's lament over Jerusalem is immediately followed by his cleansing of the temple—the same temple that provided consolation in the time of Jeremiah as well as in Jesus's day. "By alluding to Jeremiah's famous temple sermon (7:2–15) Jesus exposes the people's foolish misconception that they can commit all manner of sin and then 'flee' to the temple like a brigand to his cave."[12]

In his *Prophetic Imagination*, Brueggemann argues that critique is at the heart of prophetic ministry, and that such critique takes the form of grief. He identifies three constitutive features of what he calls the "royal consciousness," the regnant social imagination of power: affluence, oppression, and static religion. The combined effect of these features is to produce numbness, especially numbness about death and suffering. It is the task of the prophetic imagination to bring people to see and engage suffering and death. This, for Brueggemann, is the core of prophetic critique, which takes the form of grief:

> The prophet does not scold or reprimand. The prophet brings to public expression the dread of endings, the collapse of our self-madness, the barriers and pecking orders that secure us at each other's expense, and the fearful practice of eating off the table of a hungry brother or sister. . . . I believe that the proper idiom for the prophet in cutting through the royal numbness and denial is the language of grief, the rhetoric that engages the community in mourning for a funeral they do not want to admit.

Jesus's lament over Jerusalem, like Jeremiah's oracles and laments, must be seen within the context of this prophetic critique, whose intended effect is to bring the grief of a dying social, political, and religious institution to public expression. As Brueggemann notes, the prophet's unique gift is the capacity "to use the language of lament and the symbolic creation of a death scene as a way of bringing to reality what the king must see and will not."[13]

---

12. Voorwinde, "Jesus' Tears," 78.
13. Brueggemann, *Prophetic Imagination*, 46.

Mourning the Covenant

Jeremiah is not only able to perceive the grief of a dying institution and bring it to public expression; he is also able to point to the abandonment of the covenant relationship as the key reason behind Israel's impending destruction. The prophet's indictment of the city (22:3 and elsewhere) is full of specifics: injustice, corruption, violence, abuse of the vulnerable. These consistently social or "horizontal" vices can also be summarized (e.g., in 22:9) in strictly "vertical," theological terms: "They have abandoned the covenant of the lord their God, and worshiped other gods and served them."[14] Accordingly, for Jeremiah, the two evils—injustice and idolatry—are deeply connected.

In the end, greed, injustice, and the oppression of the poor reflect the broken covenant. The prophet uses various images to portray Israel's betrayal: the people have "forsaken" the covenant (2:13; 4:22), and have "rebelled," and "forgotten" God (2:31–35). They have changed course (2:36) and become rebellious (3:12–16), rejecting the living water: "they have forsaken me, the fountain of living waters and hewed out cisterns for themselves" (2:13). However, by far the most powerful image of Israel's infidelity is the one of marriage: "I remember the devotion of your youth, your love as a bride" (2:2), but now "you have played the whore with many lovers" (3:1).

Yahweh's first response is to invite the unfaithful spouse to repentance, a theme that dominates the first eight chapters of Jeremiah:

> Return, faithless Israel,
>   declares the Lord.
> I will not look on you in anger,
>   for I am merciful,
> declares the Lord;
>   I will not be angry forever. (3:12)

But as Yahweh's invitation goes unheeded and Israel persists in her shameless ways and rejects Yahweh, the prophet is commanded to announce Yahweh's judgment and the impending destruction, which will amount to a complete undoing of creation. It would be hard to find a more striking instance of that clear, painful insight, expressed in concrete images, than Jeremiah's vision of de-creation in 4:23–26:[15]

14. Frisk, "See My Tears," 162.
15. See Davis, "Jeremiah: Master of Lament." Hereafter, page references to this sermon appear in parentheses within the text.

I looked on the earth, and behold, it was without form and void;
    and to the heavens, and they had no light.
I looked on the mountains, and behold, they were quaking,
    and all the hills moved to and fro.
I looked, and behold, there was no man,
    and all the birds of the air had fled.
I looked, and behold, the fruitful land was a desert,
    and all its cities were laid in ruins
    before the Lord, before his fierce anger.

Jeremiah's tears are, as it were, the first installment of the mourning of the de-creation under way as the result of Israel's unfaithfulness, for as Yahweh vows in the verses that follow:

The whole land shall be a desolation. . . .
For this the earth shall mourn,
    and the heavens above be dark. (4:27–28)

From a peacebuilding perspective, what the foregoing discussion confirms is that there can be no genuine peace that does not have as its foundation or core the covenant relationship. Israel's attempt to secure her peace through economic and political alliances with her neighbors, while neglecting the basic requirements of the covenant relationship with Yahweh, is both misguided and dangerous. Such an attempt not only amounts to rejecting Yahweh himself, but also has dire consequences: Israel's destruction and, beyond that, the unmaking of the whole of creation. This is what Jeremiah sees and mourns.

The Prophet Jeremiah as the "Other" of Yahweh

Jeremiah's tears are not just an embodied social critique and not merely an expression of mourning for the loss of the covenant and its effects; they also reflect Yahweh's own tears. The divine laments in 4:19–21 and 8:18–9:3 set the tone of the announcement of judgment. Even as Yahweh pronounces the destruction of his people, Yahweh is the first to suffer and the first to weep: "My anguish, my anguish! I writhe in pain" (4:19). "My joy is gone; grief is upon me; my heart is sick within me" (8:18). "Oh that my head were waters, and my eyes a fountain of tears, so that I might weep day and night for the slain of the daughter of my people" (9:1).[16]

Interwoven with Jeremiah's pronouncements of the coming judgment of God are a series of personal laments that have been called the "confessions of Jeremiah": 11:18–23; 12:1–6; 15:21; 17:14–18; 18:19–23; 20:7–18. What is significant about these "confessions of Jeremiah" is that, in the midst of Jeremiah's lament, God breaks in to express his own resentment and grief over the sins of the people (e.g., 8:18–9:11; 12:7–13; 15:5–9; 18:13–17), so that it is often difficult to tell who is weeping—Jeremiah or God.

> Let my eyes run down with tears night and day,
>   and let them not cease,
> for the virgin daughter of my people is shattered with a great wound,
>   with a very grievous blow. (14:17)

The frequent difficulty of distinguishing who is weeping, Yahweh or Jeremiah (as in the above verse), means that "the tears of God exist alongside and are often mingled with Jeremiah's tears."[17] To be sure, Jeremiah's confessions reflect the prophet's rejection by his own people, and come to a climax during Jeremiah's imprisonment. He feels

> like a gentle lamb
>   led to the slaughter;
> I did not know it was against me
>   they devised schemes, saying,
> "Let us destroy the tree with its fruit;
>   let us cut him off from the land of the living,
> that his name be remembered no more." (11:19)

He laments:

> Woe is me, my mother, that you bore me, a man of strife and contention to

---

16. See Scott A. Ellington, *Risking Truth* (Eugene, OR: Pickwick, 2008), 137.

17. Ellington, *Risking Truth*, 131. Ellington cites J. J. M. Roberts, who, e.g., argues that the passages in Jeremiah that cause Jeremiah to be identified as the weeping prophet (Jer. 4:19–21; 8:18–9:3; 14:17–18) refer not to the weeping of the prophet but to the weeping of God. See Roberts, "The Motif of the Weeping God in Jeremiah and Its Background in the Lament Tradition of the Ancient Near East," in Roberts, *The Bible and the Ancient Near East: Collected Essays* (Winona Lake, IN: Eisenbrauns, 2002).

the whole land! I have not lent, nor have I borrowed, yet all of them curse me. (15:10)

At the height of his lament, Jeremiah accuses God of setting him up, for in spite of Yahweh's earlier assurances to Jeremiah (see 1:8; 1:17–19), the latter feels totally abandoned:

O Lord, you have deceived me,
    and I was deceived;
you are stronger than I,
    and you have prevailed.
I have become a laughingstock all the day;
    everyone mocks me. (20:7)

But what is interesting is that even Jeremiah's being rejected is a reflection of Yahweh's own rejection by the lover who "has played the whore with many lovers" (3:1) and who "has become to me like a lion in the forest" (12:8). Accordingly, Jeremiah suffers not simply because he represents God to the people; he participates directly in the divine experience of rejection, and thus in the divine pathos. As Ellington notes, the primary task of the prophet is first "to experience and then to express the anguish and anger of God caused by God's relationship with an unfaithful people":

Because the prophet speaks to the people out of the heart of God, "a prophetic work begins, not with hellfire and damnation, but with the picture of the pain and anguish of God." The prophet stands between God and Israel to deliver God's word. The form of the prophetic message is found not only in what he or she speaks, but in the prophet's direct participation in the pain of God. . . . The prophetic ministry is one of shared pathos.[18]

Coming from a slightly different angle, Ellen Davis arrives at a similar conclusion about the prophetic task. Prophecy, she notes, is about seeing our present situation in the divine perspective. The prophet's gift "is to see with clarity what others do not see or turn away from, and then to communicate it, framing it in words and sometimes in embodied signs/acts" (2). But since, as O'Connor notes, the God that the prophet speaks *to* and *for* is "not a Greek deity of stoic power and unchangeableness but a fluid being filled with pathos and

---

18. Ellington, *Risking Truth*, 46.

emotionally engaged in the life of the people,"[19] the prophetic task involves the "twin disciplines of bearing pain and bearing with God" (Davis, 3). Thus, Davis concludes, "the prophet is suspended in the terrible middle space between God and the doomed people, unable to turn away fully from either one" (3). Among the prophets, Jeremiah most fully expresses the pain of occupying that space.

Perhaps what needs to be highlighted in Davis's observation is the fact that the *gift* (insight, the ability to see) and the *discipline* (bearing pain, bearing God) of prophetic ministry are integrally connected. They go hand in hand. The ability to see the situation clearly from God's perspective does not come easily or naturally. It requires and involves the "twin disciplines of bearing pain and bearing with God" (2). However, it is this pain-saturated "bearing" that projects the promise of newness.

A New Covenant

Jeremiah's call to the prophetic task involves three sets of words:

> See, I have set you this day over nations and over kingdoms
> to *pluck up* and to *break down,*
> to *destroy* and to *overthrow,*
> to *build* and to *plant.* (1:10)

Jeremiah is called on not only to tear down but also to build and plant, not only to offer warning for the impending destruction (as in the first twenty-eight chapters), but also to evoke hope in the wake of destruction. The section of Jeremiah that runs from the beginning of chapter 31 to the last verse of chapter 33 is often referred to by scholars as the "book of consolation." Here Jeremiah's words to those who survived the destruction he had predicted and to those carried off into exile are filled with promises of healing and visions of return. The prophet promises not just restoration; he speaks of "a new order" in which the city will be rebuilt on its mound, the citadel set on its rightful site (30:18); the people, who were once crushed and despised, will be honored (30:19); and visions of economic flourishing will fill city and countryside:

> "He who scattered Israel will gather him,
> and will keep him as a shepherd keeps his flock."

19. O'Connor, *Jeremiah: Pain and Promise*, 65.

> For the Lord has ransomed Jacob
>   and has redeemed him from hands too strong for him.
> They shall come and sing aloud on the height of Zion,
>   and they shall be radiant over the goodness of the Lord,
> over the grain, the wine, and the oil,
>   and over the young of the flock and the herd;
> their life shall be like a watered garden,
>   and they shall languish no more.
> Then shall the young women rejoice in the dance,
>   and the young men and the old shall be merry.
> I will turn their mourning into joy;
>   I will comfort them, and give them gladness for sorrow.
> I will feast the soul of the priests with abundance,
>   and my people shall be satisfied with my goodness,
> declares the Lord. (31:10–14)

For Jeremiah, the restoration will signal a new covenant that God will make with the people:

> Behold, the days are coming, declares the Lord, when I will make a new covenant with the house of Israel and the house of Judah, not like the covenant that I made with their fathers on the day when I took them by the hand to bring them out of the land of Egypt, my covenant that they broke, though I was their husband, declares the Lord. For this is the covenant that I will make with the house of Israel after those days, declares the Lord: I will put my law within them, and I will write it on their hearts. And I will be their God, and they shall be my people. (31:31–33)

The throbbing heart of Yahweh's new covenant is the promise that "they will all know me":

> No longer shall each one teach his neighbor and each his brother, saying, "Know the Lord," for they shall all know me, from the least of them to the greatest, declares the Lord. (31:34)

Recall that the lack of that knowledge was a major theme in Jeremiah's lament against his people. He reproaches them for their failure to know the time, which, according to Jeremiah, was the result of their having set aside the covenant. The birds and the animals did better, for at least they knew the times

(8:7). It is a similar lack of knowledge ("Would that you, even you, had known on this day the things that make for peace!" [Luke 19:42]) that is at the heart of Jesus's lament over Jerusalem. Now, here in the book of Jeremiah, it is clear that the knowledge at stake is the knowledge of God. From the least of them to the greatest, "they shall all *know* me" (Jer. 31:34). The verb used here for this knowledge is *yada'*, which means to relate intimately, as in sexual intimacy. By using the same word that is used for carnal knowledge, Jeremiah plays on the marriage image noted earlier. Unlike the infidelity that led to Israel's destruction, the people will enjoy, with the new covenant, a close and intimate relationship with God or, as O'Connor notes, "they will be breathers of God's life."[20] To have knowledge of God means to participate in God's life, glimpsed provisionally and partially and practiced in community.

But if the promised restoration is founded on a new covenant and intimate relationship between God and the people, what is clear from our exploration of the book of Jeremiah is that this *renew*ed covenant is born only out of tears— Yahweh's own tears. Ellington puts it well when he notes that

> the laments of Jeremiah both give expression to divine pathos, and in doing so, create space for the notion of covenant to be conceived of in new ways. It is Jeremiah's unique contribution to see in the divine suffering the basis for a new covenant that embraces personal relationship rather than political attachment as its basis.[21]

This is what makes Jeremiah, for all his wailing, a prophet of hope—"the boldest and most inventive of all the prophets of hope."[22] Brueggemann has observed that the articulation of pathos—grieving over death—is the necessary first step of prophetic ministry. But for him, this grieving over death is not an end in itself. In view of the other crucial task of prophetic ministry, namely, the task of energizing, "it is the task of the prophetic imagination and ministry to bring people to engage the promise of newness that is at work in our history with God."[23] It is this newness that Jeremiah communicates. Out of his own pain he has come to know (to intimately participate in) God's own pathos, and thus to see the new covenant that is under way in and through God's anguished love for his wayward people.

20. O'Connor, *Jeremiah: Pain and Promise*, 112.

21. Ellington, *Risking Truth*, 136.

22. See Brueggemann, *Prophetic Imagination*, 59, referring to Thomas Raitt, *A Theology of Exile: Judgment/Deliverance in Jeremiah and Ezekiel* (Philadelphia: Fortress, 1977).

23. Brueggemann, *Prophetic Imagination*, 59-60.

I have found it necessary to explore Jeremiah's prophetic ministry of lament at length in order to lay out the full context of Jesus's wailing over Jerusalem and to make obvious the full force of its political and peacebuilding implications. Our exploration has confirmed that Jeremiah's pronouncements, critique, and lament point not only to much-needed reform and revision but to the birth of a new society founded on a new covenant. In his wailing over Jerusalem, Jesus not only casts himself as a kind of Jeremiah, but as an embodiment of the entire prophetic tradition, which is at once a form of critique and a form of energizing (to use Brueggemann's language), or which "moves from woe to blessing, from judgment to hope, from criticism to energy."[24] Accordingly, Jesus and his lament over Jerusalem—no less than Jeremiah's wailing—points to a new covenant, which Jesus was about to realize in the final week of his life. This new covenant is not going to be founded on strategic military alliances, nor simply on the false assurance of the presence of a temple, but on a new intimate relationship—indeed, a passionate relationship—that will be chiseled on their hearts ("I will write it" [Jer. 31:33]).

What Jesus's wailing points to and dramatically reenacts is the vision of a new society, a fresh vision of peace founded on a new covenant of self-sacrificing love. That is why Jesus's wailing cannot be construed as a "religious" event that might have political implications. It is a decisive political intervention—a critique of present political logic and systems built on military force, problematic alliances, an economics of greed, and an absence of truth. It is also the provision of an alternative, nonviolent form of politics. Instead of the usual self-serving schemes of political realism, Jesus offers a vision of society founded on the self-sacrificing love of God himself. This new vision of society is born of the throbbing pathos of God, which Jesus dramatically expresses in his wailing as he enters Jerusalem, but later more quietly participates in by way of his passion, crucifixion, and death.

This is the newness, the hope, that the ministry of Jesus, which is dramatically captured by Luke in the wailing scene, communicates. And just as with Jeremiah, Jesus's own knowledge of—and intimate participation in—the pathos of God is the condition of possibility out of which the vision of an alternative, nonviolent society emerges. What Brueggemann says about Jeremiah is especially true of Jesus:

The prophet is engaged in a battle for language, in an effort to create a different epistemology out of which another community might emerge. The

24. Brueggemann, *Prophetic Imagination*, 109.

prophet is not addressing behavior problems. He is not even pressing for repentance. He has only the hope that the *ache* of God could penetrate the *numbness* of history. He engages not in scare or threat but only in a yearning that grows with and out of pain.[25]

Brueggemann's observation confirms that the tears of Jeremiah and Jesus are a form of epistemology—a way of knowing. This is not the *epistēmē* of detached theoretical or analytical knowledge; nor is it merely the *technē* of peace-building skills and peace accords; it is also not merely the ethical knowledge that addresses moral and behavioral problems. It is *yadaʿ*, an intimate personal knowledge of and participation in God's anguished love for God's people. It is a form of engagement, a way of living, a kind of compassion (suffering with) that, as in the case of Jeremiah and Jesus, not only critiques forms of shallow peace that masquerade as true peace, but brings people to engage the promise of newness within those nonviolent alternatives that they discover via their journey and history with God.

Something of this knowledge is what is at work in the life and nonviolent struggle of Mama Angelina Atyam of Northern Uganda, who was willing to sacrifice her daughter, "knowing" that that is what God would have her do rather than give up the struggle on behalf of all abducted children.[26] It is this kind of knowledge that is also at work in the life and nonviolent advocacy of Archbishop Christopher Munzihirwa of Bukavu in Eastern Congo. His oft-repeated saying—"there are things that can be seen only by eyes that have cried"—points to this prophetic logic that is both a critique of the politics of violence and the promise of a new, nonviolent social reality grounded in what Munzihirwa referred to as "the way of Christ." In order to get a fuller grasp of the social and political implications of prophetic lament within the African context, let us examine the story of Archbishop Christopher Munzihirwa and his work in Bukavu.

25. Brueggemann, *Prophetic Imagination*, 55.
26. See E. Katongole, *The Sacrifice of Africa: A Political Theology for Africa* (Grand Rapids: Eerdmans, 2011).

CHAPTER 8

Christopher Munzihirwa and the Politics of Nonviolent Love

There are things that can be seen only with eyes that have cried.

Christopher Munzihirwa

Emmanuel Kataliko's predecessor as Archbishop of Bukavu was Christopher Munzihirwa mwene Ngabo. Munzihirwa had been ordained a diocesan priest for Bukavu in 1958, but he soon entered the Jesuit order. After his religious profession in 1965, he undertook a brief period of studies (social and economic science) in Belgium, before he returned to Congo to serve, first as director of social services at the Ignatian House in Kinshasa, then as rector of the Jesuit scholasticate in Kimwena, and eventually as the provincial of Jesuits in Central Africa (Zaire, Rwanda, and Burundi). In 1986 he was named coadjutor bishop of Kasongo, and eventually the titular bishop there in 1990. In 1994, Pope John Paul II named him Archbishop of Bukavu.

Munzihirwa's tenure as Archbishop of Bukavu lasted just a little over two years—two turbulent years in the history of Congo and Bukavu. At the time of his installation as archbishop (June 1994), the Rwandan genocide was still unfolding in Congo's eastern neighbor and millions of refugees were crossing from Rwanda into the city of Bukavu, located on the Zaire side of Rwanda's western border. The arrival of so many refugees there and in the neighboring villages created an immediate humanitarian crisis. The city was crowded; the countryside was overpopulated; trees were cut down for firewood and to make spaces on which to pitch makeshift tents; the population was hungry; and there was fear of an outbreak of cholera and/or other diseases. At the same time, armed gangs—made up of undisciplined, underpaid, and demoralized Zairean soldiers, plus Rwandan *Interahamwe* youth militias (many of whom had committed genocide in Rwanda)—roamed the streets, terrorizing the population, extorting money from the refugees, and pillaging the towns and homes of the local population.

In response to that refugee crisis, Munzihirwa's leadership assumed various forms. He met with military commanders and issued statements that called on soldiers to be disciplined and to avoid pillaging; he reminded them of their duty to protect people's property and lives. He also encouraged the local population to welcome the refugees. He himself did as much. On many mornings he would go across the bridge and help children, the sick, and the infirm cross over the bridge. When the genocide in neighboring Rwanda was over, he appealed to the international community to put pressure on the Rwandan government to welcome the refugees back, while at the same time protesting the forced repatriation of refugees. As Rwandan troops prepared to attack Zaire in the fall of 1996, and civil and military leaders fled the region, Munzihirwa remained the sole leader and shield between the Rwandan forces and the vulnerable populace of Bukavu. On Sunday, October 27, 1996, he issued a final plea from the pulpit to the people, encouraging them to "stand firm in charity," not to flee from their homes, and to avoid rumors and radio propaganda meant to incite panic. Two days later he drove to a neighboring parish and rescued two Rwandan nuns whose lives were threatened. In the afternoon, he held a meeting with remaining civic and business leaders to try to figure out a way to save the city.[1] As he left that meeting to return to his residence at the Jesuit Alifajiri School in the evening, he was stopped at a checkpoint and shot dead by a Rwandan military commander.

Munzihirwa's assassination was not wholly unexpected—either by his colleagues (who constantly worried about his exposure) or by Munzihirwa himself. In an Easter message that year he had written: "Despite anguish and suffering, the Christian who is persecuted for the cause of justice finds spiritual peace in total and profound assent to God, in accord with a vocation that can lead even to death."[2]

But what drove Munzihirwa to embrace a "vocation that [could] lead even to death"? What did he see? What shaped Munzihirwa's vision in the way he understood himself as a pastor and shaped his courage as well as his simple lifestyle? What was his vision of society, into which he invited the people of

1. Among other things, he recorded and sent a radio message to Rome in a bid to raise international awareness of the situation. See Christian Decker, "Voices from the Grave," http://jloughnan.tripod.com/zaire.htm (4/3/15).

2. See John Allen, *The Global War on Christians: Dispatches from the Front Lines of Anti-Christian Persecution* (New York: Image, 2013), 49.

Bukavu at this critical time? What inspired that vision of society, and what were its specific marks?

The key to answering these questions—that is, the key to the whole of Munzihirwa's life and pastoral ministry—lies in one of his favorite sayings: "There are things that can be seen only with eyes that have cried."[3] The more closely one examines this observation, the more one notes that the "seeing" that Munzihirwa refers to is the *yada'*—the intimate personal knowledge of and participation in God's anguished love for God's people that Jeremiah (and Jesus) pointed to. But just as with the wailings of Jeremiah and Jesus, Munzihirwa's anguished life points to a revolutionary social vision founded on nonviolent, self-sacrificing love. Munzihirwa not only invoked this vision, he performed it as he invited the people of Bukavu into its reality. That is why, in the face of the region's (Congo's and Rwanda's) violent politics of power and plunder, Munzihirwa's vision and "politics" could not but clash with that of the generals, and would thus lead to his inevitable assassination. However, this is what makes Munzihirwa, for all his limitations, a kind of Jeremiah and Christlike figure, whose life and ministry provides an ecclesiological illumination of the church as a nonviolent alternative and interruption of the politics of violence. The church's own ability to be such a nonviolent interruption depends on its ability to enter the "way of Christ"—to enter, that is, the way of God's self-sacrificing love that is manifested through his suffering and death. As it turns out, entering the "way of Christ" is not a mere pious or spiritual recommendation; it is an invitation into a revolutionary social vision.

The Way of Christ: A Revolutionary Social Vision

In a 1995 Advent message to the refugees, Munzihirwa wrote:

> We hope that in entering the way of Christ, in a month we will be able to wish each other a "Merry Christmas," the joy of the Son of God, who is born in the gash of human history and who knows that he will die on the Cross to save the world. It is this profound joy of true hope—that which hopes against all hope—that I already wish for you and that, in solidarity, we will construct together while waiting for the day of your return to your homeland.[4]

3. Allen, *Global War on Christians*, 49.

4. Christopher Munzihirwa, Advent Pastoral Letter, Bukavu (November 18, 1995; translation by the author).

Munzihirwa addressed this message to Rwandan refugees at the height of intense pressure being brought by the United Nations concerning the forced repatriation of the Rwanda refugees. In his message, Munzihirwa protested the decision to repatriate, arguing that "we cannot agree to the measures taken against you that violate the rights of man and especially the rights of the refugee. The refugee cannot be repatriated against his will, above all when he knows that almost certain death awaits him in his homeland."[5] Inviting the refugees to identify with the Son of God, he encouraged them not simply to accept their suffering but to see their suffering as in the spirit of Christ's, as a "purification to prepare for a better, clearer, and more united future." In that way their suffering, rather than simply being passive endurance, would become an opportunity for "conversion" and for the construction of a new society "that we will construct together as we wait for the day of your return."[6]

True, Munzihirwa understood the work of conversion to be at its core a "spiritual" message, a new encounter with God. But because it was that, it was also a revolutionary social experience. Quoting Charles Péguy, the French poet and essayist, he noted:

> Social revolution . . . will be moral or will not be revolution. . . . We cannot transform the social system without reforming ourselves first, provoking in ourselves a renovation of spiritual and moral life, digging down to the personal, spiritual, and moral foundations of human life, and renewing spiritual and moral ideas that preside over the constitution and over social life as such, and by awakening within that group a new spring. Our true battlefield is first the soul, the spirit of man.[7]

Accordingly, if the way of the Son of man, who is born "in the gash of human history," points to Christ's willingness to suffer violence rather than use violence to establish his kingdom, entering "his" way is at the same time a social vision—a vision of society founded not on war but on nonviolent love. War cannot be the foundation of true and lasting peace, Munzihirwa often reminded his audience: "We must remember that war is always something despicable. Those who love peace work to build structures of justice, forgiveness, and love."[8] As he reminded the university students of Bukavu, these structures

---

5. Munzihirwa, Advent Pastoral Letter, 1995.

6. Munzihirwa, Advent Pastoral Letter, 1995.

7. See Sébastien Muyengo Mulombe, *Christophe Munzihirwa: La Sentinelle des Grands Lacs* (Kinshasa: Afriquespoir, 2011), 17–18 (translation by the author).

8. Deogratias Mirindi Ya Nacironge, *Père Evêque Christophe Munzihirwa Mwene Ngabo,*

of peace take time to "grow" and require the necessary social, political, and economic institutions of a nation: "We need peace to grow. Not the peace of the armies of those who each day are standing at the ready for war, nor the peace of the cemetery. Rather, we want living and invigorating peace that allows economic, legal, agronomic, and medical sciences to flourish in our university."[9]

If Munzihirwa's vision of peace required the building of institutional structures of justice, forgiveness, and love, it also required and equally depended on everyday nonviolent interruptions of the business of war. Thus, in the anxiety-saturated atmosphere, as Rwanda prepared to attack Bukavu in 1996, Archbishop Munzihirwa warned the populace against rumors (warmongering) and encouraged them to go about their daily lives, cultivate their fields,[10] open the markets and shops, replant trees, protect the soil cover, and resist the temptation to flee from their homes.[11] Just as for Kataliko, Munzihirwa's everyday practices were not only an effort to resist the effects of war but were the path for the "construction of true and durable peace." For Munzihirwa, however, "the greatest weapon in the struggle for peace and resistance against violence [had to] remain solidarity and charity toward everybody."[12]

Behind Munzihirwa's call for "charity toward everybody" is a vision of shared humanity with the Son of God, who, via the incarnation, establishes our shared humanity with our suffering brothers and sisters. This is what Munzihirwa was pointing to when, in the Advent letter quoted above, he told the refugees: "Since we welcomed you, your fate has become in some ways ours. It is the same Christ who suffers in all of us." It is the same vision of our shared humanity that Munzihirwa proposes as an antidote in the highly charged and

---

Prophète et Martyr en notre temps (Bukavu: Center Interdiocésain de Pastorale, Catéchèse et Liturgie, Julie 2003), 83 (translation by the author).

9. Mirindi Ya Nacironge, *Père Evêque*, 83.

10. In an address to the students and faculty at the University of Bukavu, less than two weeks before his assassination, Munzihirwa talked to his audience about the need for medical research in preventive, nutritional, and curative medicine, but also reminded them that healthy eating is the first medicine. See "L'Université de Bukavu et la paix," Bukavu (Oct. 19, 1996), in Joseph Mukabalera Cigwira, "Monseigneur Munzihirwa Christophe, Romero du Congo? Le concept de Martyre de Béatification et de Canonization revisités à lumière de l'histoire religieuse contemporaine" (PhD diss., L'Université Libre de Bruxelles, 2003).

11. "We need the agronomic research that helps us not only to improve vegetable and animal species, but which permits ecological equilibrium through the reforestation of our hills, which were stripped in ignorance of the unpleasant consequences of deforestation or in the greedy unconsciousness of people who only cared about getting rich" (Munzihirwa, "L'Université de Bukavu et la paix").

12. "Stand Firm in Charity" (Oct. 27, 1996).

volatile "ethnic" context in Bukavu.[13] Even as people have a right to defend themselves and their property against looters, Munzihirwa warned against perpetrating ethnic violence: "Let us remember that we are Christians. We never encourage racial, tribal, or ethnic discrimination. And one who harms a human being [who is] the image of God harms God himself."[14] Behind Munzihirwa's appeal lay a vision not only of shared humanity (in the image of God) but of reconciled ethnic differences as the foundation of a new society: "Our happiness should be in seeing people of all the ethnicities around the Great Lakes Region rub shoulders like brothers, enriching themselves from their differences and from constant dialogue. The strongest countries are those who have succeeded in reconciling differences."[15]

Performing the Way of Christ

I have taken time to outline the social vision behind Munzihirwa's invitation to the refugees and the citizens of Bukavu into "the way of Christ" in order to underscore both its revolutionary and nonviolent nature. This social vision was particularly revolutionary in the context of Munzihirwa's Bukavu, as well as in the broader context of the church in Congo. For, as Prunier notes, while the Catholic church grew increasingly powerful in the wake of Mobutu's collapsing state, it was also "thoroughly Zairenized" in that it tended to reflect the ethnic and political culture of Congo society.[16] Given this observation, the radical nature of Munzihirwa's vision consisted not only in the force of his words but also in the way in which he himself embodied that vision and lived it out in his actions, actions that confirmed that the "way of Christ" was not an abstract theological doctrine, not simply a restatement of a principle of Catholic social teaching. This was no mere pastoral knowledge; this was *yada'*, the intimately personal knowledge of one born in the fracturing of human history. In order

13. For a good background to and analysis of the politics of "ethnicity" in Kivu, see Gérard Prunier, "The Catholic Church and the Kivu Conflict," *Journal of Religion in Africa* 31, no. 2 (2001): 139–62.

14. Mulombe, *Christophe Munzihirwa*, 11.

15. Munizihirwa, Letter, Sept. 27, 1996. Again, in a letter directed to all churches (Sept. 29, 1995), Munizihirwa writes: "Let us remain welcoming to strangers in order to enrich ourselves with multiplied values that bring together different ethnicities and races. . . . It is crazy to attack peaceful people just because they are of a certain ethnicity. No one among us has chosen his or her parents or his or her ethnicity."

16. Prunier, "Catholic Church and the Kivu Conflict," 156.

to get a sense of what this knowledge, or *yada'*, looked like, I will highlight four characteristics of Munzihirwa's life and ministry.

The Muhudumu of Bukavu

Soon after he was appointed bishop of Kasongo in 1990, Munzihirwa started using the title *Muhudumu*—a Swahili word that means "watchman" and is often used for a shepherd who stays out and awake at night, watching over the sheep—to refer to himself and his role as bishop. Munzihirwa saw this title as theologically fitting (a reflection of John 10:1-18) and culturally relevant, a title that described his pastoral ministry better than titles such as "bishop" or "archbishop." Thus, at the height of the tensions in Bukavu, with war looming, Munzihirwa is reported to have answered those who encouraged him to take refuge in another diocese by saying, "I am the Muhudumu of Bukavu. Yes, I have the possibility of leaving, but where will the population of Bukavu flee to?"[17] For the same reason, in the homily that he gave shortly before his assassination, he encouraged his priests to "stand firm" and not to flee from their parishes. It was Munzihirwa's self-understanding as the Muhudumu of Bukavu that gave him the confidence and courage to engage different publics and offer various messages and warnings to the soldiers,[18] the international community, the refugees, and the local populace.[19] He took his title of Muhudumu so seriously that he saw himself not simply as caring for the Catholic faithful of the

17. Mulombe, *Christophe Munzihirwa*, 15.

18. In a September 1996 letter addressed to the military, which entreated soldiers to stop pillaging the goods of ordinary civilians, Munzihirwa wrote: "Soldiers whose ideal is pillaging cannot defend the homeland. Pillaging is in the heart of the soldiers tired of themselves. . . . Discipline is at the base of military efficiency. . . . The Gospel tells that while soldiers asked John the Baptist what we should do to save our souls, he responded, 'Respect justice and content yourself with your pay.'"

19. In a letter to Cardinal Danneels and the European community (Jan. 30, 1996), Munzihirwa invited them to exert pressure on the Rwandan government to welcome the refugees back, pointing to the need to investigate the possibility that the government of Rwanda was invoking the 1994 genocide as an excuse to carry out mass killings of Hutu in the refugee camps (Mulombe, *Christophe Munzihirwa*, 10). In an October 1995 letter to the United Nations high commissioner for refugees, he warned of a new "Palestinian problem" in central Africa: "The refugees find themselves cornered. Zaire doesn't want them anymore. Rwanda doesn't want them either. . . . The situation therefore is explosive. There is urgency." In a letter to President Jimmy Carter, Munzihirwa declared: "The refugees in the camps live in a painful situation. They feel despised. . . . The health care available to them is elementary and insufficient . . . [and] the prospect of forced repatriation . . . breeds strong fear among them" (Letter, Jan. 30, 1996).

archdiocese, but also as the watchman for the entire population of Bukavu. Thus, on the afternoon of his assassination, he met with key civic and business leaders of the city to work out a plan to protect the city. A Protestant pastor captured Munzihirwa's impact in these words: "Munzihirwa . . . was a pastor for all people of Bukavu and of Kivu."[20] Another pastor I met in Munzihirwa Square (the city has so named the area where he was assassinated) concurred: "Munzihirwa was truly a Christian. Beyond Catholic, Anglican, Pentecostal. Even beyond Christian."[21]

Welcoming Refugees

Munzihirwa's advocacy on behalf of the refugees did not endear him to either the local population or the Rwanda government. Already by November 1994, public sentiment had turned against the refugees: they were seen not only as dangerous interlopers but also as the beneficiaries of help and services that the local population could not dream of receiving. Consequently, the local political parties operating in Kivu sent a memorandum to the United Nations High Commission for Refugees (UNHCR), which read in part:

> These refugees have destroyed our food reserves, destroyed our fields, our cattle, our natural parks, caused famine and spread epidemics; they benefit from food aid while we get nothing. They sell or give weapons to their fellow countrymen; commit murders of both Tutsi and local Zairians. . . . They must be disarmed, counted, subjected to Zairian laws and finally repatriated.[22]

Munzihirwa opposed this wholesale condemnation of the refugees as he also opposed the 1996 decision by the NGOs and the American government to reduce food rations to the refugee camps in order to force the refugees to return to Rwanda. "Even refugees deserve to eat," he argued. At the same time, he opposed the "humanitarian" approach of aid agencies that were giving out food rations, and he suggested that NGOs instead pay local farmers to grow the food. Otherwise, the humanitarianism of the NGOs would end up disempowering the refugees and impoverishing the local host communities.

20. Mirindi Ya Nacironge, *Père Evêque*, 30.
21. Interview, Munzihirwa Square, Bukavu (July 17, 2013).
22. Quoted in Prunier, "Catholic Church and the Kivu Conflict," 151-52.

The key to understanding Munzihirwa's radical hospitality to the refugees is that it reflects the incarnational vision of the shared humanity with one who was born "in the gash of human history" and thus calls us into the sufferings of our brothers and sisters. Even before he became the Archbishop of Bukavu, when he was still a Jesuit provincial, Munzihirwa spent time with refugees. This was particularly true in 1979, during the refugee crisis in the West Nile (Uganda) as Ugandan refugees flooded into Congo following the destruction of the town of Arua by Idi Amin's fleeing soldiers. Munzihirwa, together with a Comboni priest, set up camp among the refugees, much to the chagrin of the UN and other humanitarian agencies. But as a result of the presence of Munzihirwa and the other priest, conditions in the camps improved tremendously.[23]

A Simple Way of Life

In Bukavu, people still talk about Munzihirwa's simplicity. He dressed simply (one of his confreres at the Jesuit school said that he had two shirts, which he personally washed and hung out to dry). He never took up residence at the bishop's palace, instead staying with the Jesuit community at the Alifajiri School, where he had a simple room. He often walked to his office at the cathedral or rode in one of the community's cars. On the day of his assassination, he was dressed in a simple clerical shirt when he approached the roadblock and identified himself as the archbishop. "If he had not told them that he was the archbishop, they would not have known," one of the priests remarked.[24] When a group of young Xaverians found his dead body the following morning at the corner of the street, they laid it on a bed and carried it into the church. Later that afternoon, they made a plain coffin out of the benches from the church, and carried his body to the cathedral for a simple funeral mass, at the end of which they buried him in a simple grave outside the cathedral. He died and was buried in the same simple way that he lived.[25]

A priest summed up the significance of Munzihirwa's lifestyle well:

Munzihirwa was a simple priest, a simple bishop, with a simple yet profound message. . . . His preaching and message was always simple and concrete. . . .

23. Interview with Didier (July 2013).
24. Interview with Didier (July 2013).
25. For one who lived and died simply, he must be turning in his grave to see the expensive monument and mausoleum that has been constructed over his and his two successor bishops' graves.

It was a message of a God who cares and protects all, especially the weak and poor, and wishes everyone to experience the same freedom and dignity of being children of God.[26]

The priest's observation confirms that Munzihirwa's simplicity not only reflected the "way of Christ" but was also the source of his own freedom and courage. "He was completely free, simple, and unafraid," the priest noted. But while Munzihirwa's message and way of life struck this quoted priest (and others) as fresh, it proved to be a challenge to many other priests, who feared him and tried to avoid him at all costs. In a society known for its flamboyance (a reflection of Mobutu's *authenticité*), some priests found him and his simple lifestyle "odd" (not befitting the office of archbishop) and even an embarrassment to the church.

Sharer in the "Way of Christ"

Writing to the Christians of Corinth, Paul reminded them that we are "always carrying in the body the death of Jesus, so that the life of Jesus may also be manifested in our bodies" (2 Cor. 4:10). Death was a constant theme in Munzihirwa's preaching: he noted that "in life's death, dying is important, because all preceding existence is a preparation for this act. And the final silence is a word of great richness for the one who knows how to listen within (to the interior)." On the twenty-fifth anniversary of his ordination as a priest, meditating on the words of 1 Peter 4:13, he said: "Insofar as you share in Christ's suffering, rejoice so that on the day of his glory, you may also rejoice and be glad." Munzihirwa further noted how this was the spiritual center of his ministry: "For a long time, I have begged Christ to give me the grace to keep this message in my heart. May the memory of his cross remain at the core of my being." This was another confirmation of Munzihirwa's freedom and courage for, as he wrote, "Only free men stand upright in the face of death; only they know how to defy death."[27]

However, the true source of Munzihirwa's courage was his identification with the suffering of Christ. For Munzihirwa, that identification meant that he

26. Interview with Fr. Mukabalera, Bukavu (July 17, 2013). See also Mukabalera Cigwira, "Monseigneur Munzihirwa Christophe." This dissertation not only declares that Munzihirwa was a martyr but also compares him to Oscar Romero.

27. Mulombe, *Christophe Munzihirwa*, 8–9.

understood death not only as part of his calling but as the calling itself. "We commonly say that the deceased have been 'called to God.' In effect, death is a vocation." The calling of death is, ironically, the source of life. Only those who enter the way of Christ are able to live fully: "If we are faithful to him, we cross life and death with hope. Henceforth, instead of living to die, we die to live. Our existence then passes from life to life."[28]

As the situation in Bukavu worsened, Munzihirwa became increasingly aware of the possibility of his assassination. He also knew that if he fled or toned down his criticisms of the Rwandan government, including its policy regarding the refugees, its ideological manipulation of the genocide for political ends, and its impending military attack on the city, he could save his life.[29] But he did not. In October, two weeks before his assassination, when he attended a meeting in Kinshasa, he told his Jesuit superior: "Do not be astonished to receive bad news. Pray only for the Lord and the Virgin Mary to accompany us to the end of the path."[30] And as Rwandan forces prepared to attack Bukavu and aired announcements over the radio encouraging the residents to flee for their safety, Munzihirwa, in what would be his final message to the people, encouraged them not to flee their homes, but to "stand firm in charity." A Jesuit confrere noted that on the Saturday evening after Munzihirwa had written his "Stand Firm in Charity" homily, which he directed should be read in all the parishes the following day, he said to his Jesuit confreres at dinner: "I think I just signed my death certificate."[31]

Things That Can Be Seen Only with Eyes That Have Cried

The foregoing observations confirm Munzihirwa's short-lived but powerful and exemplary leadership and how it was intrinsic to what he came to understand as the "way of Christ." Abstracted from this theological matrix, Munzihirwa's life and agency cannot make sense. For it is this invitation into the way of Christ that provided the logic not only for the social vision (*telos*) of a nonviolent, reconciled society, but also the logic for Munzihirwa's exhortations—and his personal way of life. What is clear is that if Munzihirwa's own

28. Mirindi Ya Nacironge, *Père Evêque*, 25.

29. In a letter to Cardinal Danneels and the European community, Munzihirwa accused the Rwandan government of using genocide as an excuse to carry out their own genocide against the Hutu in the refugee camps (Mulombe, *Christophe Munzihirwa*, 10).

30. Mulombe, *Christophe Munzihirwa*, 16; Mirindi Ya Nacironge, *Père Evêque*, 25.

31. Interview with Didier (July 17, 2013).

participation in the way of Christ opened him up to embracing the vocation of death, it also freed him to speak and advocate fiercely as the Muhudumu of the refugees and the vulnerable populace of Bukavu. Three related conclusions emerge from this treatment of Munzihirwa's life and work in Bukavu, conclusions that have far-reaching implications for peacebuilding efforts in Africa and beyond.

Political Heart Transplant

The first conclusion relates to the significance of the prophetic dimension of peacebuilding. In the preceding chapter I noted that prophetic ministry is grounded in lament and that both Jeremiah's and Jesus's laments are a social critique of politics that had lost or forgotten the spiritual anchor of the covenant with God. Such politics have not only led to the exploitation of the poor, they have increasingly turned to military might and strategic alliances to secure their legitimacy. In the face of shallow visions of peace that promised "'peace, peace,' when there is no peace" (Jer. 6:14), Jeremiah pointed to the restoration of the covenant and the knowledge of God as the foundation of true and lasting peace. It was a similar prophetic moment, in its double gifts of critique and energizing, that Munzihirwa embodied in Bukavu in the context of the refugee crisis and the impending military attack on the city. But what makes prophets like Jeremiah and Munzihirwa unique is not simply their harsh critique, but also the fact that they see and stand within the reality of a completely different society, a different politics grounded within a different vision. It is this alternative vision in which they stand that makes possible and impels their critique of the reigning social and political ideologies.

Once we have grasped that conclusion, it becomes clear that prophets like Munzihirwa are not simply calling for law and order, nor merely for justice and reconciliation; they would not be satisfied with mere legal and administrative adjustments within the framework of the current politics. They invoke a totally new vision of society: in this vision it is not the generals who reign supreme, but God. For them, politics devoid of God cannot be true politics, but are a mere sham. And just as it was for Jeremiah and Jesus, a mere invocation of God—a politics in which leaders commit all manner of violence and injustice and then "flee to the temple like a brigand to his cave"—will not do, so it was for Munzihirwa. He was not merely asking that the generals become more God-fearing. It is not merely the heart of the generals that he was after; he was after the very heart of politics, seeking, as it were, a political transplant—seeking to give politics a new heart and a new spirit. This is the ambitious nature of prophets, what makes their lives and message at once a gift but also a challenge. For while they already see and stand within this new creation themselves, the reality around them reflects and operates under a different logic. The prophet's life thus becomes one great act of "groaning" in the one act of giving birth (Rom. 8:22), as the prophet takes on what might appear to be a futile attempt to build a new world within the shell of the old.

The Way of Nonviolence

As I have suggested above, the heart of Munzihirwa's message was an invitation into the way of Christ and the nonviolent, self-sacrificing love of God. A clear conclusion emerging from the story of Munzihirwa is that nonviolence is not just an ethical position one adopts from among many other options, nor is it merely a strategy for peacebuilding.[32] It is an ontological claim, a statement about the way the world really is. Nonviolence is not one among other beliefs about the world, but is a claim that this is the way God creates, rules, and governs the world.[33] The story of Munzihirwa confirms that, in order to come to this knowledge, one must surrender one's whole life to God and to a "vocation that can lead even to death." Nonviolence is a suffering love.

There is thus something inherently tragic, something inherently violent,

32. There is a renewed interest today in nonviolence as a strategy for peace. In *Why Civil Resistance Works: The Strategic Logic of Nonviolent Conflict* (New York: Columbia University Press, 2012), Erica Chenoweth and Maria J. Stephan argue that not only are campaigns of nonviolent resistance more than twice as effective as their violent counterparts in achieving their stated goals, successful nonviolent resistance ushers in more durable and internally peaceful democracies. For a good introduction and overview of this nascent area of interest in nonviolence and civil resistance studies within the broad field of peace studies, see Sharon Erickson Nepstad, *Nonviolent Struggle: Theories, Strategies, and Dynamics* (Oxford: Oxford University Press, 2015).

33. The claim seems to stand in stark contrast to the seemingly violent depictions of God in the Bible. While there may be no easy way to deal with the complex issue of violence in the Bible, the claim that God creates, rules, and governs creation in nonviolent ways requires an acknowledgment of the Christ event as the decisive hermeneutical lens through which Christ is interpreted. For if in Christ "the fullness of God was pleased to dwell" (Col. 1:19) and he is the "image of the invisible God" (Col. 1:15), then in Jesus we see God as God truly is. And in Jesus we see a God who would rather suffer violence than use violence to establish God's kingdom. For a more elaborate discussion of Christian nonviolence as an ontological claim, see Stanley Hauerwas, *With the Grain of the Universe: The Church's Witness and Natural Theology* (Grand Rapids: Brazos, 2001), esp. 205–41.

about nonviolence. This is what the slain Archbishop of San Salvador, Blessed Oscar Romero, called the "violence of love."[34] And this is what Munzihirwa meant when he spoke about "things that can be seen only with eyes that have cried." He was pointing to the circular logic involved within the nonviolent struggle for a more just and peaceful society. While such struggle may not make the world more "peaceful," and will certainly not rid the world of violence, it is a "vocation" for those willing to walk the way of Christ.

The Church's Gift and Burden: Bearing God and Bearing with God

Munzihirwa's story thus provides a compelling ecclesiological illumination of the church as a sign and sacrament of the way of Christ. In her incarnational presence in the world, and in places of conflict in Africa and elsewhere, the church remembers and bears the story of the incarnate God. In this "remembrance" the church finds herself in that "terrible middle" between an embattled and suffering people whose history she shares and the suffering God of love, whose story she bears. Her calling in that terrible middle is to offer this story of the suffering God as a gift to an embattled people, even as she carries the burden of her knowledge and participation in God's own self-sacrificing love for humanity. Ellen Davis has talked about the twin disciplines of "bearing God and bearing with God," which is both the gift and the burden the church bears.[35]

And this is the gift and burden that Munzihirwa bore as he found himself in the terrible middle in Bukavu. This is also what his names pointed to. Munzihirwa's father, Albert Ngabo, had had a number of wives before he married Elizabeth Mwa Lubongo, Munzihirwa's mother. All Ngabo's previous wives had borne children who died at birth, but Munzihirwa's mother bore five children, all of whom survived. Ngabo named the youngest of these children Munzihirwa, meaning "gift of providence."[36] At his baptism, Munzihirwa was given the name of Christophe, after Saint Christopher. According to Christian legend, Christopher was crossing a river when a child asked to be carried

---

34. "The church believes in only one violence, that of Christ, who was nailed to the cross. . . . Taking upon himself all the violence of hatred and misunderstanding, so that we humans might forgive one another, love one another, feel ourselves brothers and sisters" (Oscar Romero, *The Violence of Love* [San Francisco: Harper and Row, 1988], 10).

35. Ellen Davis, "Jeremiah: Master of Lament," Sermon at Duke Summer Institute (May 29, 2013).

36. See Mirindi Ya Nacironge, *Père Evêque*, 4–5.

across. When Christopher put the child on his shoulders he found the child was unbelievably heavy. The child was the world, according to the legend, and Christopher was Christ carrying the weight of the whole world.[37] Behind this legend of Christopher lies a deep christological mystery that came to characterize Munzihirwa's life and ministry, namely, that in order to come to know Christ and to know him as crucified (1 Cor. 2:1–2), we must carry him on our shoulders. At the same time, of course, "Jesus carries us on his shoulders."[38]

37. See, "Saint Christopher," Catholic Online: http://www.catholic.org/saints/saint.php? saint_id=36#wiki, accessed Dec. 6, 2015.

38. Jon Sobrino, SJ, comes to this conclusion with respect to the Salvadoran context, and especially in the life of Oscar Romero. Reflecting on Karl Rahner's dialectic of "carrying and being carried," Sobrino notes (quoting Rahner) that "being a Christian is a heavy-light burden, as the Gospel calls it. When we carry it, it carries us. The longer one lives, the heavier and lighter it becomes." See Jon Sobrino, "Jesus of Galilee from the Salvadoran Context: Compassion, Hope, and Following the Light of the Cross," *Theological Studies* 70 (2009): 451.

CHAPTER 9

The Costly Loss of Lament

The pathos of our condition is not that we have failed. . . . The pathos of it is that we cannot bring ourselves as a people to contemplate our failure.

Douglas John Hall, *Lighten Our Darkness*

Our discussion so far, especially in the last two sections, has increasingly pointed to the practical, social, and political dynamism of lament as confirmed through the stories of Kataliko, Nyirumbe, and Munzihirwa. We need to note that the notion and practice of lament should play a more explicit and prominent role in the theology and practice of the churches in Africa. The fact that it doesn't do so yet is, of course, unfortunate. For the loss of lament in the church today is costly not only theologically but also politically. No one has drawn our attention to the "costly loss of lament" from contemporary (Western) churches more than Walter Brueggemann. Noting the "curious fact that the church has, by and large, continued to sing songs of orientation in a world increasingly experienced as disoriented," Brueggemann discerns an underlying theological problem.[1] The loss of lament reflects "the absence of a genuine covenant

---

1. See, e.g., Walter Brueggemann, "Costly Loss of Lament," *Journal of the Study of the Old Testament* 11, no. 36 (1986): 57–71. See also Glenn Pemberton, *Hurting with God: Learning to Lament with the Psalms* (Abilene, TX: Abilene Christian University Press, 2011) on the survey in Protestant churches that reveals that, while psalms of lament constitute 40 percent of the book of Psalms, in the Protestant hymnals surveyed, songs of praise, thanksgiving, and trust (which number thirty-seven, or under 20 percent of all Psalms) are chosen over songs of lament. Moreover, absent from contemporary hymns of lament are the themes that are most prevalent in the laments of the Psalter: the problem of enemies, unmerited suffering, and

interaction since the second party to the covenant (the petitioner) has become voiceless or has a voice that is permitted to speak only praise and doxology."[2] Scott Ellington comes to the same conclusion, namely, that a relationship of trust, intimacy, and love is a necessary precondition for genuine lament. Since many of us today no longer feel that "foundational relationship that binds together the individual with the members of the community of faith and that community with God," lament becomes nothing more than a raging against the storm or a weeping in the darkness, an act of defiance against a hostile deity or a hopeless gesture that carries with it no expectation of being heard.[3]

There are other related reasons that contribute to the eclipse of lament from the church's language and practice. Pemberton suggests another (social) reason, which has to do with the social location of the church as a middle-class institution that has become increasingly embarrassed by the coarse language of lament. The reason that many psalms and prayers of lament find no place in our churches, Pemberton writes, "is because we have chosen to live pro-tected lives in insulated communities, whether our community is a middle- to upper-class neighborhood or a church with a fortress mentality. Our lack of solidarity with those in need is what causes us to wonder why these prayers are in the Bible and question who would ever need them."[4] For Ellington too, the loss of lament of the church has to do in large part with the church's increased prosperity and investment in mainstream society. Given that context, "lament sounds so dreary, negative, and unspiritual to those who do not wish to be reminded either of their own vulnerability to suffering or of the suffering of those around them."[5]

A more existential reason is given by Brueggemann, who connects the loss of lament with the inability to face suffering and embrace negativity in our modern world. The eclipse of lament reflects a frightened, numb denial, a refusal to acknowledge or experience the disorientation of life. And given the large number of psalms that are songs of lament, protest, and complaint about

---

God's failure to act. This observation is instructive as it points to the loss of the biblical notion of lament with its full texture. On attempts to reclaim language of lament, see Sally A. Brown and Patrick D. Miller, eds., *Lament: Reclaiming Practices in Pulpit, Pew, and Public Square* (Louisville: Westminster John Knox, 2005); Soong-Chan Rah, *Prophetic Lament: A Call for Justice in Troubled Times* (Downers Grove, IL: InterVarsity, 2015).

2. Walter Brueggemann, *The Psalms and the Life of Faith* (Minneapolis: Augsburg Fortress, 1995), quoted in Rah, *Prophetic Lament*, 148.

3. Scott A. Ellington, *Risking Truth* (Eugene, OR: Pickwick, 2008), 7.

4. Pemberton, *Hurting with God*, 131.

5. Ellington, *Risking Truth*, 11.

the incoherence of our experience in the world, it seems almost a willful act of blindness when Christians, especially those who engage the biblical texts so passionately, read them infrequently in their churches. I believe that serious religious use of the lament psalms has been minimal because we have come to believe that faith does not mean acknowledging and embracing suffering.

Coming from a different angle, the Canadian theologian Douglas John Hall, in *Lighten Our Darkness*, points to the same inability to embrace negativity in his apt analysis of modern society as an "officially optimistic society."[6] Hall describes the inability to deal with suffering as the defining problem of modern Western society. "The pathos of our condition is not that we have failed. . . . The pathos of it is that we cannot bring ourselves as a people to contemplate our failure" (16). Hall traces this inability to face failure to the modern (Enlightenment) positive outlook grounded in the belief of man's inherent goodness and limitless freedom. He notes: "We belong to a society that was assured it could hope. Hope would not disappoint us, for we were participants in a process and the end of the process was good. We belong to a people that were taught to think positively" (60). This positive outlook is characterized, on the one hand, by the belief in technology to solve all our problems—"it is really very difficult for many people in our society to reflect on problems that are not related to technique" (64)—and, on the other hand, by the incessant drive toward progress, which drives modern economics. The negative effect of this quest for endless progress is the colonization, pillaging, enslavement, and "death of other men and other societies" (40). "The whole world," Hall writes, "suffers today because its most powerful societies desperately retain expectations that can no longer stand the test of experience" (23).

The heart of Hall's critique in *Lighten Our Darkness* is that Christianity, which is supposed to help society face the negative experiences and darkness of its limitations, has itself become an integral part of the deafening blanket of "overt despair" that masks itself as optimism about the endless benefits of progress. "The truth of the matter," Hall writes, "is that an integral part of the problem, perhaps the most problematic part, is—Christianity itself! As it has displayed itself in the life of the New World, Christianity is the greatest barrier to its becoming a redemptive force, a light for our darkness" (74); it is now "the official religion of the officially optimistic society" (74). This, in Hall's as-

---

6. Douglas John Hall, *Lighten Our Darkness: Toward an Indigenous Theology of the Cross* (Philadelphia: Westminster, 1976). Hereafter, page references to this work appear in parentheses within the text.

sessment, is what makes our condition "all the more problematic, dangerous, and infinitely sad" (16).

I find Hall's diagnosis of the modern condition and the eclipse of lament from the church's language and practice not only powerful but profoundly relevant to our discussion of hope in Africa. Although his analyses are mostly directed to Christian churches in the West, the lack of an explicit theology and practice of lament in African Christianity is at once surprising and unfortunate. Part of the reason for this lack may be what I already pointed to as an uneasiness about the fact of a "suffering God." But another reason seems to be that African Christianity in general has yet to develop a sustained theological conversation, with the resources and capacity to sift through the many social, historical, cultural, political, and religious challenges in order to develop a unique theological voice relevant to her needs.[7] In the absence of this theological conversation, the African church quite often finds herself simply responding to one crisis after another or simply reverting to outdated ecclesiological models or prepackaged theological formulas from the West. In the current context of the "pentecostalization of African Christianity," the worship in African churches is increasingly dominated by "songs of praise."[8] Like their brothers and sisters in the West, African Christians are now more likely, in Brueggemann's words, to "sing songs of orientation in a world increasingly experienced as disoriented."

The discussion becomes particularly poignant where Brueggemann, Hall, Pemberton, and Ellington all come to the same conclusion—namely, that the loss of lament is also a loss in social and political dynamism:

7. For a more extended argument for the need for a distinct theological conversation in Africa and the direction it needs to take, see E. Katongole, "Of Coffins and Churches: Seven Marks of an Emerging African Ecclesiology," in *The Church We Want: Foundations, Theology and Mission of the Church in Africa*, ed. Agbonkhianmeghe E. Orobator (Nairobi: Paulines Publications, 2015), 190–202.

8. See, e.g., Cephas N. Omenyo, "From the Fringes to the Centre: Pentecostalization of the Mainline Churches in Ghana," *Exchange* 34, no. 1 (2005): 39–60. What Omenyo discovers as a major paradigmatic shift in the spirituality, theology, practices, and programs of mainline churches in Ghana occasioned by the migration of the charismatic features that began on the margins but have now found their way into the mainline churches (thus blurring the sharp distinction between mainline churches and Pentecostals) is true across much of sub-Saharan Africa. In an influential study, Allan H. Anderson makes a similar observation: he refers to the "pentecostalization" of African Christianity as the African reformation of the twentieth century that has fundamentally altered the character of Christianity, including that of the so-called mission churches. See Anderson, *African Reformation: African Initiated Christianity in the 20th Century* (Trenton, NJ: Africa World Press, 2001).

A community of faith which negates laments soon concludes that the hard issues of justice are improper questions to pose at the throne, because the throne seems to be only a place of praise. I believe it thus follows that if justice questions are improper questions at the throne . . . they soon appear to be improper questions in public places, in schools, in hospitals, with the government, and eventually even in the courts. Justice questions disappear into civility and docility.[9]

That is why, in the end, the loss of lament signals a loss of passion for social justice. A church that has lost its nerve to lament before God will likely lack the nerve to confront oppression and be prone to support the status quo.[10] But that is also the reason why an attempt to recover the language of lament is about solidarity with those who suffer: Hall says:

> The point of departure for this social ethic may be the only one that is finally legitimate, even in terms that secular men such as Marx can recognize: namely, a real solidarity with those who suffer. Only as the Christian community permits itself to undergo a continuous crucifixion to the world can it be in the world as the friend of those who are crucified. Apart from that, it always ends in a theology and an ethic of glory. For it imagines that it has something to bring, something to give, something that will enable it to master the situation. Real solidarity with those who suffer recognizes that their condition is our own: we are all beggars together. The possibility of community, which is the aim of Christian social ethics, is given at that point of recognition, and nowhere else. True community exists only at the foot of the cross. (152)

In view of this conclusion and the foregoing discussion in general, nothing could be further from the truth than Melissa Snarr's claim that lament distracts from and even deforms political agency rather than restoring it. A professor of Christian ethics and the academic dean at Vanderbilt Divinity School, Snarr develops her critique with regard to Emilie Townes's womanist theology.[11] In

---

9. Brueggemann, "Costly Loss of Lament," 64.

10. Pemberton, *Hurting with God*, 203.

11. C. Melissa Snarr, *Social Selves and Political Reforms: Five Visions in Contemporary Christian Ethics* (New York: T & T Clark, 2007). (Hereafter, page references to this work appear in parentheses within the text.) Snarr considers five major veins of thought in Christian ethics as represented by Walter Rauschenbush (social gospel), Reinhold Niebuhr (realist), Stanley Hauerwas (communitarian), Beverly Harrison (feminist), and Emilie Townes (womanist). I

her work, Townes focuses on the range of resources for resistance and moral agency that black women and black churches can cultivate within oppressive social structures. Comparing the context of the African-American community with the context of Israel in the Old Testament, Townes points to the power of *communal lament* to shape socially resilient selves and moral agency for liberation.[12]

Even though Snarr deems Townes's work to be on the whole quite provocative, she finds that the attention to lament and apocalyptic vision has the effect of distracting us from the task of much-needed political reform.[13]

> Unfortunately, in the end I find [Townes's] focus on lament and apocalyptic vision turning into its own "miasma of abstraction" in relation to current policy debates and strategic options. . . . My concern is that without a connection between her lament (which certainly includes structural analysis) and concrete political strategy, political formations will continue to deform moral agency and undermine even the most resilient communities. (102–3)

Part of Snarr's problem may be the narrow parameters of what constitutes the "political" (which she equates with engaging public policy through government structures). Because she thinks that Townes does not spend enough time analyzing public policy proposals or political strategies, she judges Townes's work to be insufficiently "political." For Snarr, Townes's goal of raising consciousness about injustice and inviting people into a "community of lament" over the condition of life in American society for black folks constitutes only "pre-political" agency, only a "preparatory" communal strengthening, which, even though necessary, nevertheless stops short of the real "political" task of engaging male-dominated political powers and structures. Snarr says that Townes's "socially resilient self" remains much too caught up in (womanist) "spirituality" and does not properly enter into "politics" (90).

---

am grateful to my former graduate assistant, Kyle Lembelet, for drawing my attention to the work of Melissa Snarr in the first place. See Kyle Lambelet, "'How Long, O Lord?' Practices of Lamentation and the Restoration of Political Agency" (unpublished paper, Duke Graduate Conference in Theology, Fall 2014).

12. See esp. Emilie Maureen Townes, *Breaking the Fine Rain of Death: African American Health Issues and a Womanist Ethic of Care* (New York: Continuum, 1998): "The power of lament, particularly communal lament, is that the community must recognize its condition and act in faith-filled ways" (25).

13. Snarr is more sympathetic to Townes's work than she is to the social visions of the others she discusses (Rauschenbush, Niebuhr, Hauerwas, and Harrison).

Where I find Snarr's critical assessment of Townes misplaced is in the fact that it does not take into account the overall import of Townes's work, which is to call into question the narrow range of what constitutes "politics" so as to recover fresh forms of belonging and identity grounded in a theological framework. For, in the end, as Snarr rightly notes, Townes sees womanist social ethics as "challenging the master narrative and analyzing social structures, processes, and communities, and ask[ing] the question of how we all belong together under God and what our responsibilities are for one another because of this soul-deep relationship with the divine."[14] Given this concern, even though Townes does not explicitly spell out her definition of "politics," what that theo-political vision of "belonging together under God" implies is that black political engagement "cannot be simply about tinkering with the current system. It must be about dramatic overhaul . . . [as] salvific redemption and liberation from unjust structures require more than just fixing the system. They require transforming the system."[15]

Moreover, if one takes into full account the dynamic connection between lament and apocalyptic vision in Townes's work, one realizes that what drives her womanist ethics is the search for a new society altogether. "The role of the apocalyptic," she writes, "is not to point to a future outside history; it is to offer an alternative picture of reality and point the community in that direction."[16] The apocalyptic "suggests a new heaven and a new earth. One in which dominant norms are challenged and debunked. One in which a new reality and project for all humanness emerges."[17] Given this agenda, her womanist theology involves nothing less than a reinvention of politics from a cultural and theological base.

Once we take this overarching goal of Townes's work into consideration, it becomes obvious that "inviting people into a community of lament" constitutes not only a form of political agency, it is a decisive and subversive form of political agency through which a new social reality is envisioned and enacted. This is the vision and performance of a revolutionary nonviolent social vision that Munzihirwa's life and ministry were about. But it is also the birth of a new social reality that Matthew's Gospel announces via the story of the slaughter of the innocents and the memory of Rachel's tears. This latter story

14. Snarr, *Social Selves*, 98, citing Townes, *In a Blaze of Glory: Womanist Spirituality as Social Witness* (Nashville: Abingdon, 1995), 183.

15. Snarr, *Social Selves*, 102-3, citing Townes, "Searching for Paradise in a World of Theme Parks," *Lexington Theological Quarterly* 33 (Fall 1998): 139, 146.

16. Snarr, *Social Selves*, 101, citing Townes, *Blaze of Glory*, 123.

17. Townes, *Blaze of Glory*, 122; Snarr, *Social Selves*, 98.

finds much resonance in Africa through the agency of faith activists such as David Kasali in Congo, Maggy Barankitse in Burundi, and the various martyrs of peace. In their lives and stories one can discern something like the form, shape, and impact of a new social reality born from lament. In the last section of *Born from Lament*, let us look more closely at the biblical imagination, as well as the sociopolitical implications of this politics of lament, in the context of Eastern Africa.

PART FIVE

The Politics of Lament

CHAPTER 10

Rachel's Cry in the Gospel of Matthew

A voice is heard in Ramah.

Matthew 2:18

Near the beginning of his Gospel, Matthew invokes the memory of a woman's lament:

> Then was fulfilled what was spoken by the prophet Jeremiah:
> "A voice is heard in Ramah,
>   mourning and great weeping,
> Rachel weeping for her children;
>   she refused to be comforted, because they are no more." (2:17-18)[1]

We can make a number of observations about this text, but they must be made within the overall goal of Matthew's Gospel: that is, to present Jesus as the promised Messiah, whose coming heralds the arrival of God's reign. Therefore, for Matthew, Jesus's birth reveals the *fact* of God's reign coming into being as much as the *how* of its realization. Lament is at the heart of this story.

---

1. Even though lament language is often used with respect to Matt. 2:18, "the passage is not a lament in the strict Old Testament sense of the term" (D. Keith Campbell, "NT Scholars' Use of OT Lament Terminology and Its Theological and Interdisciplinary Implications," *Bulletin for Biblical Research* 21, no. 2 [2011]: 213-26, at 219). The reason is that it does not fit the identifiable literary genre and structure of Old Testament laments, which have the following elements: address, complaint, request, motivation, and confidence (see Chapter 5 above).

This Is How Jesus Came to Be Born

At least three observations are relevant to the story of Rachel's weeping at the beginning of Matthew's Gospel. First, the obvious political overtones of the story. For Matthew, God's reign is not a spiritual province, but a social and political reality that establishes here on earth the same conditions of justice, righteousness, and mercy as they hold in heaven. Matthew's distinctive way of speaking about this sociopolitical reality is by using the phrase "the kingdom of heaven" (twenty-two times). What is particularly telling is that Matthew announces the proclamation of the kingdom with a story of lament; also, toward the end of Matthew's proclamation of the Good News, he offers another cry of anguish as Jesus on the cross utters, *Lama, lama, eli sabachthani* ("My God, my God, why have you forsaken me?" Matt. 27:46). These two cries of anguish—by Rachel and by Jesus on the cross, one a mother, the other a son—serve as the bookends of the proclamation of the Good News. Matthew thus succeeds in showing that lament impels, accompanies, and consummates the messianic reign.

Second, the context of Rachel's cry is Jesus's birth. Here it is instructive to show a contrast to Luke's Gospel: Matthew's account of the birth of the Messiah contains not an account of Mary's joy, as in Luke's Gospel, but a report of Rachel's tears. The reason for this, scholars suggest, is that Matthew "is casting the birth of the Messiah in terms of a new Exodus with a new Joseph to dream dreams, a new pharaoh to slaughter babies, and a single child who escapes to become savior."[2] Within this Exodus context, Rachel's cry is significant. The Exodus begins with such a cry: "The people of Israel groaned because of their slavery and cried out for help. Their cry for rescue from slavery came up to God. And God heard their groaning, and God remembered his covenant with Abraham, with Isaac, and with Jacob" (Exod. 2:23-24). Thus Ellington notes:

2. See Scott A. Ellington, *Risking Truth* (Eugene, OR: Pickwick, 2008), 174, with reference to Frederick Niedner, "Rachel's Lament," 412. By connecting Rachel's lament to the prophecy of Jeremiah, Matthew also invokes the exile context. From the very beginning, Matthew presents Jesus as the one who announces and ushers in the eschatological end of Israel's exile. Matthew's genealogy itself portrays the life of Jesus as the story of Israel, and presents Jesus as the Messiah who will bring Israel's exile to an end. Within the framework of Matthew 1-5, Jesus's "genesis" (1:1), his announcement of Good News (4:23), and his promise of blessing on those who mourn (5:4) are God's response to Rachel's plea and represent the promised consolation of Israel (see Rebekah Ann Eklund, "Lord, Teach Us How to Grieve: Jesus' Lament and Christian Hope" (ThD diss., Duke University, 2012), 228.

Just as the cry of Israelite slaves initiated God's deliverance in the Exodus, so too the initiation of his Exodus of all creation through the birth of Emmanuel finds its genesis in the tears brought about by innocent suffering, obscene corruption, and inconsolable loss. Matthew though, insists on reminding us that, just as with the Exodus, so too with the coming of Messiah, the first word in God's salvation is not a shout of joy, but a cry of pain.[3]

Third, the immediate context of Rachel's cry is the story of the slaughter of the innocents in Matthew 2. But this story is itself located within the larger story of the birth of Jesus. "The birth of Jesus Christ took place in this way," Matthew announces in 1:18, before he tells the story of how Mary, who had been engaged to Joseph, was found to be with child of the Holy Spirit. Then, in the first verses of chapter 2, Matthew describes a series of events that happened after Jesus had been born at the time of King Herod (the visit of the Magi, the flight into Egypt, and the slaughter of the innocents).

Drawing attention to this immediate context helps to highlight the fact that, if the birth of Jesus is the in-breaking of a new social reality (the kingdom of heaven), Matthew's infancy stories now provide not simply the context but the conditions of possibility for the new social reality. Three elements stand out here: First, the birth does not come without a struggle between the old and the new, between the world of Herod and the world of the newborn king. The rage of Herod that results in the slaughter of the innocent children is the last gasp of the old order in its desperate attempt to hold on to the old way.[4] Second, while Herod and the chief priests and scribes have no clue as to where the birth has taken place (and are, in fact, frightened by the news of it), the birth is recognized and welcomed as a gift by those at the margins of Herod's empire: an innocent young virgin (Mary); a simple and obedient carpenter (Joseph); and the magi—the outsiders who come searching for the child.[5] Third, the birth of a new social reality does not come without a price, in this case the slaughter of the innocents (Matt. 2:1-17). Thus does the new social reality emerge by way of lament.

However, the realization that the newness comes from God is equally important to Matthew—thus the story of the young virgin who was "found to be with child from the Holy Spirit" (1:18). For Matthew, this "fact" is important and worth repeating—"that which is conceived in her is from the

---

3. Ellington, *Risking Truth*, 174.

4. Walter Brueggemann, *The Prophetic Imagination* (Philadelphia: Fortress, 1978), 82.

5. Brueggemann, *The Prophetic Imagination*, 103.

Holy Spirit" (1:20)—because he recognizes that newness from God is the only serious source of energy for a new social reality.[6] It is, in fact, the total astonishment at the newness of what God has created in the midst of grief that Matthew wishes to capture by introducing the story of Rachel's lament with these words: "Then was fulfilled what was spoken by the prophet Jeremiah" (Matt. 2:17). In order to capture the surprise—and thus the gift of a new social reality that emerges through the pain and tears that accompany the slaughter of the innocent—we need to attend in detail to the text of Jeremiah, of which Matthew 2:18 is presented as a fulfillment.

The Memory of Rachel's Tears

According to Matthew, the slaughter of the innocent children is a fulfillment of a prophecy:

> Thus says the Lord:
> "A voice is heard in Ramah,
>   lamentation and bitter weeping.
> Rachel is weeping for her children;
>   she refuses to be comforted for her children,
>   because they are no more." (Jer. 31:15)

These words are found in part 3 (the "book of consolation") of Jeremiah's prophecy, more specifically in chapter 31, which promises the "return" of the exiles and a new covenant:

> "For the Lord has ransomed Jacob
>   and has redeemed him from hands too strong for him.
> They shall come and sing aloud on the height of Zion,
>   and they shall be radiant over the goodness of the Lord,
> over the grain, the wine, and the oil,
>   and over the young of the flock and the herd;
> their life shall be like a watered garden,
>   and they shall languish no more.
> Then shall the young women rejoice in the dance,
>   and the young men and the old shall be merry.

6. Brueggemann, *The Prophetic Imagination*, 78–79.

I will turn their mourning into joy;
 I will comfort them, and give them gladness for sorrow.
I will feast the soul of the priests with abundance,
 and my people shall be satisfied with my goodness,
declares the Lord." (Jer. 31:11–14)

It is within this context that the memory of Rachel's tears is invoked—as part of the consolation and promise of return. And to register both the promise of the return and the return as a totally surprising gift that can be realized only by God, Jeremiah invokes the memory of Rachel: he begins with a woman's anguished voice (v. 15) and ends with a promise of a "new thing" that the Lord has created in the land (v. 22). In order to get a clearer sense of the movements that lead to this wonderful and totally unexpected pronouncement, we need to look at the full section of Jeremiah 31:15–22, which has as its central focus the memory of Rachel's cry.

Thus says the Lord:
"A voice is heard in Ramah,
 lamentation and bitter weeping.
Rachel is weeping for her children;
 she refuses to be comforted for her children,
 because they are no more."

Thus says the Lord:
"Keep your voice from weeping,
 and your eyes from tears,
for there is a reward for your work,
declares the Lord,
 and they shall come back from the land of the enemy.
There is hope for your future,
declares the Lord,
 and your children shall come back to their own country.
I have heard Ephraim grieving,
'You have disciplined me, and I was disciplined,
 like an untrained calf;
bring me back that I may be restored,
 for you are the Lord my God.
For after I had turned away, I relented,
 and after I was instructed, I struck my thigh;
I was ashamed, and I was confounded,

because I bore the disgrace of my youth.'
Is Ephraim my dear son?
   Is he my darling child?
For as often as I speak against him,
   I do remember him still.
Therefore my heart yearns for him;
   I will surely have mercy on him,"
declares the Lord.

"Set up road markers for yourself;
   make yourself guideposts;
consider well the highway,
   the road by which you went.
Return, O virgin Israel,
   return to these your cities.
How long will you waver,
   O faithless daughter?
For the Lord has created a new thing on the earth:
   a woman encircles a man."

When we look at the memory of Rachel's cry in its entirety, it becomes clear that it is not only the conclusion, the promise of a new thing in the land, that is surprising, but also the steps leading to it. To get a sense of the surprise or amazement at play, one needs to follow the movements in the text. There are at least five key moments in the poem:[7]

Rachel weeps (v. 15)
Yahweh consoles her (vv. 16–17)
Ephraim confesses (vv. 18–19)
Yahweh contemplates (v. 20)
Jeremiah commands (v. 21) and announces (v. 22)

What the movements show is that Rachel's wailing (and refusing to be consoled) moves Yahweh, who consoles Rachel; but it also moves Ephraim

7. I am grateful in this section for the work of the internationally renowned biblical scholar Phyllis Trible, esp. her essay "The Gift of a Poem: A Rhetorical Study of Jeremiah 31:15–22," *Andover Newton Quarterly* 17 (1977): 271–80. Hereafter, page references to this essay appear in parentheses within the text.

(Joseph's younger son, Rachel's grandson), who confesses and repents (vv. 18–19). In turn, Ephraim's confession and repentance move Yahweh to console Ephraim and promise a return.

> There is hope for your future,
> declares the Lord,
>> and your children shall come back to their own country. (v. 17)

Another way to capture the surprise is to note how Rachel's wailing sets in motion a series of movements of anguish. If Rachel's anguish is her refusal to be consoled by anything other than God, God's consolation of Rachel is nothing other than God's own anguish, not only for Rachel but also for Ephraim (who is in exile). This anguish is what triggers Ephraim's own anguish and repentance (vv. 18–19), which he addresses to God.

Having heard Ephraim's grief, Yahweh responds (v. 20) with a question that combines both intimacy and distance. According to Phyllis Trible, what the hesitation shows is how Rachel's weeping is really Yahweh's weeping (274). Are not the children whom Rachel weeps for also Yahweh's children?

> Is Ephraim my dear son?
>> Is he my darling child?
> For as often as I speak against him,
>> I do remember him still. (v. 20a)

In the end, the text suggests, the cry of Rachel for her children is really Yahweh's cry. Yahweh is the woman crying for her children:

> "Therefore my heart yearns for him;
>> I will surely have mercy on him,"
> declares the Lord. (v. 20b)

Trible translates:

> "My womb trembles for him, I will surely show motherly compassion for
>> him." (279)

Thus there is a parallel between Rachel and Yahweh. The voice of Rachel is the voice of God the mother. As Rachel mourns the loss of the fruit of her womb, so does Yahweh, from the divine womb, mourn the child of her womb. It is within the context of this parallel, this reversal between Rachel and Yahweh, that we appreciate a number of other reversals that are triggered by Rachel's anguish.[8]

First, the human mother (Rachel) refuses to be consoled; but the divine mother consoles her. As a result, the poem moves from the desolate lamentation of Rachel to the redemptive compassion of God, as the divine mother changes grief into grace. This reversal is confirmed by the verbal link between "bitterness" and "guideposts." It is the same word, *tamrurim*, that is used in both verses 15 and 21:

> The nouns *tamrurim* appear in the end of the first line of both strophes. In the former instance the word means bitterness, in the latter, guideposts. A poem that begins with the mother bitterly crying for her lost children concludes with the prophet commanding them to make guideposts for their return home. Despair becomes hope. (276)

Another significant reversal is also under way in the poem:

> Along the way a new thing has happened to the children. They change sex. At first male; at last female. Ephraim the son becomes Israel the daughter. Jeremiah speaks to the daughter. This change of imagery converges upon the center of the poem to surround male with female. (276)

The overall effect of these reversals is not only to point to the "new thing God is creating in the land," but the urgency of the new creation. Therefore, Jeremiah speaks with urgency—and with impatience. Since restoration has been promised by God, the children ought to return immediately:

> Set up road markers for yourself;
>   make yourself guideposts;
> consider well the highway,
>   the road by which you went.
> Return, O virgin Israel,
>   return to these your cities. (v. 21)

---

8. According to Brueggemann, the poet's gift and task is to communicate the reversal, or "inversion," that God promises and brings about in the midst of Israel's suffering and exile. In 2 Isaiah, three key images—"new song," "birth to the barren," and "nourishment"—communicate the reversal that God will soon accomplish (Brueggemann, *Prophetic Imagination*, 74ff.).

A third significant reversal connected with the promise of return is that the promised return to the land is, in fact, a return to the Lord:

How long will you waver,
O unfaithful daughter? (v. 22a)

Finally, the new creation is "in the land"! Yahweh, who promised that the children will return from the land of the enemy (v. 16), now creates a new thing in that very land (v. 22).[9]

The cumulative effect of these reversals is to lead to the final, climactic line, according to which the "the new thing" is not simply a promise but a reality that God has already realized:

The Lord has created a new thing on the earth:
a woman encircles a man. (v. 22b)

In the end, this is what the prophet Jeremiah announces: what God has done—a new creation. As Trible notes, "this new thing requires a new verb, *bara*, a verb that is used throughout the Old Testament (as in Gen 1:27) only for the creative work of God" (277). In fact, the new thing is like the original creation, a totally unexpected, underived, surprising reality, the source of both irony and delight. Thus the image: "a woman encircles a man."

> Accordingly, female surrounding the male is Rachel the mother embracing her sons with tears and with speech; it *is* Yahweh consoling Rachel about Ephraim; it *is* Yahweh declaring motherly compassion for Ephraim; and it *is* the daughter Israel superseding son Ephraim. And it is more than these images. Female surrounding man has power to dry up the tears of Rachel; to fulfill the compassion of Yahweh; and to overturn the apostasy of Israel. And it is other than all these images, for it is Yahweh's creation of a new thing in the land. (279)

I have found it helpful to draw extensively from Trible's work because it clearly shows that the new future—"a new thing in the land "—that God prom-

---

9. An event quite consistent with Jer. 29:5-7: "Build houses and settle down; plant gardens and eat what they produce. Marry and have sons and daughters; find wives for your sons and give your daughters in marriage, so that they too may have sons and daughters. Increase in number there; do not decrease. Also, seek the peace and prosperity of the city to which I have carried you into exile."

ises is triggered by and realized in the midst of Rachel's anguished lament. To be sure, it is not Rachel's tears that generate the new thing. It is God who creates (*bara*) it via a number of totally unexpected reversals, and is thus the cause of amazement. Therefore, for Matthew to introduce Rachel's lament with the words "Then was fulfilled what was spoken by the prophet Jeremiah" is to remind his audience, all of whom are familiar with the Old Testament tradition and the full context of Rachel's cry, of both the surprise and irony of Herod's slaughter of the innocents. Matthew's invocation of Rachel's lament is a veiled doxology with regard to the surprising new reality that is being created through the messianic event.

From this point of view, Rachel's lament in Matthew fulfills the same function as Mary's Magnificat does in Luke (1:46–55), where Mary is filled with amazement at the incredible reversal accomplished by God: "He has brought down the mighty from their thrones and exalted those of humble estate" (Luke 1:52).[10] Thus, by connecting the birth of the new reality to Rachel's tears, Matthew helps to show us that lament and doxology belong together. They cannot be torn from each other, because "only those who anguish will sing new songs. Without anguish the new song is likely to be strident and just more royal fakery."[11]

What Matthew's memory of Rachel also does is deny any sociological reductionism whereby lament inevitably leads to newness. Rather, critique and newness, lament and hope are connected through divine agency and grace. Rachel's tears do not lead to a new thing. Through her tears she enters into the dynamic and creative movement (set of movements) through which she is carried forth into an unexpected new future as her grief turns into hope.

---

10. In the medieval world, Rachel's lament for her children was seen as a type for the grieving Mary. See Donald G. La Salle, "Liturgical and Popular Lament: A Study for the Role of Lament in Liturgical and Popular Religious Practices of Good Friday in Northern Italy from the Twelfth to Sixteenth Centuries" (PhD diss., Catholic University of America, 1997), 246. This link between Rachel and Mary has been lost to many churches, and that has serious negative effects, as Kathleen B. Billman and Daniel L. Migliore note: "Rachel and Mary are thus bound together as sisters of faith in the biblical tradition. Even though the church has often remembered Mary but forgotten Rachel, the two belong together in the prayer and practice of Christian faith. Together, they remind us that the danger of praise without lament is triumphalism, and the danger of lament without praise is hopelessness. . . . Christian prayer is whole and strong only when it includes both Rachel's cry of sorrow and protest and Mary's cry of joy and praise" (*Rachel's Cry: Prayer of Lament and Rebirth of Hope* [Cleveland: United Church Press, 1999], 4).

11. Brueggemann, *Prophetic Imagination*, 79.

That hope, the new future, is God's creation—thus the use of the verb *bara* in verse 22.

Rachel's experience has been proven true in other historical circumstances where lament has turned into hope—or where, to quote Brueggemann,

> funeral becomes festival, grief becomes doxology, and despair turns into amazement. Perhaps it is no more than a cultic event, but don't sell it short because cult kept close to historical experience can indeed energize people. For example, witness the African American churches and civil rights movements or the liberation resistance in Latin America. The cult may be a staging for the inversion that the kings think is not possible.[12]

This is definitely true in the African context, where one witnesses similar transformations of grief into hope in the lives of many faith activists. In this connection, the story of Rachel's weeping "explodes" with rich theological and practical, peacebuilding reverberations.[13] In the next three chapters, I will trace some of these explosions through some portraits of nonviolent change in Africa. The overall goal of my effort will be not only to display the many parallels between Rachel's tears and the experience in Africa, but to locate the agency for nonviolent change within the scriptural-theological matrix of lament. Moreover, doing so helps to confirm that lament is a gift—an odd gift, to be sure—that does not simply have far-reaching practical implications but is a decisive political reality. The practice of lament is a political practice.

---

12. Brueggemann, *Prophetic Imagination*, 74.

13. On the notion of scriptural "explosion," see Brueggemann's essay, "Texts That Linger, Words That Explode," in Walter Brueggemann, *Texts That Linger, Words That Explode: Listening to Prophetic Voices* (Minneapolis: Fortress, 2008).

CHAPTER 11

David Kasali and the Université Chrétienne Bilingue du Congo in Beni

The Lord has created a new thing on the earth.

Jeremiah 31:22

But coming here to UCBC . . . we have learned a whole new way of seeing the world. We have come to believe that even simple people can effect change. We will be the change.

UCBC student

It is Saturday afternoon. The entire town of Beni in the Congo seems to be on the move: men, women, and children on foot; young men on bicycles and boda bodas (motorcycles); a few families in cars. Everyone is moving toward the basketball court in the center of the town to watch and cheer on the men's basketball team of the Université Chrétienne Bilingue du Congo (UCBC) as they take on a team from Goma for the regional championship. The mood during the game is tense, but as UCBC begins to pull away in the final quarter, residents of the entire town are singing, dancing, and waving their hands in the air. And when the final buzzer goes off, signaling that UCBC has won the regional championship, the crowd of students storm the basketball court, and, led by their academic dean, celebrate with the slogan they have adapted from the movie *Remember the Titans*, which captures UCBC's distinctiveness expressed through its name and in its traditional anthem: "Everywhere we go—people want to know—who we are—and we tell them—We are bilingual—We are Christian—UCBC, UCBC, UCBC power!" The anthem of UCBC, composed by the school choir, "Ebenezer Worship Team" (a name that emphasizes how far the Lord has brought not only the school but also the nation of the Democratic Republic of Congo [DRC] out of the many perils it has suffered) highlights the mutually constructive marriage and interaction that exists between UCBC and the community. It says: "Nous sommes UCBC . . . la Communauté c'est notre force; la Communauté ça nous renforce; la Communauté nous transforme. Nous sommes UCBC." (We are UCBC. . . . The community is our power; the community is our strength; the community transforms us. We are UCBC.)

The rector steps onto the court, congratulates the team, and talks about the significance of sports in building character, morale, and identity. Promising to build a basketball court at UCBC, he reminds the team and the cheering students to always struggle for excellence, adding that this is what UCBC is about.

The winning of the regional basketball championship is yet another remarkable accomplishment by this relatively young (only seven years old) and relatively small (489 students) college, whose campus sits just four miles outside the town of Beni. Even though not every student who attends UCBC is Christian, its mission is unabashedly Christian: "To train and develop strong, indigenous Christian leaders to transform their communities and their nation, the DRC."

It is quite an ambitious mission. But the fact that just seven years into existence, UCBC is already making significant local, regional, and national impact confirms that the university represents a unique sign of hope, something of a fresh new future in this beleaguered region and nation. Much of that freshness and much of UCBC's mission and work are connected to the story of David Kasali, the college's founder and president, who resigned his position as president of the prestigious Nairobi Evangelical Graduate School of Theology (NEGEST) to return to his native Beni and found a university there in the midst of the war. But the more closely one pays attention to Kasali's story, the more one realizes that UCBC is not only born from lament, but is a work of lament, a work that has turned into one of the most visible signs of hope in Beni and Eastern Congo. In fact, UCBC points to a number of striking similarities between Kasali's story and the story of Rachel, who in the midst of her tears is promised a "return" for the children and a "new thing in the land."

In order to highlight the Rachel-like reversals of Kasali's tears, one has to place his dramatic decision to return to Beni within the broader story of Kasali's relationship with God—or what he describes as his "love affair" with God.

A Love Affair with God

David grew up in a Christian family. His father, Zephania, one of the early Congolese converts to Christianity, had become a pastor in the interdenominational missionary society, Africa Inland Mission (AIM). Although their home was next to the church, just across from the missionary compound, and often served as the guesthouse of the mission station, the Kasalis did not have much by way of earthly goods. His father's Christian zeal, as well as much of the Christianity woven into David's upbringing, was focused on the promise of heaven. David's early memories are filled with the prayers of his father, who prayed every day, at five in the morning, for the salvation of each of his nine children. He would pray: "Lord, I do not want to be in heaven one day and hear the voice of one of my children crying out from hell because he did not believe in you." David remembers how sometimes he would feel like yelling to his father to remind God that "we have no shoes."

It was not only shoes they lacked; they also struggled with school fees for their education. Therefore, from an early age, David was determined not to be like his father. He would study hard, he thought, get a good job, and be successful in life. "I believe in God, but I will not work for God. God does not pay well. That is why my brothers and sisters could not go to school, because my father could not afford it. I will get a job, and I will pay for my children to go to school."[1]

Soon after graduation, and after he had married a beautiful nurse, Kasali settled down to the task of making money and becoming someone important in the community. He worked hard, was honest, and was soon entrusted with handling the finances of the company that employed him. All this time, David saw Christianity as a kind of insurance policy: he respected and feared God and lived according to the strict requirements of his Christian faith. He expected God, in turn, to bless him with success and, of course, the eternal rewards of heaven. Though this relationship worked, it did not have much joy or love in it.

However, that was soon to change when David became a friend of the manager of the bank where he regularly deposited the company's money. The manager invited David to his home, and as the latter came to know the manager better, he discovered not only that he was a man of prayer, but that his version of Christianity was different from what David had known:

1. Interview with David Kasali at Entebbe, Uganda (Dec. 13, 2010). Unless otherwise stated, all direct quotes in the text are taken from this particular interview.

For him, Jesus was a friend. Christianity was a love affair; you could fall in love with Jesus the way you fall in love with your wife. You could be in love with Jesus . . . with God. I had a Christianity where God was good but he was tough and demanding. And there were regulations, so one had to be careful. But for him Christianity was a love affair.[2]

David was not only fascinated by this new version of Christianity; he became hooked. He joined a group of friends who regularly met with the bank manager for prayer—and for the first time he started "enjoying God."

When I started praying with them—wow, I discovered that actually prayer is just the way we are talking . . . it is talking with someone you love. It is sharing your life and worshiping and appreciating. . . . This was different. . . . I stayed with them. For the first time I started fasting. For the first time, I started spending the whole night in prayer. Overnight would seem as if it were not long enough. (21)

This was not only a turning point in David's relationship with God; his whole life was turned upside down. One day during one of the overnight prayer sessions, a woman told the prayer gathering: "I have a message from the Lord. . . . David, the Lord wants you full-time. The Lord has been calling you. It seems that you have not been ready. It seems that you have been running away. The Lord has been calling you."

David did not know what to say, yet some words were coming out of his mouth: "I feel like Jonah; I *have* been running away." Then he pulled out his wallet and said:

This is why I have been running away. I wanted to work for my own life, to earn my own money. I wanted to be able to send my children to school. It is as though, when I was baptized, I pulled my wallet out of my pocket and said, "Don't baptize my wallet." Today, I want my wallet to be baptized with me. I surrender it. (21)

The effect on David's life was immediate and total:

2. Sharon Atkinson Shehan, *This Is for You: The Story of David Kasali and the Congo Initiative* (self-published), 20. Hereafter, page references to this work appear in parentheses within the text.

It was as if a huge weight went off my heart. My pursuits seemed meaning-less. It was as if I had been working hard to find a dream that was so small. And now God was giving me a bigger dream. A bigger vision. My vision was just around me.

If he had felt that his father's work as a pastor was insignificant and un-rewarded before, he now found himself wishing to imitate his father's selfless service: "No, no, I *want* to be like my father." He resigned his position with his company and moved from Beni to Aungba to teach high school geography and mentor young people in Christian discipleship.

Expanding Horizons

Everyone in Beni thought David was crazy to resign from a top-paying job and move to an unpaid position in rural Aungba (it was akin to resigning from Goldman Sachs and moving from New York to Artesia in rural Mississippi). But for David, given his new love affair with God, the two years at Aungba were among the happiest years of his life: "High school kids would be in my house all the time. It was the best time of my life. And, oh my goodness, I would be tired by the end of the day. It was the most difficult and the best at the same time" (24).

Ironically, it would be from backwater Aungba that David would be of-fered an opportunity to do a master's degree in divinity at the Nairobi Evan-gelical Graduate School of Theology, a journey that would thrust him onto a global platform, while expanding the horizon of his vision, connections, and leadership.

During his graduate studies at NEGEST, David's passion and skills brought him to the attention of the Association of Evangelicals in Africa (AEA), who invited him, after his graduation, to work for them and build up their depart-ment of "Ethics, Society and Development" (the department constituted the evangelistic arm of social engagement). The position gave Kasali an oppor-tunity to travel across Africa, which in turn opened him up not only to the immense gifts and potential of the continent, but also to its deepest challenges: widespread violence, poverty, ethnicity, and a general sense of helplessness. In the many parts of Africa that he traveled to, Kasali encountered a mindset of fatalism and hopeless resignation: "This is who we are and we can do nothing about it; we cannot change our condition" (29).

What was particularly disheartening was to see that this widespread sense of helplessness often went hand in hand with an otherwise widespread, even lively expression of the Christian faith and worship. It was then that Kasali began to question the gospel of "evacuation" that seemed predominant in Africa. "What is the role of the church? What hope are we giving to people? Just hope to go to heaven? Yes, we do have that hope. But what about the hope to live on earth?"

He was beginning to believe that Christianity needed to be grounded in African soil. For if the church could not address the everyday problems that African men and women experienced, then why was Christianity here? As he questioned and thought about the difference Christianity should make on the African continent, he became more aware of his need for further theological education. In 1989, after working for AEA for three years, he applied to and was admitted into the graduate program at Trinity Evangelical Divinity School near Chicago. Kasali's research for his doctoral dissertation would focus on hope in Paul's letters, thereby attempting to seek answers to the general sense of hopelessness he had witnessed in Africa.

The five years that David spent in Deerfield, Illinois (1989–94), were challenging for him and his family (his wife, Kaswera, and their three boys accompanied him to the United States). In the cold of Deerfield and the loneliness of working on his PhD, he often found himself homesick. "God," he prayed, "I want to go home. I want to be with my people." What kept him going was a sense that the doctorate was something that he would need in order to serve God's mission in Africa; and meanwhile, the church community where he and his family worshiped became a much-needed network of support. Before he had left for his studies at NEGEST, David's father had advised him and Kaswera: "When you go, find a church; stick to a church. There God will give you brothers and sisters, fathers and mothers." This proved particularly true in Deerfield, Illinois, where Western Springs Baptist Church became their home away from home.

At the end of his studies at Trinity Evangelical Divinity School, Kasali was offered a faculty position at his alma mater. But the NEGEST he returned to was a very different institution from the one he had graduated from just a few years earlier. A number of faculty members had resigned; the remaining faculty members were divided; student morale was down; the administration was in disarray; funding was dwindling, and the buildings were crumbling. Hope, his dissertation subject, was to get its first major practical challenge at NEGEST itself.

Resurrection Garden

David called together several faculty members to try to salvage the situation. They wrote a memorandum to the trustees (AEA), who convened the governing board, which approved all the faculty recommendations, including the need for a new vice-chancellor. However, when no candidates applied for the advertised position, the head of the board of trustees and several faculty members proposed David's name for the job.

David's immediate response was clear. There was no way he could accept the position. Not only was he a young faculty member (newly returned with his PhD), but he was averse to conflict (and this was a conflict-laden context); and furthermore, he had no fundraising experience. But as more colleagues encouraged him to apply for the position, he asked Kaswera whether they should give the invitation more prayerful consideration. Close to NEGEST was a Catholic retreat center, the Resurrection Garden. Here David would spend hours, walking the Stations of the Cross. Here he prayed and struggled with the decision. His prayer was simple and direct: "God, dare not put me there if it is not your call. Dare not let me run away if it is your call."

One day, as he was driving home from Resurrection Garden, an SUV came from behind and overtook him (50). As it passed him, David saw a bumper sticker on the back of the Land Rover: "Expect Miracles!" it said. Even though he was ordinarily not the kind of person who believed in random signs from God, he took this to be one. Thus, in August 1996, after a month of agonizing prayer, after entering his name for nomination, he was appointed vice-chancellor of NEGEST.

David soon set to work: meeting with various people; leading faculty and staff retreats; establishing new partnerships. Colleagues began to feel a sense of belonging as David met with them, listened to them, and encouraged them. And as the financial health of the school began to stabilize, faculty, staff, and student morale rebounded, new programs and buildings were added, and enrollment rose. Within a few years of David's leadership, the school's physical, spiritual, academic, and financial future was on a secure footing.

There might be a number of reasons to explain Kasali's success at NEGEST, not the least of which was a spirit of shared vision and ownership. According to one assessment, "people began to feel like they were part of a movement— like something exciting was going to happen anytime." For David, however, the secret of NEGEST's rebounding lay in the Resurrection Garden, to which David regularly returned for prayer, for clarification of his vision, and for consolation when things were not going well. He was leading NEGEST from the Resurrection Garden, and in the end, NEGEST's rebirth reflected the same spirit of surprise ("expect miracles") as Jesus's own being raised from the dead, which David contemplated on his regular walk of the Stations of the Cross. And just as God raised Jesus from the dead, it was God who turned NEGEST around: "We had a lot of fun. God just turned *everything* around. Hope and passion were like drops of water in a dry land where people were just waiting for the rain to fall and ready to take part" (55).

Then, just when things seemed to be going extraordinarily well, David resigned his position as president of NEGEST to return to Congo in the midst of the war. This was more than surprising; it was shocking. But his decision to leave was not an arbitrary one: it was grounded in lament in the wake of the fighting in Eastern Congo, in the midst of which David felt God "calling" him—in fact, "ordering" him—to return to Beni. That is why the decision to return to Beni needs to be located within the context of David's ongoing relationship ("love affair") with God. Within that context, the violence in Beni and the loss of his close relatives brought David to a breaking point, to an unprecedented moment of "turning" in and around God.

How Long, O God!

The second Congo war broke out in 1998 and would not only lead to the occupation of Eastern Congo by Rwandan and Ugandan forces, but it would trigger a number of armed conflicts by local groups, the most deadly of which was the so-called Ituri conflict, which pitted Lendu and Hema ethnic groups against each other. One day in 1998, David Kasali received a note from Lyn Lusi, a British missionary (cofounder with her Congolese husband, Joe Lusi, of Heal Africa[3] in Goma) with a question: "How should I respond to Christians who constantly ask whether they should take up guns and machetes to defend themselves and their families against enemies who are killing them and raping their wives and daughters?" (70). Lyn also wanted to know if David could recommend books (preferably written by Africans) that could throw some light on how Christian faith intersected with tribal loyalties and witchcraft and fighting over land in the African context.

Lyn Lusi's question brought David's long-felt desire to apply the Bible to the African context into dramatic focus. He had received an outstanding theological education, he was a professor of theology, and he was building one

---

3. Heal Africa, "History": http://www.healafrica.org/history (accessed Dec. 17, 2015).

of Africa's leading theological institutions. But here he was without a good answer for Lyn. As he prayed and anguished over this, an answer began to emerge in the form of a Bible verse from one of Paul's letters. Yes, Christians should and must take up weapons and defend themselves—but weapons that are stronger than guns and machetes. Paul had written to the Ephesians that we fight "against the spiritual forces of evil in the heavenly places. Therefore, take up the whole armor of God, that you may be able to withstand in the evil day, and having done all, to stand firm" (Eph. 6:12–13).

David Kasali had found an answer to Lyn's question in Scripture. But the answer raised far more questions than it answered. For while Paul had reminded the Ephesians that "we do not wrestle against flesh and blood, but against the rulers, against the authorities, against the cosmic powers over this present darkness, against the spiritual forces of evil in the heavenly places" (Eph. 6:12), it was not clear how Paul's recommendation that the Christians put on the full armor of God could be "enfleshed" in the midst of Congo's history and politics of war and fighting. How would it become incarnated in Eastern Congo? And how does that "armor" address the problems of rebel militias, dictatorship, poor governance, poverty, ethnicity, and witchcraft in Africa? These and similar questions pointed to the need for concrete practices and institutions through which the gospel of God's armor would come into being and would be incarnated into everyday patterns of peaceful living.

While Lyn's questions troubled David and raised additional persistent questions about the incarnation of peaceful practices and institutions in the midst of war, the personal loss of David's relatives during the war was what triggered his deepest lament and eventually led to his decision to return to Congo. News of the growing toll of casualties from the fighting in Eastern Congo was filtering out every day. Soon he received news that his pregnant niece had been killed and the baby in her womb cut into pieces. A few months later, it was the news that his twenty-eight-year-old sister Jeanyne had died in the hospital at Oicha when all the nurses and doctors had run into the forest to escape the fighting. Not long after, he received the news of the death of his older brother Josias, who had died in the forests as he fled from the fighting militias.

The news was devastating, and David was inconsolable. This was no longer about abstract statistics of 5.4 million victims of the Congo wars. "This was *my* beautiful twenty-eight-year-old sister Jeanyne; this was *my* big brother Josias; this was *my* niece." "Why, O God? How long, O God?" he cried, groaned, and prayed as his world changed completely. He could not eat; he could no longer concentrate on his work at the university. He shared with Kaswera the growing realization that "we need to go home to be with our people. . . . Our people are dying. Why should they be dying for us, when we are safe and secure here?" Kaswera was concerned not only about returning to Congo in the midst of the war but also about abandoning the work of rebuilding NEGEST that God had entrusted to David. "I still have many dreams for NEGEST," David replied to Kaswera's concerns: "I need two lifetimes to realize those dreams, but God gives us only one lifetime. He did not call us to finish our dreams; he called us to be faithful in what he wants from us and in the time he gives us" (72). As in the past, Kaswera was willing to give her full support: "If you are confident that this is God's will, I will support you. Whatever it is, I am with you," she assured him. So they decided to leave NEGEST and to return to Congo, without even having a clear plan of what to do once they were there. "We went to Congo without knowing what [we would do]. We just wanted to be with the people. . . . I went as a broken man just to be with the people . . . to mourn with them."[4]

Université Chrétienne Bilingue du Congo

Road Markers for a New Future

In response to Rachel's tears, God promises that "the children shall return" and the prophet urges the children to "set up road markers for yourself, make yourself guideposts" for the return (Jer. 31:21). These signposts were, to use the image from Jeremiah, the road markers of the "new thing" that God was about to create in the land.

As if David Kasali had been reading Jeremiah's text, he and Kaswera had started setting up road markers two years before they left NEGEST, which pointed to the vision of a new initiative in Congo. In 2002, they traveled to Beni to meet with key leaders and pastors in the community. In the course of three days they engaged those pastors with three questions: (1) What had gone wrong in the DRC? (2) Where was the church in the midst of such widespread suffering and violence? and (3) What does the future look like, and what is the role of the church in that future? They placed large pieces of paper on the wall and wrote ideas on them. Then they grouped those ideas into six categories, which would form the core programs of the "Congo Initiative."

The initial workshop was followed by a number of other workshops, in-

4. Interview, Notre Dame University, Notre Dame, IN (Sept. 11, 2014).

cluding the "Pastoral Ministry in Times of Crisis" (2003), which was held in Beni and was also attended by Paul and Dick Robinson, who had grown up as missionary kids in Congo and were now David Kasali's friends and key partners for the future. A vision for holistic transformation began to emerge from these workshops, with a number of significant components. The vision was that there should be:

(1) a deeper understanding of Congo's problems coming from Congolese men and women who analyzed their own context.
(2) an acknowledgment and lament over the church's complicity in the violence that had ripped their communities apart. (In one seminar, pastors cried and wrote letters of confession and repentance on behalf of the members of their congregations who had killed and raped. In another seminar [on the book of Revelation] the pastors responded to the spirit's letters to the seven churches [Rev. 2–3] by writing a letter to all the churches in Congo, calling them to repent, to ask for forgiveness, and to live out their mission as "redemptive communities" in the midst of the fighting.)
(3) a shared vision of a restored Congo, in which pastoral leadership was at the heart of that transformation. This would require, among other things, a vision of the church as an agent and catalyst for social healing and reconstruction after the model of Nehemiah, who undertook the rebuilding of the city in the midst of war and violence.
(4) training and development of strong indigenous Christian leaders to transform their communities and their country (more on this below).

Another crucial element, as significant as the local conversations, was the mobilization of a network of global conversations and partnerships. As soon as David's term at NEGEST ended, he and Kaswera relocated, with their family, to the United States for three years to allow Kaswera to complete her doctorate (in education) at Trinity Evangelical Divinity School, and for David to work on an initiative that would bring together the visions, dreams, and sentiments of the local Congolese leaders and pastors. Dick Robinson connected the Kasalis to his calling church, Elmbrook Church in Milwaukee, which became the springboard for new relationships. During that time Kasali made several trips to Congo, met with local leaders and pastors, and, in the meanwhile, held numerous conversations with members of his Elmbrook congregation. Out of these efforts, the Congo Initiative was formed as a 501c3 nonprofit, with both a US and Congo board, and a clear mission "to train and develop indigenous Christian leaders to transform their communities and their nation, the DRC."[5] The Université Chrétienne Bilingue du Congo at Beni would serve as the catalyst and the heart of Congo Initiative's (CI) mission for holistic transformation. With the vision and mission in place, as well as the legal and institutional infrastructure of the CI established, the Kasalis relocated to Beni permanently in 2007 to formally inaugurate the university.

A New Thing in Eastern Congo

Paul Robinson's parents had come as missionaries to Congo, and Paul was raised there. He has worked closely with David Kasali on their project at UCBC, and he now serves as president and CEO of Congo Initiative. Asked why he had resigned his faculty position at Wheaton College in Illinois two years before in order to spend more time at UCBC, he had this to say: "I have never been involved in anything that I felt had as much potential as UCBC. There is so much hope at UCBC."[6] Pressed on what the hope is, he answered, "Students want to see something different, to develop something new." It is this vision and expectation of something new that resonated within the people from the start and touched a deep sentiment in a community that was experiencing profound war fatigue and a sense of helplessness. It is not surprising, then, that when Kasali convened the local leaders and pastors and invited them to dream of a new church and a new society in Eastern Congo, their excitement was palpable. The vision and expectation of something new not only got everyone in the community excited; it unleashed, in turn, a new spirit of generosity. The tribal chief donated the land for the campus, and men and women from the community came to clear the bush, burn weeds, dig the foundation, and plant the compound. From the very beginning, UCBC has been seen as the "people's university": thus the people of Beni refer to UCBC as "our university" and speak of building a new future for "our children."[7]

UCBC and CI also represent a new model of partnership. For even as the visions and dreams shaping UCBC and CI are the dreams of people in Congo, David Kasali served as a key bridge, inviting his American friends into the vision and mission of the university. This was, of course, a radical departure

5. Congo Initiative at http://www.congoinitiative.org/.

6. Interview with Paul Robinson, Wheaton College, Wheaton, IL (Feb. 28, 2015).

7. Recall the words of UCBC's anthem: "La Communauté": "La Communauté / C'est notre force / La Communauté / Ça nous renforce (2x) / La Communauté / Nous transforme / Nous sommes UCBC."

from standard mission development practice, in which the needs of Africa are often figured out by Western experts, and Africans are only brought into the picture as recipients or implementers of those plans and programs. The fact that Congolese and American Christians are working together on this exciting project—and they are saying, "This is what *we* are doing"—this represents a unique "Ephesian moment."[8] The moment illumines not merely a model of collaboration; it is an ecclesiological radiance that reveals the church as a new community drawn from all nations, tribes, and tongues, where these different cultural fragments are brought together to reveal the "measure of the stature of the fullness of Christ" (Eph. 4:13). This sense of a "new we" is also reflected at UCBC, with students coming from different faiths and different ethnic backgrounds, and living and working together in the different university programs.

There is also something new in the education model that UCBC is setting in place. First, it is bilingual, which is distinctive for a Congolese university, but which offers the prospect of orienting graduates toward East Africa and the greater English-speaking world. Second, its focus on female leadership is explicit throughout its programs and enrollment: the female population is 46 percent of the current enrollment, which is a marked difference from the national average of only 10 percent. Third, while the university offers the traditional staples of applied sciences, communications, economics, and theology, service learning and community work are also incorporated into the curriculum. Students are expected to participate in the surrounding community through service activities. Fourth, and by far the most striking aspect of UCBC, is the way faith inspires and shapes the ethos, programs, and activities of the university, whose mission is "to nurture and shape an authentic, redemptive community of Christ's followers." What this means is that faith does not exist in its own realm of "spiritual" matters; rather, it is seen as the reason and the glue that holds together the different traditional course offerings. Behind this determination to hold faith at the heart of the programs is a robust theological vision of reconciliation—of God reconciling all things "visible and invisible . . . [for] in him all things hold together" (Col. 1:16–17). Given this overarching theological vision, the goal of UCBC is not simply

8. For more on the Ephesian moment of World Christianity, see Andrew Walls, "The Ephesian Moment: At a Crossroads in Christian History," in *The Cross-Cultural Process in Christian History: Studies in the Transmission and Appropriation of Faith* (Maryknoll, NY: Orbis, 2002), 71–81. For an elaboration on the "Ephesian moment" within an African context, see E. Katongole, "Mission and the Ephesian Moment of World Christianity: Pilgrimages of Pain and Hope and the Economics of Eating Together," *Mission Studies* 29, no. 2 (2012): 183–200.

to *train* students to think, reflect, analyze, and give practical solutions to the challenges facing society; the goal is far more ambitious. The goal is to *form* students, as Paul would say, through the "renewal of [their] mind" (Rom. 12:2), so that they can live out their new sense of identity and confidence in God's new creation in concrete and visible ways. The goal is the realization of a new creation in Congo, for which the students are both the first fruits and the agents (ambassadors). Thus UCBC's motto: "Being transformed to transform."

Community engagement is another distinctive feature. In addition to its degree programs, UCBC promotes holistic transformation and renewal in DRC by engaging the wider community through five community centers. These community centers facilitate a variety of conferences, workshops, and training programs for pastors and church leaders, legal professionals, and vulnerable women and children.[9]

These factors, together with the fact that UCBC was the very first university in Beni, contribute to the general sense that the university is something new and exciting, especially since UCBC was founded in the middle of the war. In addition, the boldness of the enterprise was underscored in 2007, when UCBC "opened its doors" to its first enrollment of seventy-seven students— even though there were no buildings yet, let alone any doors to open! It is this madness that makes UCBC a unique story of hope in Africa. As Paul Robinson points out: "I have never been involved in anything that I felt had as much hope and potential as UCBC."[10]

A New Way of Seeing the World

The key Scripture text that frames and shapes the work of UCBC is Isaiah 43:18–19:

---

9. For example, the Center for Development and Partnership teaches income generation, micro-finance, resource mobilization and development, partnership building; the Center for Church Renewal and Global Mission emphasizes teaching and equipping servants and leaders to promote reconciliation, healing, and restoration; the Center for Community and Family Renewal includes a women's rehabilitation center, child development, health center, and hospital partnership, athletic facility, micro-enterprises, counseling seminars and conferences; the Center for Professional Development and Vocational Training emphasizes skills training, professional development, HIV prevention and counseling, church mobilization, vocational training (carpentry, construction, etc.); and the Center for the Creative Arts includes music and worship, radio/TV, recording, and art (performing arts, art therapy).

10. Paul Robinson interview, Wheaton College, Wheaton, IL (Feb. 28, 2015).

Forget the former things;
do not dwell on the past.
See, I am doing a new thing!
Now it springs up; do you not perceive it?
I am making a way in the wilderness
and streams in the wasteland.

This text hangs in David Kasali's office within a framed image of the map of Africa, with a river emerging out of its southern tip, lush fields and vegetation all around; and inside Africa, from Congo, radiant beams are refracted through UCBC's signature buildings, engulfing village communities and families in its brilliant light. The artwork provides not only a visual commentary on UCBC as a fulfillment of Isaiah's promise, but also serves as a constant reminder of the vision of hope that the university is invited to live into. In this passage Isaiah offers a message of hope to a people who had given up hope.[11] He depicts the hope—the new thing that God is doing—as a stream in the wasteland, and equally important as a seed that "springs up" unexpectedly. Isaiah 43:18–22 offers the same message as Jeremiah's promise of God creating (*bara*) a new thing in the land (31:22). But the fact that Isaiah uses the image of seed springing up points to an interesting quality of hope as being both a promise and reality. For as John and Angela Lederach observe with regard to the seed-like quality of reconciliation and social healing, "the metaphor of seeds contains simultaneously fruit and generative potential."[12]

This observation is extremely helpful in highlighting the hope that UCBC represents. On the one hand, the institution is still very young and small: from the initial seventy-seven students, it has grown to a current enrollment of 489 students, with an alumni community of under 300. But like a seed that is just springing up, though it is still small, it holds a lot of future promise. However, on the other side of its relative smallness, UCBC has already produced fruit, and its impact can already be felt by its students and by the local community in and around Beni—and even beyond. More than anything else, the impact is a new lens, a whole new way of seeing and living in the world. This is witnessed

11. The message of Deutero Isaiah (Isa. 40–55) was the message of consolation for an oppressed people languishing in exile. The book's first three chapters open with the words "Comfort my people." They have lost hope. Their deliverance is foretold as a new thing, with respect to which the deliverance from Egypt (the former things) will appear as naught. The restoration will be like a new creation.

12. John Paul and Angela Jill Lederach, *When Bones and Blood Cry Out: Journeys through the Soundscape of Healing and Reconciliation* (Oxford: Oxford University Press, 2010), 53.

to by the students themselves. Jimmy, one of the first graduates, captures the institution's impact on students:

> I transferred from another university, which was considered to be one of the best. . . . I could fill my head with theories. . . . I had very good teachers. But coming here to UCBC . . . we have learned a whole new way of seeing the world. We have come to believe that even simple people can effect change. We will be the change.[13]

That positive impact has already been recognized by the Congolese ministry of education. When David Kasali went to Kinshasa to register for a charter for UCBC in 2007, the minister of education listened attentively as David shared his vision. "This is exactly what we need," he said. "This is what is going to change our country and break the cycles of poverty, violence and corruption. We are going to watch you."[14] And watch they did. In 2008 the government was beginning the process of changing the entire curriculum of higher education for the whole country. They asked two universities to be the first institutions of higher education to put the new system in place. One was the famous Catholic University of Kinshasa (formerly known as Louvanium), one of the oldest, largest (c. 27,000 students), and preeminent institutions of learning in Congo. The other was an unknown start-up, in a tiny place out in the middle of a war zone in Eastern Congo—the Université Chrétienne Bilingue du Congo.

The impact on Beni and the local community has been even more immediate and powerful. In the fall of 2014, the massacre of over 250 people in and around Beni by unknown gangs sent over 80,000 people fleeing their homes and threatened to close down the city. The mayor and the city's civic and political leaders sent a message to UCBC urging them not to close the university, but to go on with classes. Closing the university, they said, would be like shutting down the city. And so, UCBC remained open, and, with time, a modicum of peace has returned to Beni. This story, like the story of the basketball game at the beginning of this chapter, underscores the political significance of the university in terms of holding the city together, especially during a critical time of war, insecurity, and violence.

In chapter 9 I offered a theoretical argument that, while Melissa Snarr

13. http://archive.constantcontact.com/fs112/1101863034612/archive/1116089229603.html.

14. Shehan, *This Is for You*, 96. See also my interview with Paul Robinson at Wheaton College (Feb. 28, 2015).

is right to be concerned with the everyday practices (such as maintaining a school), she is wrong to suggest that lament is a distraction from everyday life. I argued, contra Snarr, that lament is not mere "spirituality," a mere pre-political strengthening or preparation. It is a decisive form of political agency and engagement. The story of David Kasali and UCBC confirms that. But what the story also confirms is that lament constitutes a form of "repair" and a "gathering" of the individual, social, and political community that has been devastated and scattered by poverty, civil war, and the politics of greed. And if one is to correctly view UCBC as both the fruit and work of lament, then one can see the potential for a politics of lament in reconstituting and redirecting politics toward its true *telos* of serving and enhancing human dignity. This is what makes UCBC a unique peacebuilding initiative; but it also brings the intersection of theology and peace studies into sharper focus. In order to explore these connections, we need to highlight a number of significant points that emerge from the story of David Kasali and the founding of the UCBC.

UCBC as Peacebuilding Initiative

Hope in the Midst of the War

The first significant point to note is that UCBC was founded in the midst of the war and continues to operate in such a context. For as the last story illustrates, the violence and resulting insecurity in and around Beni continues to be high. The process of social healing and peacebuilding does not wait until war ends and the conflict abates. As the Lederachs note, "local communities face the ongoing challenge of how to nurture spaces for healing and reconciliation not as 'post' violence products, but as . . . permanently available and challenging innovations that must give birth and be reborn in the midst of less than ideal conditions."[15] UCBC is such an innovation that not only provides an "interruption" in the reality and logic of war in Eastern Congo, but exists as a "permanently available innovation" where hope is reborn.

Even without a background in peace studies, Kasali's theological sensibility had led him to see the need for a university in the midst of the war zone as a way of giving and nurturing hope. As we have seen in citing 1 Peter 3:15, hope, by its very character, exists in the midst of tribulations. It is a similar character and logic of hope that Isaiah describes as "rivers in the desert" (Isa. 43:19) and

---

15. Lederach and Lederach, *Bones and Blood*, 53–54.

the psalmist portrays as a "table [prepared] before me in the presence of my enemies" (Ps. 23:5).

Forming a New Generation of Leaders for Congo and Africa

Another crucial peacebuilding dimension of UCBC is its explicit mission of forming a fresh generation of leaders for Congo and Africa. The absence of credible leadership in Africa has been well noted. Writing in 2009, the late Kenyan Nobel laureate and environment activist Wangari Maathai observed: "What has held Africa back, and continues to do so, has its origins in a lack of principled, ethical leadership."[16] Kasali's travels through the continent had also revealed the crisis of leadership as one of the root causes of Africa's problems. UCBC's focus on leadership formation is a way to get to the root of such problems:

> You have to go to the roots. The root for me is leadership. Our suffering in Congo is dependent on the type of leaders that we have. If we can prepare a new generation of leaders who are critical in their thinking, who are grounded in ethics of love your enemies and love your neighbors, and who say, "Enough is enough," then in the long run we will change to a sustained development that will do away with the relief work.[17]

One must be careful, however, even while noting the crisis of leadership in Africa, not to surrender to despair. As Jason Stearns, toward the end of *Dancing in the Glory of Monsters*, suggests, with a certain note of resignation: "Perhaps the most nagging, persistent problem I have witnessed . . . has been the lack of visionary, civic-minded leadership."[18] But what the story of David Kasali confirms is that visionary and civic-minded leadership is not totally absent in Africa. The challenge, as is often the case, has been how to look for it and where to find it. Most discussions about leadership in Africa have tended to focus on the "formal" sector of government and nation-state actors. David Kasali's story points to the need to pay more attention to the so-called informal

16. *The Challenge for Africa* (New York: Pantheon, 2009), 25.
17. "David M. Kasali: Being Transformed to Transform," *Faith and Leadership* (Sept. 19, 2010): http://www.faithandleadership.com/multimedia/david-m-kasali-being-transformed -transform (accessed Dec. 9, 2015).
18. Jason K. Stearns, *Dancing in the Glory of Monsters: The Collapse of the Congo and the Great War of Africa* (New York: PublicAffairs, 2011), 328.

sector, more specifically to the range of faith-inspired activists for nonviolent change in Africa. Kasali is one such leader, but not the only one. For as our discussion in this book shows, leaders like Kataliko, Munzihirwa, Nyirumbe, Barankitse, Angelina Atyam, Taban, Odama, Nyiritegeka, and many others are part of that cloud of witnesses. And this is a sample from just the East African region.

The Agency of a Christian Faith Activist

Kasali's story provides an insider perspective of the way faith activists come to practical conclusions—such as founding a university in the midst of war in Congo. Whereas the public initiatives of Christian faith activists often receive widespread admiration, the process and theological reasons that motivate them quite often remain hidden.[19] And to the extent that this is so, the agency of the faith activists remains opaque. In taking this opportunity to tell Kasali's story, I hope that I have succeeded in making that agency transparent and the extent to which it is grounded not so much in the calculated logic of utilitarian or strategic peacebuilding agendas, but in something like a logic of "obedience" on the part of one who feels *led* to do what she or he does.

Since offering his wallet to be baptized, David has understood his agency as a response to what he feels God is calling him to do: he is a participant and

---

19. This is true even of leaders like Desmond Tutu, whose stellar leadership of the Truth and Reconciliation Commission in South Africa has been well noted (see, e.g., Daniel Philpott, *Just and Unjust Peace: An Ethic of Political Reconciliation* [New York: Oxford University Press, 2012]). The "public" Tutu is very rarely connected to the Tutu that is aptly captured by a picture, alone in a chapel, looking at the cross, presumably praying (see in John Allen, *Rabble-rouser for Peace: The Authorized Biography of Desmond Tutu* [New York: Free Press, 2006]). Without an understanding of what Tutu sees in this quiet turning toward the suffering God, any story about him remains incomplete. Perhaps that is the reason that Tutu wrote *Made for Goodness* (see Desmond Tutu and Mpho Tutu, *Made for Goodness: And Why This Makes All the Difference* [New York: Harper One, 2010]). In the preface, Tutu writes: "I speak to audiences across the world, and I often get the same questions, 'Why are you so joyful?' 'How do you keep your faith in people when you see so much injustice, oppression, and cruelty?' 'What makes you so certain that the world is going to get better?' What these questions really want to know is, What do I see that they're missing? How do I see the world and my role in it? How do I see God? What is the faith that drives me? What are the spiritual practices that uphold me? What do I see in the heart of humanity and in the sweep of history that confirms my conviction that goodness will triumph?" (ix). *Made for Goodness* offers a glimpse into the hidden Tutu—and thus into the rich theological matrix of his agency.

"servant" within the drama God is writing in the Congo. "My life—the way I wanted it—was to be for the first few years in the university and in the business world. But from then on, my life was as the Lord wanted it, everything I was and everything that came to me was not me fighting for it, it was just God."[20] For David, surrendering to God's will turned his life into something far richer than he would have imagined. "My life was surrendered to God, and then he gave me back what I was passionate about. . . . If I belonged to myself I would still be struggling and sitting somewhere doing what, I do not know."

This is an important observation that illuminates the logic of how faith activists see and understand their agency for nonviolent advocacy. Of course, one can say that by the same logic faith activists might be led to militant and violent activism, even terrorism. There is no way to assume that faith activism in and of itself will lead to nonviolent activism. That is why it is important to take seriously the thesis of the "ambivalence of the sacred" and the conditions that distinguish "strong" from "weak" religion.[21] But even more importantly, that is why a theology of peace depends on narrative more than on abstract principles or strategies. For it is only by telling the individual stories of the faith activists that one is able to lay open the full context of their agency and its peaceful prospects. As I noted above, a key mark of the truth and power of Christian social activism is the consistent

---

20. Shehan, *This Is for You*, 105.

21. On the distinction between "strong" and "weak" religion, see Scott Appleby, *The Ambivalence of the Sacred: Religion, Violence, and Reconciliation* (Lanham, MD: Rowman and Littlefield, 2000): "A religion is strong, first of all, if its institutions are well developed and secure and its adherents 'literate' in doctrinal and moral teachings and practiced in its devotional, ritual, and spiritual traditions. . . . A weak religion is one in which the people retain meaningful contact only with vestiges of the broader religious worldview and network of meanings and resources, in which they are isolated from one another and from educators and spiritual moral exemplars, and in which ethnic, nationalist, secular-liberal, and other worldviews and ideologies have a free rein to shape the meaning of those vestiges" (77). Commenting on Yugoslavia and on the failure of Christian leaders to stem the spate of ethnic violence, Appleby describes factors that contributed to make Christianity a "weak" religion. In general, "inadequate or nonexistent programs of religious education, politically unprepared religious leaders and the lack of viable ecumenical and interreligious structures conspired to limit the religious potential for peacemaking" (75). More specifically, "religious leadership led too little and followed too much. Preoccupied with the state, religious leaders did not attend sufficiently to the task of sharpening the attitudes and behaviors of their 'natural constituencies.' By and large the faithful, the potential base of the independent political power of the churches, were not mobilized for nonviolent forms of religious activism, such as conflict mediation and healing and reconciliation ministries" (74).

commitment to nonviolent social change and the invitation into the story of a loving and peaceful God.[22]

The Work of Lament

In Jeremiah 31:16, in response to Rachel's tears, Yahweh consoles her with these words:

> Keep your voice from weeping,
>   and your eyes from tears,
> for there is a reward for your work,
>   declares the Lord,
>   and they shall come back from the land of the enemy.

The prophet refers to Rachel's tears as work whose reward is the return of the children—and, in the end, the creation of a new thing in the land (v. 22). This observation finds a lot of reverberations in David Kasali's story. His lament for the loss of his relatives in the Congo did trigger his decision to return to Beni, which, as his story shows, is what led to the formation of the founding of UCBC. What the story confirms is that lament is not merely a

---

22. For this reason, the rather widespread assumption among many secular peace scholars that religion leads to violence can both be historically misleading and ideologically driven. For a good historical, philosophical, and ideological analysis of the "myth of religious violence" that I find compelling, see William T. Cavanaugh, *The Myth of Religious Violence: Secular Ideology and Roots of Modern Conflict* (Oxford: Oxford University Press, 2009). Without denying historical cases where violence *has* been perpetrated in the name of religion, to always associate religion with violence can have the ideological effect of blinding us to other more prevalent forms of violence. As Cavanaugh argues in his latest book, *Field Hospital: The Church's Engagement with a Wounded World* (Grand Rapids: Eerdmans, 2016), people kill for all sorts of things: gods, oil, Jesus, Jihad, land, flags, the invisible hand of the market. The challenge, Cavanaugh notes, is one of idolatry, which transfers worship and allegiance from the one true God to all sorts of false gods (idols), in whose name we are willing to kill. From a Christian point of view that one true God, is the "crucified God"—a God who responds to an excess of evil through an excess of love (Kataliko). As I see it, the challenge is for the church to make this clear and explicit—and thus offer a constant reminder that her engagement in the world is grounded in the story of this crucified God. The witness of Christians such as Kataliko, Munzihirwa, Nyirumbe, Angelina, and others profiled here not only reflects this story of a God willing to suffer rather than use violence; they also remind and call back the church to her role as a field hospital to bind and heal wounds in the midst of the world's violence.

sentiment, but a set of practical commitments—indeed, a form of work. In Kasali's case, this work revolved around four key markers.

First, it was the work of *presence*, or what I have referred to above as the capacity to stand on the ground of pain and suffering. Kasali felt a need to return to Beni, just to be there, to stand with them in lament. As he noted, "I just went as a broken man just to be with my people . . . to mourn with them." Second, it was the work of *gathering* community. As I have noted above, the seminars and workshops with the community leaders were not simply for analyzing Congo's history; they were also opportunities of repentance and forgiveness. Like the prophet Joel, who instructs the priests to "call a solemn assembly" (2:15) for a period of fasting, weeping, and mourning, the workshops in Beni turned into similar gatherings of lament. But just as in Joel's case, with the gift of fresh dreams and vision ("Your sons and daughters shall prophesy, your old men will dream dreams" [2:28]), the seminars turned into rich dreaming and visioning sessions for a new future. Third, it was the work of *mobilizing* different resources, partners and resources that were needed for setting up the Congo Initiative and building the university. And finally, it is the *ongoing* work of *running* a university. In the context of Eastern Congo, such quotidian activities have proved the most challenging. Kasali says: "There are so many unfinished buildings; unfinished programs; we have shortage of faculty; very little funding, a lot of things to do . . . and a lot of suffering; many funerals to attend . . . the security situation continues to be uncertain. . . . I have to constantly remind myself that it is not me."

If these challenges often prove "overwhelming, they keep [David] under the cross of Jesus Christ, and keep [his] faith going, and keep John 15 very real: 'Remain in me and me in you; without me, you cannot do it. Being there, I have to depend completely on God, and that without him we can do nothing.'"[23] At the same time, the challenges keep David grounded in Beni.

Many people in the Congo have never heard of the small town of Beni in North Kivu, on the eastern fringes of the DRC, over one thousand miles from the capital, Kinshasa. Like most other towns in Eastern Congo, Beni has few schools, its infrastructure is undeveloped, and its roads unpaved—all of which are the legacy of Mobutu's thirty-two years in power and his intentional marginalization of Eastern Congo. Mobutu lived in constant fear of an uprising and the possible secession of Eastern Congo, a prospect that would be increased if the region had more schools, a developed infrastructure, and a thriving economy. This is what makes Kasali's ambitious goal of transforming

---

23. "David M. Kasali," *Faith and Leadership*.

the DRC and Africa from this small town out in the middle of a war zone in Eastern Congo all the more remarkable. Ambitions of that magnitude are normally expected to come from places like Kinshasa, or, even better, from New York, London, or Paris! But this is where Kasali's Beni finds reverberations with Ramah in Rachel's story. "A voice is heard in Ramah . . . Rachel is weeping for her children" (Jer. 31:15).

In Jeremiah's time, Ramah was a town about six miles north of Jerusalem, on the main road leading north to Samaria, Syria, and Babylon (scholars identify the place as present-day Ramallah). In 587–586 BCE, when Jerusalem was destroyed by the Babylonians, the Israelites taken captive were assembled in Ramah before being deported to Babylon (Jer. 40:1). Thus Ramah not only lies "outside" Jerusalem; its memory evokes bondage, exile, and death. Rachel's weeping at Ramah evokes the fate of her children there. But by placing Rachel's cry at Ramah, Jeremiah also invokes another tradition, according to which Rachel, who died in childbirth, was buried in or near Ramah (1 Sam. 10:2).[24] In earlier times, Ramah was also the center of Samuel's prophetic activity (1 Sam. 7:17), the point from which he went throughout the land reproving, rebuking, and exhorting people to repentance. It is also said that Samuel anointed Saul king at Ramah.

The overall effect of these historical memories and traditions is to point to Ramah's location outside Jerusalem as a significant factor in thinking about the prophetic role of the church in the search for peace. For as Brueggemann reminds us, while God can raise up prophets and authorize prophetic voices and deeds from anywhere, anytime, and under any circumstance, "subcommunities that stand in tension with the dominant community in any political economy" are the "natural habitat" of the prophetic imagination.[25] Prophets not only stand outside the dominant political economy; it is from within this outside location that they critique the reigning social visions while offering alternative visions for a new future. The margins are important for this prophetic task because it is here that they are able to see, stand within, and express

24. According to Genesis 35, Rachel died in childbirth on the road from Bethel to Bethlehem. This is perhaps the main reason why her official tomb is outside Bethlehem ("Rachel's Tomb," *Life in the Holy Land*: http://www.lifeintheholyland.com/rachel_tomb_bethlehem.htm [accessed Dec. 9, 2015]). Matthew brings together the two traditions of 1 Samuel and Genesis, and so Matthew pictures Rachel weeping in her grave at Ramah over the horrific events taking place in Bethlehem (the slaughter of the innocents)—the destination she was looking toward while dying (see David Lang, "Why Is Rachel Weeping at Ramah?" December 18, 2012: http://www.accordancebible.com/Why-Is-Rachel-Weeping-At-Ramah (accessed Apr. 20, 2015).

25. Walter Brueggemann, *The Prophetic Imagination* (Philadelphia: Fortress, 1978), xi.

pain without giving way to despair, and at the same time draw from a different "long and available memory" to energize a new future.

Another way to make this observation is to note that "prophetic" does not simply mean being over and against, even though critique is an essential aspect of the prophet's work. Being prophetic is also about energizing and preparing for the birth of a new social reality in the land. Lament is at the heart of this double task. This is what is going on in the story of Rachel's tears at Ramah, which are transformed into the guideposts for a new thing in the land. This is what the story of Kasali at Beni is about. In telling Kasali's story, I have tried to make explicit the "long and available memory" that energizes and inspires Kasali and the UCBC, and how that memory stands in tension with the dominant social imagination that drives Congo. It is because of this difference that UCBC stands as a surprising new thing in the land. But what I have also tried to show is the lament that is at the heart of this reality, and which thus makes UCBC a work of lament.

In the previous section, I displayed this work of lament as revolving around four tasks: of *presence*, of *gathering* community, of *mobilizing* resources, and of the daily ongoing effort of *running* an institution. The more closely one examines these tasks, the more one discovers that they are an outline of a robust ecclesiology. The four tasks point to four essential ecclesiological marks: (1) the church as an incarnational presence; (2) the church as a community of forgiveness and repentance; (3) the church as a catholic community; and (4) the church as a sacrament of daily sanctification engaged in the very practical exigencies of healing and binding wounds. In view of the current discussion, what we need to highlight is that "Ramah" is the church's unique location and mission. The church, in the words of Pope Francis, is a "field hospital" whose mission is "to go forth from [her] own comfort zone in order to reach all the 'peripheries' in need of the light of the Gospel."[26] That is to say, marginality is essential to the very nature and mission of the church. The church is born and lives in "Ramah"—on the "outside" of dominant political and economic structures, shaped by a long and distinct memory of a loving and suffering God, and in the business of energizing and receiving the gift of

26. Pope Francis, *Evangelii Gaudium*, §20. See also Pope Francis, "A Big Heart Open to God," interview with Antonio Spadaro, SJ, *America*, September 30, 2013: http://americamagazine .org/pope-interview. For an extended and illuminating explication of this ecclesiological vision articulated by Pope Francis, which lies behind what I try to show in *Born from Lament*, see Cavanaugh, *Field Hospital: The Church's Engagement with a Wounded World* (Grand Rapids: Eerdmans, 2016).

a new social reality in the world.[27] It is this ecclesiological vision that drives David Kasali and reveals UCBC as an exceptional ecclesial radiance of a new future—born from lament.

27. For a further elaboration of this claim in the light of Pope Francis's vision of "a poor church for the poor," see Stan Ilo, "The Church of the Poor: Towards an Ecclesiology of Vulnerable Mission," *Ecclesiology* 10 (2014): 229–50. Commenting on Pope Francis's address to journalists, March 16, 2013 (*Zenit*: http://www.zenit.org/en/articles/pope-francis-address-to -journalists), Ilo writes: "The church bears the marks and carries in her womb the brokenness of our wounded humanity and has a summons to discover, in the pains and sufferings of those on the margins, the voice of God who calls us again and again in mystery" (232–33).

CHAPTER 12

Maggy Barankitse and the Politics of Forgiveness in Burundi

> *And so . . . we women began to look for our children. . . . Such intense sorrow, such a depth of pain, as one by one we found our children, . . . broken . . . ravished . . . wounded . . . the children the children . . . searching searching. . . . We found our children, battered . . . bloodied . . . crushed . . . violated. Gathering them to us, gathering them to us. And so we women began our grieving for our children, with our children.*

Judy Atkinson

The story of Rachel weeping for her children that we examined in chapter 10 explodes with rich reverberations within the African context in a way that confirms the gendered, generative, and political dimensions of lament.

Rachel Weeping

The Gendered Dimension of Lament

The voice of Rachel is the voice of an anguished *woman*. Feminist and womanist theologies have drawn our attention to the experience of the suffering of women in various contexts, including within the biblical story. Elizabeth Johnson identifies four ways in which women participate in the reality of suffering: (1) through labor and childbirth; (2) in the struggle against injustice and domination; (3) in the grief that attends to injury or loss of a loved one; and (4) through physical and emotional suffering arising out of radical evil.

"This is the suffering that does not come about because a woman has chosen to birth new life, or stand up for justice, or love someone. It is forced upon her by men, against her will, robbing her of everything, even life itself."[1]

Nowhere is this fourth reality of gender violence more evident than in Eastern Congo, which has come to be known as "the rape capital of the world"—a place where over 200,000 women have been raped.[2] As noted elsewhere, the factors behind this widespread violence against women in Eastern Congo are complex, and this book's scope does not allow for the opportunity to enter that discussion.[3] However, I do want to make the point here that Rachel's weeping finds a great deal of resonance in the African context, where women quite often bear much of the pain and suffering that come with Africa's violent convulsions.

The Generative Dimension of Lament

The voice of Rachel is the voice of an anguished *mother*. Rachel, Jacob's wife, desperately wanted to have children, but for many years she could not, until finally "God remembered Rachel . . . and opened her womb" (Gen. 30:22), which is when she gave birth to Joseph. Though she experienced the joy of seeing her barrenness end with the birth of Joseph, her happiness came to an end when she hemorrhaged to death in giving birth to her second child, Benjamin (Gen. 35:16-21). She named her son Ben-oni (son of my sorrow), but Jacob, unable to endure this painful reminder of his wife's death, renamed the child Benjamin (son of the right hand).

Rachel's weeping as a mother finds considerable resonance with many of the weeping mothers of Africa. For Rachel, as for them, the connection between birth and death perhaps helps to explain why women, more than men, play the key role in mourning the dead, for the same reason that they play the key role in giving birth to new life. Birthing and mourning are both affirmations and confirmations of life cycles, and they reflect the "womb," from whose depth the pangs of both new life and lament spring.

1. Elizabeth A. Johnson, *She Who Is: The Mystery of God in Feminist Theological Discourse* (New York: Crossroad, 1992), 262, quoted in Kathleen B. Billman and Daniel L. Migliore, *Rachel's Cry: Prayer of Lament and Rebirth of Hope* (Cleveland: United Church Press, 1999), 71.

2. Jo Adetunji, "Forty-eight Women Raped Every Hour in Congo, Study Finds," *The Guardian*, May 12, 2011: http://www.theguardian.com/world/2011/may/12/48-women-raped-hour-congo (accessed Apr. 8, 2014).

3. See above, Chapter 1.

But there is another crucial dimension to Rachel's motherhood: Rachel stands in the tradition of biblical women whose barrenness is transformed into fruitfulness, women such as Sarah (Gen. 11:30), Rebekah (Gen. 25:21), Hannah (1 Sam. 1:2), and Elizabeth (Luke 1:7).[4] The gift of new life is miraculously given to these barren women. Even more importantly, their giving birth becomes a metaphor for the opening of a new future and the generation of an alternative way of being by the miraculous power of God. Rachel not only stands within this tradition; she extends it by pointing to the reality of divine motherhood itself. In her tears she becomes a metaphor for God as a grieving mother. For, as I have noted earlier, given the reversals under way in Jeremiah 31:15ff., Rachel's lament points not only to Rachel but to God as the mother who weeps for her children, and whose womb trembles for Ephraim, "my dear son" (Jer. 31:20).

Dangerous Lament: The Political Dimension of Female Lament

As I have suggested above, the reason that Matthew invokes Rachel's lament at the beginning of his Gospel is to present the birth of Jesus as a *political* event that fulfills the promise of a "new thing in the land." Thus, for Matthew, the birth of Jesus is the birth of a new social reality—the kingdom of heaven—and one that happens to be a threat to the reigning political order, as shown by Herod's panic when he received news of Jesus's birth and his response of ordering the slaughter of the innocents. For Matthew, of course, that massacre was nothing but the last gasp of the old order in its desperate attempt to hold on to the old way.

In *Dangerous Voices*, Gail Holst-Warhaft confirms this political—and thus dangerous—dimension of lament in her study of the laments of women in Greek literature.[5] Holst-Warhaft shows that, as an essentially female form, lament gave women considerable power over the rituals of death in ancient Greece. However, from the sixth century onward, legislation was introduced in Athens and a number of other city-states to curb the use of lament, largely because women's power over mourning challenged the social order at a time when the emergent city-states needed to recruit standing armies to bolster their political and military ambitions. For such

---

4. Tellingly, Rachel's grandson (Joseph's son) is named Ephraim, which means "fruitful."

5. Gail Holst-Warhaft, *Dangerous Voices: Women's Laments and Greek Literature* (London: Routledge, 1992).

a project, it was politically important for death in war to be glorified, not lamented.[6]

This political and dangerous dimension of female lament finds resonance in the African context. In Liberia, for instance, Leymah Gbowee and her fellow women ignited and led a movement that saw as its goal an end to war and the restoration of peaceful, democratic politics.[7] It is the same dangerous politics that is displayed in the story of Angelina Atyam, whose daughter was abducted by the Lord's Resistance Army, and who, out of that experience of lament, led a passionate campaign of forgiveness, advocacy (for the release of all the abducted children), and a nonviolent end to war. It is a similar form of politics of lament that is the key to Maggy Barankitse's Maison Shalom and her determination to invent a new future in Burundi, one founded on love and forgiveness. In my previous work, especially *The Sacrifice of Africa*, I have depicted both Angelina and Maggy as part of the broader argument for the invention of a new political future.[8] Because Maggy's story brings out the interconnections between the gendered, generative, and political dimensions of lament so clearly, and because her story helps to display, in a very lucid way, the inner logic of hope as a discipline that is born of, deepened through, and carried forth by lament, it is important to retell it here.

Maggy Barankitse and Maison Shalom

Born from Lament (Sunday, October 24, 1993)

Before the events of 1993 in Burundi, Maggy, a Tutsi, had already adopted children—three Tutsi and four Hutu. Following the assassination of the first democratically elected Hutu president, Melchior Ndadaye, on October 21, 1993,

---

6. The attempt to limit the clan cults (of mourning women) coincides with "the establishment of state-sanctioned cults and a new attitude toward the mourning of the dead, one demanded by a state that must recruit a standing army if is to survive . . . it is suggestive, to say the least, that restrictions on female mourning occur at the same time as these new cults offer promises of rewards for dying in the service of the state. . . . Restrictions on women are another sign of incipient democracy" (Holst-Warhaft, *Dangerous Voices*, 116–17).

7. See Leymah Gbowee, *Mighty Be Our Powers: How Sisterhood, Prayer, and Sex Changed a Nation at War—A Memoir* (New York: Beast Books, 2011). See also the documentary *Pray the Devil Back to Hell* (2008): http://praythedevilbacktohell.com/.

8. *The Sacrifice of Africa: A Political Theology for Africa* (Grand Rapids: Eerdmans, 2011), 148–92.

the country erupted in Hutu-Tutsi ethnic massacres and counter-massacres. Together with her seven children and a number of Hutu families, Maggy hid in the local bishop's residence. But on October 24, soldiers, led by some of Maggy's Tutsi family members, attacked the bishop's house, stripped and tied Maggy down on a chair, set the building on fire, and killed seventy-two people. Among them was Maggy's friend Juliette, a Tutsi married to a Hutu. Juliette was going to be spared, but she offered herself to be killed with her husband, saying, "I married not a Hutu but the man I love. If you are going to kill my husband, you might as well kill me." She took her two children—Lysette (almost four years old) and Lydia (one and a half)—laid them at Maggy's feet, and asked Maggy to take care of them. Then they killed her.

After the massacre, Maggy crawled into the chapel. She prayed as she cried: "My mother taught me that you are a God of love. She lied to me. You are not love . . . . God, why was I not killed? Why am I here? Why, O God?"[9] As she prayed and cried, she heard Chloe, one of her seven children, calling from the sacristy, "Mama, we are here. All of us are here." The children had escaped by hiding. Bribing the militia with money, she managed to save another twenty-five children from the burning building and hide them in the cemetery, and as night fell she sought refuge at the home of a German development worker.

The significance of this story is that, by means of this painful event, Maggy recognized a calling to look after the children and raise them in a spirit of love—beyond the hatred she had witnessed in the killers' eyes:

> I felt this incredible resistance inside me, like strength . . . as soon as I knew that my children had survived, I felt a strong will to live. I could think of one thing and only one thing: taking care of them, raising them beyond this hatred and bitterness that I came to see in [the soldiers'] eyes.

Three aspects stand out about Maggy's life and work in response to the call that emerged from the tragic events of 1993. First, it was the incredible energy that Maggy miraculously felt following the massacre:

> I always felt called to a mission, but I did not know exactly what that mission was—until then. I was always afraid of failing, of not having the strength

9. Interview, Entebbe Bethany House, Uganda (Jan. 19, 2015). I am particularly grateful to David Toole and Jessica Shewan, who conducted the interview, and to David Toole for the transcriptions of the interview. References to the interview will hereafter be cited in parentheses as EBH.

to do what I need to do, of being unfaithful to myself. I was afraid of being judged. Before it was me, Maggy, that helped a few children, but in 1993, after such great pain, I felt the call to leave it all behind and count on God's mighty power. I devoted everything to their service. I was driven by this inexplicable strength. I had not eaten anything in two days, but I wasn't the least bit hungry. I had plenty of energy.[10]

The boundless energy translated into setting up Maison Shalom and various programs and activities for the children. As the massacres turned into a full-fledged civil war, the work of Maison Shalom was extended. First, when a German NGO closed as a result of the fighting, Maggy settled the children in an abandoned school building in Ruyigi. She had over a hundred children by May 1994, when she started taking in child survivors from the Rwanda genocide. She was then invited by Italian volunteers running an Internally Displaced Persons (IDP) camp at Butezi to open a center for the children there—at Casa della Pace—which she did in October 1995. Later that year, she opened up another center for the children, Oasis de la Paix, in Gisuru, near the border with Tanzania. She also founded a place for mothers near the border with Burundi, and then near Butezi she took some houses that belonged to an Italian congregation (who had fled) and turned them into houses for nurses and social workers. And then they started to cultivate fields.

Second, determined to succeed at all costs, Maggy gave her all to the work of looking after and setting up programs for her growing number of children. The result was she would not only go for hours without food, but she also had very little time for prayer. At times she would spend a night at Maison Shalom in Ruyigi, the following night at Casa della Pace, then at Oasis de la Paix. "I wanted to serve the children," she said. "I was determined to show Burundi-ans, and the international community, that Burundians can think and work for peace" (EBH).

Third, behind Maggy's fearless and determined effort for the children was a seething anger. Still enraged by the massacre of 1993, she was determined to fight anyone in her way. On October 25, when she came to bury the people massacred in the bishop's compound, she asked a priest to help her. When the priest refused, Maggy angrily told him to his face, "Hell will not be hot enough for you." Another time she fought a military man who called her children "snakes." She also confronted a person in church who was wearing the clothes

10. Katongole, *Sacrifice of Africa*, 171.

of her friend Juliette's husband. Pictures at this early phase of Maison Shalom show a sour-looking but determined Maggy. But this changed in May 1996, when Maggy witnessed still more violence.

Deepened in Lament (May 28, 1996: Breakdown)

In Butezi, Maggy's Casa della Pace was situated just outside an IDP camp of Tutsi refugees. One day Maggy received word that Hutu militias were planning to attack the camp, and she called the regional military commander (a Tutsi) to warn him of what was about to happen. The military command met and decided to send only a few soldiers to the camp, judging that they should let the attack happen in order to expose the savagery of the Hutu militias to the international community. They also wanted to use the Hutu attack as an excuse for military takeover (Buyoya was to come back to power following the IDP camp massacre). During the night the Hutu militias entered the camp and massacred over 400 people. The following morning, as Maggy walked through the dead bodies, she could not believe that the Tutsi military would sacrifice even "their own" people for political purposes. She was filled with rage, pain, and a sense of total helplessness. She broke down and literally lost her voice.

She withdrew to a Polish Carmelite monastery in Musongati, where she spent a month, doing nothing but crying, resting and praying. Looking back at this time, Maggy remembers it as a period of "mourning" and of "abandoning myself into the hands of God" (EBH). Here she would confront her naiveté. "Before 1993, I was naive in thinking that my family could not kill, that my family would protect me." She had come to the realization that she had been naive to believe that she would be able, through her own efforts, to "stop the war and bring sense to [her] brothers and sisters" (EBH). If she had emerged from the events of 1993 with an overwhelming determination and boundless strength, she now felt weak and powerless. If after 1993 she was determined to fight her family, countrymen, and all the criminals in Burundi, she was now feeling an invitation into a deeper and more enduring way of realizing peace in Burundi—the way of forgiveness and love:

> But in this moment, I wanted to forgive myself for my weakness, and also accept that the others are weak, and accept that I belong to this people, not having been born in the USA or Belgium. I was born in this village, and I must also love those criminal brothers. (EBH)

The decisive factor in this newfound and strange gift of forgiveness was the encounter with the suffering God. Before going to Musongati, she could not understand the hatred in men's hearts; but at the Carmelite monastery, "I began to understand God on the cross" (EBH). If, after 1993, Maggy had depended on a powerful God to support her efforts, now she realized that God is powerful, but also that "God is love, God is tenderness, God forgives all of us" (EBH). In meditating on the cross, Maggy felt as though she had encountered the face of a loving and forgiving God for the first time.

> When Jesus was on the cross, there was the thief who said, "Please, remember me when you get to heaven." Imagine Jesus saying, "This evening you will be with me." How? He was criminal. He didn't say, "You must pass in hell, this evening." Who are we to judge, to say, "You can't be with me; you are a criminal." We have a noble vocation, which is to go to them, to say to them, "You are not a criminal only." (EBH)

The effect of Maggy's one-month stay at the Carmelite monastery on her life, her understanding of her call, and the mission of Maison Shalom was extraordinary. First, she saw clearly that Maison Shalom was not so much about the projects and programs. It was not even about the children. It was about the message of a loving and forgiving God who invites us into the embrace of love as our true identity and calling. "Love is the most beautiful calling of human beings. We are created out of love and to love."[11]

Second, she was now able to see more clearly that, because God's love is a reconciling and forgiving love, forgiveness and reconciliation must be at the heart of Maison Shalom. She would not only bring up the children into this spirit of forgiveness, she would organize events, feasts, and programs to which she would invite the community, including the killers.

Third, the effect on Maggy's own life was immediately visible. Not only did she recover her voice, but a new Maggy emerged from the Carmelite monastery. If before Maggy was angry, tense, and determined to fight, she was now relaxed and wearing an irresistible smile. She started dressing in beautiful bright costumes, walking elegantly, and joking more readily. "It is like a weight was taken off my back. God is God. . . . I wanted to be a little instrument to love, to denounce, to tell the truth, but not to accuse, and not to lose tenderness" (EBH).

11. Katongole, *Sacrifice of Africa*, 176, citing Maggy's speech given at the 49th International Eucharistic Congress, Quebec City, Quebec, Canada (June 21, 2008).

Determined to sustain the "tenderness" she had encountered in the crucified God at the Carmelite monastery, Maggy now made prayer a central and regular discipline of her work: "Each year, I take two weeks of retreat; each month one day off to pray; and each day, at least one hour. . . . It is now I have discovered—this was a reason for me—that without him, we can't do anything" (EBH).

Ironically, her desire to be just a "little instrument for love" unleashed some of the most ambitious, audacious, and impressive visions for Maison Shalom. Soon after the monastery experience, she set out to build her home village of Ruyigi into a "city of angels" that would serve as an exhibit of God's tender and forgiving love and a demonstration of what Burundi should be. She set up houses for the children, farms, businesses, and in this remote village, she built a swimming pool (1996), a cinema (1997), a hospital (2008), a nursing school (2010), a microfinance credit union (2011), and, most recently, a university (2014). Reflecting on the connection between these audacious dreams and her Carmelite monastery experience, she observes:

> I was a new person. . . . I began to dream good things for my children. . . . Even the children began to dream. We were dreaming together. They began to say, "Oh, when I finish my studies, I will buy a jet, a private jet for you. . . ." And I'd say to them, "I will build schools for you, cinema, swimming pool, we will have our restaurant." (EBH)

At the same time, Maggy's advocacy for peace took on an even more urgent, determined, and national—even international—character. After the monastery,

> I began to meet all those ministers, and I also visited the rebels and said to them, "Oh, no, you must stop killing!" But I also told the World Food Bank, "No, we do not need food from the UN. You will see that we can cultivate our own food. . . ." We began to cultivate some vegetables. (EBH)

True, Maggy and Maison Shalom cannot be understood outside the painful events of 1993, when Maggy "received her call" to raise the children beyond the spirit of hatred and revenge. However, it was the breakdown at the Carmelite monastery following the 1996 massacre in Butezi, and the month of "mourning" and "abandoning" herself to the hands of God, that clarified the call—and thus came to define both Maggy and Maison Shalom as we know them today. Without this event, Maggy's life and work, the hope that she and

Maison Shalom represent, do not make full sense. In *The Sacrifice of Africa*, I completely missed this decisive event, and so, though my assessment of Maggy and Maison Shalom as a political alternative to the tribalism, violence, and poverty of Burundi was valid, I did not fully account for its inner logic.

Carried Forth in Lament: Sustaining the Daily-ness

Visitors to Ruyigi are always eager to see Maison Shalom's impressive projects and programs and to discover the reasons behind their success. However, Maggy always insists on taking visitors to the bishop's house and the gravesite where she buried the seventy-two people from the 1993 massacre. She cries as she tells the story. Asked why she must insist on taking people to the gravesite and why she doesn't simply tell the story, Maggy responds: "The reason I must return to the gravesite is not to relive the trauma but that I may see the future more clearly."[12] This response implies a number of significant points that confirm lament as the underlying practice that carries the work of Maison Shalom forward.

First, Maggy's returning to the gravesite to see the future more clearly reminds us of Munzihirwa's claim that there are "things that can be seen only with eyes that have cried." What Munzihirwa and Maggy are pointing to is lament as a way of knowing, an "epistemology" out of which another community might emerge. The ethnic hatred that led to the slaughter of Juliette and the other people buried in the graveyard stands in sharp contrast with the all-inclusive family of Maison Shalom, where all—Hutu, Tutsi, Congo, Twa—are members of God's family. It is as if Maggy has to stand at the gravesite to see the depth of the hatred, and thus to remember the magnitude of God's love into which she has been drawn and out of which she improvises a new future beyond ethnicity, hatred, and violence.

Second, Maggy's practice of visiting the gravesite presses against any lineal conceptualization of hope, of lament as a stage on the way to hope. Standing on the ground of lament to see the future clearly confirms that hope requires lament, and that lament and hope go hand in hand. If, as Clifton Black has observed, "the spine of lament is hope," Maggy's practice of visiting the gravesite confirms that the inverse is also true: the spine of hope is lament.

Third, her practice confirms memory as a guide to the future. This observation is particularly true within the biblical tradition: the Israelites are constantly being exhorted to "remember" and not to forget (Deut. 5:15; 6:20–23;

12. Interview, Ruyigi (January 2010).

8:18; Num. 15:38–40; 1 Chron. 16:15) as a way of moving into the future. Within the biblical story, remembering the past (what God has done) provides the anchor—and the reason—for any future promises. Seen against this biblical framework, Maggy's practice of revisiting the gravesite is indeed a way of remembering. It is not simply the past that is remembered, but the future. Her lament "remembers" the future.

Fourth, Maggy's visits to the graveyard are "eucharistic" in that they illuminate an ecclesiological reality of the church as a community that lives by constantly remembering the night Jesus was betrayed. And just as in eucharistic practice, what makes the visits to the grave salvific is the fact that, instead of unleashing vengeful terror, they release a superabundance of love and forgiveness, and thus the promise of a qualitatively different future.

Finally, it is this last aspect that makes Maggy's visits to the gravesite a practice of "dangerous memory." For as the German theologian Johannes Metz has noted, the memory of Jesus and of human suffering can and does interrupt the "logic of 'the way things are' and 'reveal[s] new and dangerous insights for the present.'"[13] For Metz, what makes the memory of Jesus's suffering dangerous—which is to say, subversive—is that it "illuminate[s] for a few moments and with a harsh and steady light the questionable nature of things we have apparently come to terms with."[14] For Christians, the memory of suffering is particularly dangerous in that these memories are not simply a matter of looking backward "archeologically"; but they are also future-oriented "forward memories," in which we remember the promises made by God and the "hopes that are experienced as a result of those promises."[15]

The significance of this last observation carries implications for the role of memory in reconciliation. In the context of suffering, the question is not whether to remember or not to remember, but *how* to remember.[16] More specifically, the crucial issue is whether a particular memory of suffering can be located within a more determinative memory. For Metz, it is the memory of Jesus's suffering that is determinative and is thus able to transform other memories of suffering into "dangerous" memories. This means that the memory of

---

13. Johannes Metz, *Faith in History and Society: Toward a Practical Fundamental Theology* (New York: Crossroad, 2011), 171.

14. Metz, *Faith in History and Society*, 109.

15. Michael Iafrate, "Rock as 'Interruption' and Bearer of Dangerous Memories," *Rock and Theology*, July 4, 2010: http://www.rockandtheology.com/?p=2171 (accessed Apr. 29, 2015).

16. For a more extended discussion of the significance of memory in healing the wounds of history, see Miroslav Volf, *The End of Memory: Remembering Rightly in a Violent World* (Grand Rapids: Eerdmans, 2006).

suffering does not lead to healing in and of itself. In fact, outside the context of a more determinative and truthful memory, the memory of suffering can lead to retraumatization and thus can become an unbearable burden or an occasion for vengeful mobilization. Only to the extent that that memory can be located within a more determinative memory of love and forgiveness can it have the promise of being healed.

That is the reason why, for Maggy, important as her visits to the graveyard are, it is the more determinative story within which she locates the particular memory of 1993 that is significant. For Maggy, that more determinative story is not the history of Burundi, but the story of the crucified Son of God, who responds to violence through self-giving love. Accordingly, every time she visits the gravesite, Maggy spends an entire afternoon alone in the chapel in front of the blessed sacrament and before the cross. Only by being remembered within the memory of the cross and Eucharist has the memory of 1993 become a truly "dangerous" memory for Maggy and Maison Shalom.

Writing about the civil rights movement in America, Charles Marsh observes that, for the civil rights activists, "the hardest part was not envisioning the end but living in the sluggish between."[17] This is true in many ways for Maison Shalom.

The Politics of Forgiveness and Reconciliation

Judy Atkinson's extraordinary work on healing the transgenerational effects of trauma among indigenous Australian peoples begins with a dream.[18] In the dream, Judy and her people are running in terror through the bush, hunted down by the thunderous horses and guns of the white settlers. In the terror of the flight, they lose the children. They begin to look for the children, and as they find them one by one, they begin the slow, difficult, and painful work of repairing the wounded girls and boys:

> And so . . . we women began to look for our children. . . . Such intense
> sorrow, such a depth of pain, as one by one we found our children . . . bro-

17. Charles Marsh, *The Beloved Community: How Faith Shapes Social Justice* (New York: Basic Books, 2005), 5.

18. Judy Atkinson, *Trauma Trails, Recreating Song Lines: The Transgenerational Effects of Trauma in Indigenous Australia* (North Melbourne: Spinifex, 2002). Atkinson employs Dadirri, a unique method of storytelling adopted from indigenous Australian culture, as a way of healing the transgenerational effects of trauma.

ken . . . ravished . . . wounded . . . the children the children . . . searching searching . . . We found our children, battered . . . bloodied . . . crushed . . . violated. Gathering them to us, gathering them to us. And so we women began our grieving for our children, with our children.[19]

In many ways, these words capture the work of Maison Shalom, where Maggy is involved in the similarly slow, difficult, and painful work of healing the lives of children, as well as the social fabric of Burundi rent by ethnic hatred and violence. And just as in the case of the indigenous Australian people of Atkinson's work, Maggy's work is simultaneously the work of "grieving" and "repairing," whose effects are evident in the lives of the children. Juliette's two daughters are now beautiful young adults. Lysette is finishing a master's degree in international law in Canada. Lydia is a secretary at Maison Shalom. Chloe, one of the first children adopted by Maggy, is now a medical doctor in Burundi. Richard, whose parents were killed and who narrowly survived himself after being badly scarred in their smoldering house, is now the administrator of Maison Shalom.

Exhilarating as these biographical stories are, what is even more impressive is the forgiveness and reconciliation through which Maggy has tried to stitch back together the shattered lives of the children.[20] Justine's story, while not unique, captures the real possibility of a new generation who have broken the cycle of violence through forgiveness. Justine's parents were killed, and she was raised by Maison Shalom. At the dedication of eighty-five new houses for the children in 2001, Justine was asked to address the invited dignitaries on behalf of the children. At one point in her speech she addressed Maggy: "Oma, you cried like a mother for seven years. This is the moment to console yourself and dry your tears. We learnt from you to respect and forgive those who killed our parents, who looted our goods, who violated our rights, or who physically and morally beat us."

Calling on the adults present to change their "irresponsible behavior" and embrace the spirit of forgiveness, she continued: "Maggy gave us love and the grace with which we can overlook our sad experiences. She was not obliged to do it. We ourselves were not part of her family. If I hadn't found her, I myself would in time have become a killer."[21]

19. Atkinson, *Trauma Trails*, 2.

20. For more stories and images of Maison Shalom children, which are captured by Belgian photographer Fabrice Moteiro, see *Wind of Change*: http://fabricemonteiro.viewbook.com/wind-of-change.

21. Katongole, *Sacrifice of Africa*, 192, and Christel Martin, *La haine n'aura pas le dernier*

The work of social repair through love and forgiveness has extended beyond the children to the local community. Perhaps no story captures this impact more dramatically than the story of Gaspar, who had killed Maggy's two aunts. Maggy's family paid to have him tortured in prison, where he languished and was about to die. But Maggy visited him and washed his wounds and asked the police commander to have him taken to the hospital. Surprised that Maggy would do this, Gaspar asked her why she was treating him differently than the rest of her family had. Maggy's response: "Because you are not a criminal only, Gaspar. With forgiveness, you can do good things in your life." Gaspar died as Maggy was still washing his wounds. But as he lay dying he said, "Your forgiveness has resurrected me. Now I die like a human person" (EBH). Forgiveness had restored Gasper's true identity.

Maggy's decision not to set up orphanages for the children of Maison Shalom, but instead to build houses for the children in their original communities, was another distinctive aspect of social repair through forgiveness. In this case, the children's homes became both a catalyst and hub for a new social life in the village, as the case of Dieudonné illustrates. Maggy found Dieudonné the morning after the Massacre of Butezi in 1996. He was just a baby and was still strapped on the back of his dead mother, who had been killed by a grenade. His mouth was gone. She took him in and after three years of reconstructive surgery in Germany, Dieudonné returned home. He now lives in his original village, where his home has become the central site for reconciliation:

When we built his house, we took a mason from this village. And the women were paid for fetching water. The men made the bricks. The whole village [would] build this house. Among those people, there are criminals sometimes. And social workers are [sometimes] among those people. There are Hutu and Tutsi in the village. [Dieudonné] lives with his grandmother, who is very old. So we bring a notebook, and seeds, or a cow. What we do with the notebook—we don't give it away. We have a community link in each village who asks about the situation of other children and makes a list of other needs. We bring what they need to the school. We cultivate the land of the grandmother, we pay the village, and they give seeds to others [who are] vulnerable in the village. We profit from this to do peacebuilding. We do this in 3,000 villages. (EBH)

---

mot: *Maggy la femme aux 10000 enfants* (Paris: Albin Michel, 2005), 155. For more stories about the children of Maison Shalom, see Judith Debetencourt Hoskins, *Hummingbird, Why Am I Here? Maggy's Children* (Charleston, SC: CreateSpace, 2012).

What Maggy's comments reveal is the catalytic role of Maison Shalom in the community: the Maison Shalom children and programs become a leaven for the transformation of the surrounding villages. This is already evident at Ruyigi, which has now been transformed into "La Cité des Anges" ("city of angels")—with its satellite of Maison Shalom-operated businesses, including a mechanic's shop (offering apprenticeships for former child soldiers), a swimming pool, cinema, radio station, and university. As a result of the transformation, Ruyigi has now become a major hub and catalyst for the social, political, and economic life of the region. But even as this slow, quiet revolution is going on, Maggy and Maison Shalom are involved in a more explicit engagement of political processes on the national level. Every day at six o'clock a radio program explains the work of Maison Shalom. Maggy visits and speaks at diocesan and national events. She is a regular visitor and speaker at the national university and other youth forums. She meets political and civic leaders, including the president himself. In fact, as recently as January 2015, she had to cut short her participation at a workshop in Entebbe in order to return to Burundi to meet with various civic leaders in an attempt to pressure Nkurunziza to abandon his bid for a third term, and to launch a new radio program for civic education ahead of the 2015 national elections.

In the recent past there has been a renewed interest in the politics of reconciliation and forgiveness.[22] In narrating the work of Maggy and Maison Shalom in the way I have done, I aim to show what a politics of forgiveness and reconciliation concretely looks like. The politics of forgiveness is not simply a work of principles and platforms (national platforms of reconciliation); it is the slow, painful work of repairing shattered lives and communities rent by hatred and violence. But my goal is also to show that it would be completely misleading to characterize the work of people like Maggy and communities like Maison Shalom as essentially "humanitarian'" (which happens to have political implications). For Maison Shalom's work of forgiveness is an alternative to the politics of ethnic hatred, violence, and war. And as a political alternative, it "illuminate[s] . . . with a harsh and steady light the questionable nature of things we have apparently come to terms with."[23] It is this illumination of the questionable nature of the way things are, via the provision of a concrete non-violent alternative, that makes Maison Shalom a dangerous—that is, subversive—form of politics threatening the political status quo. Therefore, it is not

---

22. See, among others, Daniel Philpott, *Just and Unjust Peace: An Ethic of Political Reconciliation* (New York: Oxford University Press, 2012).

23. Metz, *Faith in History and Society*, 109.

surprising that Maggy's work has quite often not only been met with suspicion and resistance, but has generated outright opposition and even animosity.

In 2008, Maggy found herself the object of an assassination attempt and a bogus court case. The fact that she built a hospital in Ruyigi had the unintended consequence of exposing the corruption and inefficiency of a number of institutions. The government-run dispensary was in a sorry and dilapidated state; the diocesan health unit was crumbling and inefficient. Some of the embarrassed leaders schemed to kill Maggy. But their plan failed. Instead, a French social worker, whose car had been mistaken for Maggy's, was killed by a car bomb. Realizing their mistake, the local government officials accused Maggy of killing the French woman and brought charges against her. At the bogus trial, Maggy was shocked to see that even people she had helped turned against her and provided false evidence. She had naively thought that everyone would rise to her defense. The case was eventually thrown out, but it left Maggy completely discouraged. She made plans to quietly leave Burundi for good.[24]

But perhaps the narrative that metaphorically best captures both the promise of Maison Shalom's politics of healing and forgiveness and its dangerous possibilities is Bosco's story. Bosco was five when his entire family was killed. He had not been born blind, but the trauma of seeing his family slaughtered in front of him turned him blind. The missionaries brought him to Maggy because no one else wanted him. She, in turn, took him to Germany to see whether a doctor could help him recover his sight. The doctor could not help him, but he said that if Bosco felt confident that there might be peace, he might be able to see again. Back at Maison Shalom, Bosco mentioned that he wanted to be a musician, so Maggy found a musician in Bukavu and brought him to Maison Shalom to teach Bosco and other children to play the guitar. The young musicians began to sing about peace and forgiveness. Bosco's sight gradually—though only partially—returned (he can see in one eye). He now lives in Bujumbura and is one of the most popular musicians in Burundi, singing songs of lament, healing, and reconciliation (EBH).[25] A key civic leader in Burundi, a person who knows Bosco, says:

24. At the check-in counter at the airport, a clerk recognized her and asked why she wanted to leave. She told Maggy that she had almost failed to recognize her because she looked so sad and had lost her smile. This brief conversation touched Maggy so deeply that she began to cry, took back her luggage, and thanked the clerk, Felicity, for the prophetic message. She returned to Ruyigi determined not to let opposition derail her mission (EBH).

25. For the story of Bosco, see also: http://vimeo.com/32100757.

When I think of their music, it is about peace and love. They sing about the beauty of the country, but they go beyond that; not only to see what is there, but of something better. . . . It is more of a prophetic message . . . pointing out what is wrong (and thus causing a lot of trouble for the government), but it's also about what the country can become. You find a lot of naming . . . of what is going on . . . putting in words what many of us feel . . . . He names the president, politicians, but also the prosperity gospel, the preachers and priests. One of the songs denouncing the government was recently banned. (EBH)

Bosco's story illuminates three clear insights about the politics of forgiveness. First, it points to the slow, difficult, and painful work of repairing the wounded, ravished, and broken children at Maison Shalom. Second, the partial restoration of Bosco's sight confirms the promise and reality of healing through forgiveness. Third, the government's banning of one of his songs testifies to the politically subversive possibilities of Maison Shalom's work.

The Mother of Burundi

In the biblical story, the tears of Rachel are the tears of the grieving mother. Rachel had been barren for a long time, but eventually she became a mother, even though she died giving birth to her second child. The child was both the cause of her grieving and the hope for the future. He was both *Benoni* (child of my sorrow) and *Benjamin* (son of God's right hand). It is this same reversal that we noted is under way in the text of Jeremiah 31:15–22 as Rachel's bitterness (*tanturim*) was transformed into guideposts (*tanturim*) for the return (restoration) of the children of Israel.

Maggy's story is filled with similar dramatic reversals. Her grandfather insisted that she take on the name Barankitse ("they have hated me"), even though her mother had given her the name Habyonyimana ("it is God who helps me"). Maggy does not have any children of her own. But the fact that this "barren" woman would become the mother of over 30,000 children—indeed, the "Mother of Burundi," as she is popularly known—is a confirmation of a miraculous "new thing in the land" within the ethnic and violent politics of the country.[26] And that Maggy's sorrow would, through the ongoing work

26. This is true not only in Burundi, but internationally, as reflected in the number of awards she has received, including French Government Human Rights Award (1998), the

of lament, turn into the healing gifts of forgiveness and reconciliation, again confirms the dangerous, subversive politics at work in Maggy's story. I have suggested that the evangelist Matthew does not include the narrative of Mary's Magnificat because the memory of Rachel that he invokes is itself a veiled Magnificat. Maggy's story points in the same direction, for in the end it is a Magnificat that issues from Maggy's womb of lament:

> If I die today, for me, I think my mission is finished. I admire what God has achieved through a little woman like me. It's so—for me, I don't know how to explain that. Sometimes now when I cry, *I cry out of joy*. How it's possible that we suffered so much—and to see Dieudonné today, to see Richard, to see Lysette, Lydia, Bosco . . . to see them all. (EBH)

There have been significant developments in Maggy's life and Maison Shalom's ministry since this interview was recorded. In the summer of 2015, the controversial decision by President Pierre Nkurunziza to run for a third term plunged the country into political crisis. Tens of thousands of people have fled the country, hundreds of people have been arrested, and several protesters and police have been killed while dozens more have been injured. Maggy had spoken out strongly against the so-called third term project—and for this she was targeted. She fled into exile, where she still lives. The government has shut down Maison Shalom programs, including the schools and hospital in Ruyigi, closed all their bank accounts, and confiscated all their assets. They also started targeting Maison Shalom children, including Bosco, who was killed. These developments have obviously deepened Maggy's lament. They have also made even more evident the parallel between her and biblical Rachel, who refused to be consoled because of the death of her children. This calls for a closer exploration of the interconnections between lament and martyrdom in order to highlight the (strange) hope that the death of the innocent, like Bosco, offers to Christians in their struggle for peace in Africa. To this task we now turn in the last chapter of *Born from Lament*.

World Children's Prize (2003), the Nansen Refugee Award (2006), the Opus Prize (2008), and a number of honorary doctorates, including those from the Catholic University of Louvain (Belgium) and Duke University (2013). More recently she received the 2016 Aurora Prize. See Katongole, *Sacrifice of Africa*, 191.

CHAPTER 13

Refusing to Be Consoled for the Death of the Martyrs

. . . lamentation and great weeping,
Rachel is weeping for her children;
*   she refuses to be comforted for her children,*
*   because they are no more.*

Jeremiah 31:15

It is something within us
that doesn't let us sleep,
that doesn't let us rest,
that won't stop pounding
deep inside . . . .
What keeps us from sleeping
is that they have threatened us with Resurrection!

Julia Esquivel[1]

In Matthew's Gospel, the slaughter of the innocents in Bethlehem is the final event that marks the end of the old order (represented by Herod) and the

---

1. Julia Esquivel, *Threatened with Resurrection: Prayers and Poems from an Exiled Guatemalan*, 2nd ed. (Elgin, IL: Brethren, 1994).

An original version of this chapter was published as "'Threatened with Resurrection': Martyrdom and Reconciliation in the World Church," in *Witness of the Body: The Past, Present, and Future of Christian Martyrdom*, ed. Michael Budde and Karen Scott (Grand Rapids: Eerdmans, 2011), 190–203. It is reproduced here with substantive revisions, and with permission.

inauguration of the new one (represented by the birth of the child Messiah). Within the Catholic tradition, these "holy innocents" are commemorated on December 28, three days after Christmas.[2] The holy innocents are regarded as "martyrs" (Greek: *martys*, meaning "witness"); this confirms that in their death they bear witness to the new social reality that, in one sense, is yet to be fully realized. But in another sense, that reality is already manifested through the birth of Jesus. Therefore, their slaughter is an occasion for great mourning—and simultaneously a sign of hope for the future. But we must be careful not to jump too quickly to the hope. Rachel's weeping is real, and it is deep. Thus in Jeremiah, with Rachel's great-grandchild in captivity, Rachel mourns and refuses to be comforted because the "children are no more." And nothing short of Yahweh's own consolation can comfort her; nothing short of the promise of the children's return and of a new thing in the land will wipe away Rachel's tears.

That is the strange gift that the slaughtered innocents were to Matthew's community, the gift that martyrs in general are to the church. But even as the martyrs are a hope for the future, the church, like Rachel, continues to mourn their untimely passing. The memory of martyrs thus represents a determined effort by the church to refuse easy consolation; that is, to resist shallow promises of "'peace, peace,' when there is no peace" (Jer. 6:14). Nothing short of God's new creation, for which the martyrs gave their lives, will satisfy. No cheap imitations, no counterfeits of God's total and true shalom will do.

When the connection between the holy innocents and Rachel's weeping is explicit, then the image of Rachel weeping for her children and refusing to be consoled explodes with rich theological and practical reverberations in the African context via the stories of martyrs—the holy innocents of Africa's violent history. In order to understand that African martyrdom, I have found it helpful to think about it hand in hand with the work of Julia Esquivel, especially her book *Threatened with Resurrection*.[3] This will not only enable us to make explicit the strange hope that martyrs represent; it also provides us with an opportunity to make explicit the ecclesiological assumptions at the heart of this study. The account of hope I have sketched out here both reflects and requires a vision of a community of faith that knows something about what it means to lament, to "turn toward and around God" in moments of suffering. While this should be obvious by now, reflecting on the memory of martyrs

---

2. Even though Stephen is often noted as the first martyr, the holy innocents were regarded by the early church as the first martyrs.

3. Esquivel, *Threatened with Resurrection*.

provides an opportunity to make explicit *why* the church is needed and what *kind* of church is needed for an account of hope and peace in the world.

Dangerous Memory

In remembering martyrs, the church celebrates the lives of men and women who have lived in an exemplary way and have paid the ultimate sacrifice as *living* witnesses—that is, as witnesses who are, though dead, still with us. While this is a sign of hope, one must be careful not to romanticize the fact that the martyrs are still with us. Their presence, though celebrated, is also to be feared. For while, to the extent that they are still with us, they are "our friends"—part of the cloud of witnesses (Heb. 11) who inspire us, support us, encourage us, and journey with us—they also *threaten* us with resurrection, and they constantly invite the church into a life of vigil, to a life of social struggle, and to a new and resurrected community.

A school teacher forced into exile from her native Guatemala, Julia Esquivel used her writing to tell of the immense suffering of her people. In one of her most famous poems, "Threatened with Resurrection," she speaks about "the endless inventory of killings since 1954" through which thousands of Mayan, Quichez, and other indigenous groups were savagely murdered by the military regime in control of Guatemala. Those slain not only witness to the pain of those still alive, but their memory keeps them (the living) from sleeping and "threatens" them with resurrection.

> There is something here within us
> Which doesn't let us sleep, which doesn't let us rest,
> Which doesn't stop pounding deep inside,
> It is the silent, warm weeping of Indian women without their husbands,
> It is the sad gaze of the children
> Fixed there beyond memory,
> In the very pupil of our eyes
> Which during sleep, though closed, keep watch
> With each contraction of the heart
> In every wakening . . . .
>
> Now six have left us,
> and nine in Rabinal,
> and two, plus two, plus two,

and ten, a hundred, a thousand,
a whole army
witness to our pain,
our fear,
our courage,
our hope!

What keeps us from sleeping,
Is it that they have threatened us with resurrection![4]

In his discussion of "Threatened with Resurrection," Parker Palmer rightly notes that it is not immediately clear who "threatens us with resurrection."[5] On the one hand, Esquivel seems to be speaking of the killers: the "demented gorillas" who have killed hundreds of peasants and who threaten those still alive. On the other hand, however, it seems that the threat of resurrection comes not from the killers but from the dead themselves. In the end, Parker concludes: "The poem imitates life, in which the 'threat of resurrection' comes from both those who dispense death and those who have died in the hope of new life" (147). The implications are significant:

> If it is true that both killers and the killed threaten us with resurrection, then we are caught between a rock and a hard place. On the one hand, we fear the killers, but not simply because they want to kill us. We fear them because they test our convictions about resurrection; they test our willingness to be brought into a larger life than the one we now know. On the other hand, we fear the innocent victims of the killers, those who have died for love and justice and peace. Though they are our friends, we fear them because they call us to follow them in the "marathon of Hope." If we were to take their calling seriously, we ourselves would have to undergo some form of dying. (148)

Caught between the killers and the killed, Palmer continues, we

> huddle together in a conspiracy of silence, trying to ignore the ambiguous call of the new life that lies beyond death. Julia Esquivel is trying to break up our

4. Esquival, *Threatened with Resurrection*, 59–61.
5. Parker J. Palmer, *The Active Life: A Spirituality of Work, Creativity, and Caring* (San Francisco: Jossey-Bass, 1990), 139–57. I am grateful to Palmer's work for first drawing my attention to Esquivel's poetry. Hereafter, page references to this work appear in parentheses within the text.

little huddle, I think, trying to inspire our active lives, calling us to engage the demented gorillas as well as our martyred friends, calling us to walk into our fear of resurrection and to open ourselves to the life on the other side. (148)

I find Parker's observations about Esquivel's poem particularly helpful in understanding the dangerous hope exemplified by the martyrs. The odd gift that martyrs are to the church and to the world lies precisely in their ability to break "our little huddles of fear." In doing so, the constant "pounding" of their memory not only keeps the church from sleeping, it re-energizes the church into a life of struggle and invites Christians into a new communion—a community of the resurrected living on this side of death. This is another reason why the church can offer no more determinative sign of hope in the world than to name and celebrate the memory of martyrs. For in so doing the church is drawn into at least three critical practices in the search for peace in the world: vigilance, social struggle, and resurrected living.

Vigilance: The Politics of Naming

In many places in "Threatened with Resurrection," Esquivel speaks of being kept from sleeping by those slain; what Esquivel is obviously referring to is not the lack of sleep otherwise known as insomnia, but a form of watchfulness. She speaks about "the whirlwind which does not let us sleep," and "while sleeping, we keep watch." It is through such watchfulness that one is able to keep an eye on the "demented gorillas"—the Herods of this present world who readily slaughter the innocent in their desperate attempt to hold onto their political and economic acquisitions.

Apparently, the early church knew something of this watchfulness, for they had no illusions that the world they lived in was hospitable to the Christian way of life. That is one reason why Christian feast days and holy days were marked by a vigil service. The vigil was not simply a way of anticipating the celebration of the martyrs' feast day with prayer and other liturgical commemoration; it was a metaphor for Christian living, a reminder that, even in the midst of celebration, the church must "keep vigil." But this is also why, as Pope John Paul II noted, the church of those first centuries, despite considerable organizational difficulties, took meticulous care to write down the witness of the martyrs in special martyrologies.[6] The cultivation of vigilance as a way of

---

6. John Paul II, Apostolic Letter, *Tertio Millennio Adveniente* (1994), §37: https://w2.vatican

life requires and involves memory, and keeping the memory of martyrs alive by retelling their stories was at least one way the church had of remembering its calling as maiden of God's gift of peace—while also naming specific threats, dangers, and temptations that threaten that gift of peace.

That is why, for example, in the context of the 1994 Rwanda Genocide, where Christians killed others in the name of ethnicity, telling the story of Chantal Mujjawamaholo and her friends not only calls the church to a life of vigilance in the face of so-called natural identities, but it reminds the church of the true goal of Christian living.[7] On March 18, 1997, three years after the genocide, *Interahamwe* militia attacked a secondary school at Nyange in Rwanda. The students had finished supper and their evening prayer, and they were in the classrooms doing their homework. The rebels attacked two of the classes and demanded that the students separate into Tutsis and Hutus. The students refused, saying that they were all the same. The rebels shot at them indiscriminately and threw grenades into the classroom. All thirteen students were killed. Afterwards, the victims were reclaimed by their families and buried at their homes, all except one girl, Chantal Mujjawamaholo, who is buried at the school.[8]

What is remarkable about this story is not simply the fact that Chantal and the other students refused to betray their friends by separating along ethnic lines—thus exposing the idolatry of tribalism—but also the meaning of her name: in Kinyarwanda, Mujjawamaholo means "maiden of peace." In refusing to separate, Mujjawamaholo and her friends made visible another community founded not on tribal identity but on reconciled friendship. This is the "gift" of peace—to which Mujjawamaholo and her friends understood themselves as ambassadors or maidens. It is important that Mujjawamaholo's name points to this gift, because, while the students' refusal to separate into tribal groups points to the possibility of resisting the idolatry of ethnicity (as well as the courage to stand firm), without a clear sense of the goal of that resistance, even courage can turn into a form of reckless self-sacrifice or an expression of radical fundamentalism.[9] In the end,

.va/content/john-paul-ii/en/apost_letters/1994/documents/hf_jp-ii_apl_19941110_tertio -millennio-adveniente.html (accessed Dec. 10, 2015).

7. For a more extended reflection on the Rwanda Genocide, see E. Katongole, *Mirror to the Church: Resurrecting Faith after Genocide in Rwanda* (Grand Rapids: Zondervan, 2009); see also Katongole, "Christianity, Tribalism, and the Rwanda Genocide," in *A Future for Africa: Critical Essays in Christian Social Imagination* (Scranton, PA: University of Scranton Press, 2005).

8. Notes taken during the author's visit to the school (Dec. 21, 2004).

9. This marks the difference between a life of martyrdom, as understood by Christians, and terrorism that may involve suicide. Martyrs do not want to die, and there is the paradox

remembering the story of Chantal Mujjawamaholo and her friends becomes both a gift and a threat to the church: it is a gift in that it reminds the church of her calling in the world; it is a threat in that it is a critique—a most decisive critique—of shallow forms of ecclesiology that assume that the blood of tribalism is deeper than the waters of baptism.[10]

In naming her martyrs, however, the church not only names her own identity as maiden of peace, she learns to correctly name the "spells" that would have us live as if conflict, war, and violence are inevitable.[11] This is what the memory of the Congolese martyr Annuarite Nengapeta (who was beatified by Pope John Paul II in 1985) points to. As a young girl, Annuarite joined the convent of the Holy Family Sisters in Isiro-Wamba in Eastern Congo, where she spent her religious life as a nun and a midwife. In 1964, when the Mulele rebellion broke out, Simba rebels invaded the convent. Annuarite was murdered when she resisted the sexual demands of the rebel leader.[12] Her encouragement of her other sisters during the siege, as well as her courage during the ordeal, is noteworthy. But what is also striking is the witness of her names. At birth she received the name Nengapeta, meaning "wealth is deceptive." When she started primary school she was erroneously registered with the name Annuarite (her sister's name), which means, "I laugh to myself about war."[13]

In remembering Annuarite Nengapeta, therefore, one learns to define

---

that even if they are willing to sacrifice their own lives for the gift, they believe that the gift is not in their own power to realize. Accordingly, they can never sacrifice others in order to bring about the peace for which they are willing to die. In fact, their willingness to die is a confirmation of their belief that such peace has already been given by the one whose death and resurrection we remember. All we are called upon to do as Christians is to witness that peace, which might involve surrendering our own lives—a strange kind of peace indeed.

10. Thus the school at Nyange where the students were killed stands in sharp contrast to the church of Nyange (on the opposite hill), which was bulldozed to the ground during the 1994 genocide that killed more than 1,200 people. The destruction of the church was led by none other than the parish priest himself (see *Mirror to the Church*). That priest was found guilty by the International Criminal Court and sentenced to fifteen years. For the story of Fr. Seromba, see Marc Lacey, "Rwandan Priest Sentenced to 15 Years for Allowing Deaths of Tutsi in Church," *The New York Times*, December 14, 2006: http://www.nytimes.com/2006/12/14 /world/africa/14rwanda.html?_r=0 (accessed Dec. 10, 2015).

11. For the language of "spells" as it applies to modern ideologies, see E. Katongole, "Violence and Christian Social Reconstruction in Africa: On the Resurrection of the Body (Politic)," *The Other Journal*, August 8, 2005: http://theotherjournal.com/2005/08/08/violence -and-christian-social-reconstruction-in-africa-on-the-resurrection-of-the-body-politic/ (accessed Dec. 10, 2015).

12. http://nbsc68.tripod.com/id90.htm.

13. http://nbsc68.tripod.com/id90.htm.

war and wealth as false consolations; and thereby one learns to cultivate the necessary habit of vigilance that we need to resist, despise, or laugh at the greed and the ideologies that seek to secure peace through fighting. Annuarite Nengapeta's names and her courage serve as powerful geographies of memory and provide one of the most telling embodied critiques of the fighting in Eastern Congo, where a number of local militias and international forces seek to control Congo's mineral and natural resources.

Pushed to its logical conclusion, naming "spells" is really about resisting or refusing to be comforted by shallow visions of peace. The story of Sr. Felicitée Niyitegeka offers a good example of what this "refusing to be comforted" looks like within the context of the Rwanda Genocide. A member of the Auxiliaries of the Apostolate, Felicitée was in charge of an orphanage in Gisenyi, where she cared for children, most of whom were Tutsi. When the news of the genocide spread to Gisenyi, Felicitée hid more than thirty Tutsis in her home and helped many more flee over the border into the Congo. When her brother, who was a colonel in the Rwanda military, asked her to stop protecting Tutsis, she refused, writing him the following letter:

> Thank you for wanting to help me. I would rather die than abandon the forty-three persons for whom I am responsible. Pray for us, that we may come to God. Say "goodbye" to our old mother and our brother. When I come to God, I shall pray for you. Keep well. Thank you for thinking of me. If God saves us, as we hope, we shall see you tomorrow.[14]

When the *Interahamwe* (the Hutu military force) came to Gisenyi, they told Felicitée that she would be spared because she was Hutu and because of her brother, but she would have to surrender all the others in her household. She answered that her household would stay together—in life and death. The commander pleaded with her, urging her to "be reasonable" in order to save her own life. But she would not comply. When all her companions had been killed before her, Felicitée asked to be killed. The militia leader told her to pray for him before he shot her.

Felicitée's willingness to be killed together with her charges rather than succumb to promises of personal security reflects her immersion in the story of the self-sacrificing love of the God she vowed to serve when she entered religious life. But the fact that the *Interahamwe* commander would ask her to

---

14. See Jean d'Amour Dusengumuremyi, *No Greater Love: Testimonies on the Life of Felicitas Niyitegeka* (Lake Oswego, OR: Dignity, 2015), 16.

pray for him before he shot her confirms what even he had come to recognize: that through Felicitée's willingness to die, she not only revealed the salvation of her God but also showed that God, not the military commanders, controls the future of history.

Social Struggle: Gestures of Peaceableness

There are two other ways in which martyrs keep the church from sleeping and call her into a life of commitment and work toward a peaceful future. First, martyrs fertilize the church's struggle by drawing the church into endless forms of advocacy and improvisations for peace. In "Threatened with Resurrection," Esquivel notes:

> They have threatened us with resurrection,
> because they are more alive than ever before,
> because they transform our agonies,
> and fertilize our struggle . . .[15]

What Esquivel points to is that, even though those slain natives in the Guatemalan civil war are dead, they "are more alive than ever before." This is especially true of martyrs: though they are dead, their witness is still alive. They may "rest" in God, but they are restless in their lament—in their struggle for nonviolent change. It is this restless lament that Saint John speaks about in the book of Revelation.

> When [the angel] broke open the fifth seal, I saw under the altar the souls of those who had been slain for the word of God and for the witness they had borne. They cried out with a loud voice, "O Sovereign Lord, holy and true, how long before you will judge and avenge our blood on those who dwell on the earth?" (Rev. 6:9–10)

Commenting on this passage, Brian K. Blount notes that in this vision of Revelation, the slaughtered souls are at the breaking point. They are mad. They are ready for God to do something (John uses the Greek word *ekdikeō*—"to vindicate"); they do not want their deaths to be for nothing. That is why their restlessness is to spur on their earthly compatriots to continue the transfor-

---

15. Esquivel, *Threatened with Resurrection*, 63.

mative efforts they began. They want those compatriots to come to the same fury, and thus the same breaking point, which is the irreplaceable condition for nonviolent resistance:

> We need people like those slaughtered souls. For them, for people like them, lament turns to anger and the anger turns to resistance, because when these people reach the breaking point, they do not break down, they break back and hard. They do not follow down, they stand up. They do not whine, they whet their appetite for struggle and nonviolent resistance. They do not give in, they give everything they have.[16]

That is why, in reading John's text of Revelation 6:9-10 in the context of Africa, one cannot but begin to see that the innocent victims of Africa's civil wars (over 5.4 million in the DRC alone in the last twenty years) constitute a cloud of witnesses whose endless cry of "how long, O God?" brings the African church to the "breaking point" that Blount speaks about—to the point where "we cannot take it anymore." This is the breaking point that Munzihirwa was illustrating when he spoke of "things that can be seen only with eyes that have cried." This is the breaking point that drove his fiery, compassionate, and non-violent advocacy on behalf of the embattled people of Bukavu. At this breaking point, he gave everything he had, including his life.

Munzihirwa's assassination was not unexpected—either by his conferees or by Munzihirwa himself. It was evident in his simple lifestyle, his watchfulness as the "Muhudumu" of Bukavu, and his fiery and compassionate advocacy on behalf of the refugees and the embattled population of his region, that he had already embraced the breaking point of lament. These were the everyday forms of living that constituted entering the "way of Christ." Thus, while martyrs are honored for the ultimate sacrifice of their lives, the significance of their "witness" directs our attention to everyday forms of living and peaceableness that constitute the shalom of God's love.[17] For this reason, the memory of martyrs cannot take an abstract or generic form; it requires the telling and retelling of the thick narrative of their stories, for the power resides in the details of how they lived.

When I visited Nyange Secondary School in December 2004 and heard

16. Brian K. Blount, "Breaking Point: A Sermon," in *Lament: Reclaiming Practices in Pulpit, Pew, and Public Square*, ed. Sally A. Brown and Patrick D. Miller (Louisville: Westminster John Knox, 2005), 152.

17. For more on this, see Katongole, *A Future for Africa*, 86–88.

the story of Chantal Mujjawamaholo and her friends, I asked why the students were willing to risk their lives rather than separate themselves into Hutus and Tutsis. Where did such courage come from? A teacher at the school suggested that, since the students had just finished their evening prayers, they could have drawn spiritual strength from that. But he also spoke about another teacher, who had since left the school, who had taught a course in unity and nonviolence. Such simple acts—praying and teaching—show that in a world so enamored with grand strategies (to end poverty, eradicate terrorism, and so on), it is often through ordinary, everyday practices that the work of peace is carried forth, and martyrs such as Sisters of the Resurrection in Busamana are formed.

The Busamana community, close to Nyondo in Rwanda, consisted of seven sisters serving a community that was reeling from the trauma of the genocide and the war across the river in neighboring Bukavu. Every week the sisters would go to the parish to obtain consecrated hosts for communion for the Christians in their community. In December 1997, the bishop, seeing the situation deteriorating, wrote to the superior, asking her to leave Busamana and return to Nyondo with her sisters. Sister Epiphanie (the superior) called her sisters together, and after praying and discussing the matter, they wrote to the bishop:

> We have received your letter and we thank you for your fatherly concern. For the present we are afraid, but we do not yet feel ourselves to be in immediate danger. There is no priest in the parish; the people have no one but us. And to leave these Christians without Communion and to flee—when we are not in grave danger—this we cannot do. We have decided to stay with our people. We are not playing politics: we do no harm to anyone. We hope that nothing will happen to us.[18]

During the night of January 7, 1998, militias attacked. Five sisters were killed, together with the guard and a catechist's sister and brother-in-law, who were staying at the convent. In many ways this story is similar to the story of Brother Christian de Chergé and his fellow Trappist monks of the Tibhirine, who decided—despite the obvious danger to their lives—to stay, in solidarity and friendship with their Muslim neighbors in Algeria.[19] For just as Christian

---

18. http://jloughnan.tripod.com/nunmartyrs.htm (5/10/15).

19. See Christian de Chergé, "Last Testament: A Letter from the Monks of the Tibhirine," *First Things* (August 1996): http://www.firstthings.com/article/1996/08/006-last-testament (accessed Dec. 11, 2015). See also the movie based on the story of the monks: *Of Gods and Men* (2011).

de Chergé had prayed for forgiveness, even for one who would strike him down, the sisters of Busamana, on Christmas day, two weeks before they were to be killed, wrote to their prioress in Bukavu: "May God free us from all fear and break the chains of hatred."

Resurrected Living: A Communion of Witnesses

If the memory of martyrs fertilizes the soil of the Christian struggle for a more peaceful world, the gift of "dreaming" is what sustains that struggle. While dreaming might strike some as an invitation into a life of fantasy (as in day-dreaming), the kind of dreaming that the martyrs call the church to is a very concrete discipline of resurrected living. In "Threatened with Resurrection," Esquivel speaks about this way of living as a form of odd existence marked by a set of apparently contradictory postures: "To dream awake, to keep watch asleep, to live while dying, and to know ourselves already resurrected!"[20] What I take from Esquivel's observation is that "resurrection" is not merely a belief about the future (an afterlife), it is a unique form of living—a way that does not fully conform to the logic of the present because it is premised on the logic of a different order. It is a way of living in the present with dreams drawn from a future beyond. Wendell Berry speaks of this odd existence as a form of art that has to be practiced, and a performance that won't compute.[21] Thomas Sankara spoke of it as a kind of "madness," a nonconformity and a willingness to turn one's back on old formulas so as to "invent the future."[22]

This is the kind of madness—of daring to invent the future—that the martyrs threaten the church with. And it is what makes resurrection both a gift and a threat. In a world built on assumptions of life as the ultimate good—and thus that nothing is worth dying for—martyrs live with an "excess of life" that confirms that some things *are* worth dying for, and because they are worth dying for they are worth living for. By living within this excess, the martyrs embody a radical sense of flourishing that cannot be threatened, not even by death.[23] Thus, in the words of Esquivel, they know themselves "already resur-

---

20. Esquivel, *Threatened with Resurrection*, 63–65.

21. In "Manifesto: The Mad Farmer Liberation Front," *Reclaiming Politics* (Fall/Winter 1991), Wendell Berry equates the logic of this resurrected living with doing "something that won't compute": "Ask the questions that have no answers . . . Be joyful though you have considered all the facts."

22. See E. Katongole, *Sacrifice of Africa* (Grand Rapids: Eerdmans, 2011), 91.

23. See D. Stephen Long and Geoffrey Holsclaw's wonderful essay "Is Anything Worth

rected." Esquivel also speaks about this excess of life as a form of "living while dying" and as an adventure, a marvelous adventure. She writes:

> Join us in this vigil
> and you will know what it is to dream!
> Then you will know how marvelous it is
> to live threatened with Resurrection![24]

What makes it marvelous is the fact that resurrected living both requires and creates a community. And so, even when martyrs die alone, what makes it possible for them to willingly accept death is their sense of belonging and participation, of being part of a story and struggle bigger than they are; it is a story into which they have been called, but one that does not fully depend on them. Accordingly,

> [I]n this marathon of Hope,
> there are always others to relieve us

Dying For? Martyrdom, Exteriority, and Politics after Bare Life," in Budde and Scott, *Witness of the Body*, 171–89. To live well, Long and Holdsclaw argue, requires knowing what is worth dying for. However, among the many innovations of modern political life has been the desire to dispense with metaphysical questions—questions of goodness, truth, and beauty—and to replace them with a new approach to politics focused exclusively on the preservation of human life. This new form of "exclusive humanism," i.e., biological life stripped from goodness and truth and coordinated by social, political, religious, or cosmic life—what Agamben calls "bare life"—fundamentally shifted the understanding of politics. "Once politics becomes grounded solely in human nature and human needs as bare life, it no longer asks what is worth dying for. Instead, a different question emerges in the formation of human politics: 'How do we avoid dying?'" (174–75). The overall effect of this shift is a form of (modern) secular politics that allows for nothing external to this exclusive humanist foundation: "The only thing worth dying for is the preservation of the conditions for a politics where nothing is worth dying for." In response to the "exclusive humanism" of modern political life, Long and Holdsclaw propose a version of "genuine humanism" and an "excess of life" that alone accounts for life. But affirming this excess invokes "truth" as a transcendent reality—as something worth living for, and thus worth dying for. Long and Holdsclaw's argument and analysis are powerful. I also find their proposal for a "genuine humanism" quite compelling. The only thing I miss from their analysis might be narratives that could display the excess of life. The stories of the martyrs in this chapter display the "excess of love" that Long and Holdsclaw talk about. So does the story of Robert Sobukwe, one of the early resisters of apartheid in South Africa, who, though imprisoned on Robben Island and banished to solitary confinement, nevertheless remained hopeful and committed to the anti-apartheid struggle. His biography is appropriately entitled *How Can Man Die Better?* See Benjamin Pogrund, *How Can Man Die Better? Sobukwe and Apartheid* (London: Peter Halban, 1990).

24. Esquivel, *Threatened with Resurrection*, 63.

who carry the strength
to reach the finish line
which lies beyond death.[25]

In a world not only marked by individualism, but one where ethical, political, and all practical considerations operate within the bounds of an "immanent frame," the stories of martyrs point to a necessary transcendental and eschatological horizon, a horizon necessary to sustain Christian engagement and struggle for peace.[26] In a world marked by the deep divisions of racial, national, and ethnic loyalties, martyrs point to a communion that cuts across these boundaries. Martyrs define the church as a resurrected community, beyond the boundaries of geography and time. In the end, this is what the story of Buta in Burundi points to.

In the early hours of one morning in the fall of 1997, a milita group attacked Buta, a high school seminary. They roused the students from their sleep and ordered the high school students to separate—Hutu on one side and Tutsi on the other. Three times the order was given, but the students refused to separate. So, the commander ordered the rebels to open fire. Some students were felled by the gunfire, while others tried to escape. In all, forty students were killed. One of the wounded students ran to the rector's house and called for the rector to open the door. When the rector opened the door, the boy dashed inside and, gasping for breath, cried out: "Father, we have won. They told us to separate and we refused. We have won." Then he collapsed and died.[27]

The mural in the cemetery where the forty seminarians were buried bears the inscription "Martyrs of Unity": it depicts the young martyrs holding palms as a sign of the victory ("we have won"). But whereas the refusal to separate

25. Esquivel, *Threatened with Resurrection*, 61.

26. This, according to Charles Taylor, is the true essence of secularism—not the explicit denial of theism or God's existence, but reducing and inscribing theistic practices, considerations and reasoning within an immanent—i.e., nontranscendental—world, a world that encounters "no echo outside," a world that is viewed and engaged *etsi Deus non daretur* [as if God did not exist]." See Taylor, *A Secular Age* (Cambridge, MA: Belknap, 2007).

27. Author interview with Fr. Zacharie Bukuru, who was rector at the time of the attack on Buta (Aug. 13, 2009). For an extended reflection on this story, see E. Katongole, "On Learning to Betray One's People: The Gospel and a Culture of Peace in Africa," the Luzbetak Lecture in Mission and Culture delivered at Catholic Theological Union, Chicago, September 29, 2014: http://learn.ctu.edu/luzbetak_lecture_2014 (accessed Dec. 11, 2015). See also E. Katongole, "Odd Bodies—A Sermon," Capital Christian Fellowship, Washington, DC (May 22, 2011): http://emmanuelkatongole.com/wordpress/wp-content/uploads/2013/11/ODD-BODIES-CCF .pdf (accessed Dec. 11, 2015).

and their subsequent martyrdom was the final sign of the victory, their triumph over the idolatrous politics of ethnicity was already evident through a number of everyday practices of "resurrected" living in the Buta community. In fact, by 1997, as ethnic tension mounted, Buta was not only one of a few schools that remained open, it was the only one where students from both ethnicities lived together and continued to study as normally as possible. This was in great part due to the leadership of the rector, Fr. Zacharie Bukuru, and his staff, who not only encouraged the students to remain at the school, but also, by way of a number of programs, helped shape the students into a rare community whose sense of solidarity superseded ethnic tags. The programs included nightly dialogue sessions, where the students were encouraged to air out hearsay and speculations and openly discuss Burundi's history and ethnic prejudices. The goal was to wage "a merciless war on lies and rumors" that were the source of much fear and anxiety in the student community. The sessions were also a way of taking the sting out of the "verbal violence" of the ethnic prejudices.[28] The overall effect was that a culture of truth, truth-telling, and trust began to form. Whereas the students were at first quiet and suspicious of one another, they now "debated all political issues, taking care to name them and to seek their origins without trying to hide anything" (35). As a result, "there was no need to dream of taking up arms, like other youths in the country, in order to find justice." Consequently, as Fr. Bukuru notes:

> We welcomed everything that might promote laughter and relaxation between the two ethnic groups: sporting competitions, matches between classes, between students and teachers, between seniors and juniors, cross-country races, manual labor that offered the chance to sing together, games, theater, dance, lectures, and festive meals shared by teachers and students. All these things changed the face of the seminary. (37)

Dance played a particularly significant role in healing, but also in cementing the unity between ethnic groups. The Kirundi traditional dance, as Bukuru notes, "called us beyond ourselves into generosity, joy, relaxation, sharing, dialogue, and purity" and "brought us together in a single culture, uniting

28. Zacharie Bukuru, *Les quarante jeunes martyrs de Buta (Burundi 1997): Frères à la vie, frères à la mort* (Paris: Karthala, 2004). Page references refer to the unpublished English translation by Jodi Mikalachki: *The Forty Martyrs of Burundi*, 33–34. (The translation has been published under the title *We Are All Children of God: The Story of the Forty Young Martyrs of Buta-Burundi* [Nairobi: Paulines, 2015]; hereafter, page references appear in parentheses within the text.)

us in something beyond our differences in ethnicity, age, or social status." In fact, dance became another form of prayer, and so on weekends the seminary "alternated modern dance, traditional dance and song, and night prayers" (38).

Through these and many other shared activities, the young men were so imbued with a spirit of fraternity that they began to create their own clubs and associations, including a local chapter of Music for Hope International.[29] They also founded an AIDS awareness organization and an environmental club, which they used to organize lectures at the seminary and practice outreach to the surrounding local communities.

I draw attention to these practices for two reasons. One is, again, to point to the everyday practices that build a culture of peace—and thus they constitute Christian peacemaking. The second is to confirm that, even before the martyrdom of these young men, they, in the words of Esquivel, "knew themselves as already resurrected." And it is this resurrected living that they now threaten the African church with, inviting us to join them "in this vigil and to . . . know what it is to dream . . . to know how marvelous it is to live threatened with Resurrection!"[30]

The Hope of Martyrs: Naming and Remembering Martyrs

Other than Annuarite Nengapeta, who was beatified in 1985, those I have discussed here—the young seminarians at Buta, the sisters of Busamana, Christian de Chergé and the Trappist monks in Algeria, Chantal Mujjawama-holo and her companions at Nyange, Munzihirwa—none have been formally recognized as martyrs by the church. However, referring to these "holy innocents" within Africa's turbulent history as martyrs fits well with the exhortation anticipated by Pope Benedict's *Africae Munus*, "to recognize among servants of the Gospel in Africa those who could be canonized according to the norms of the Church."[31] This exhortation in *Africae Munus* is timely. For a true appreciation of the hope embodied by martyrs calls for the recovery

29. Inspired by the Argentinian pianist Miguel Ángel Estrella, one of the objectives of the *Musique Espérance* is to promote equal opportunities and access to a culture of peace mostly for children and teenagers through music programs that can raise active participation and solidarity awareness. See information for Music for Hope International Federation at: http://federation-musique-esperance.org/EN/index_en.html.

30. Esquivel, *Threatened with Resurrection*, 63.

31. Pope Benedict XVI, *Africae Munus* (2011), §114: http://w2.vatican.va/content/benedict-xvi/en/apost_exhortations/documents/hf_ben-xvi_exh_20111119_africae-munus.html.

of a vibrant conversation about why and whom the church should name as martyrs.[32]

If such a conversation were to become lacking or uninteresting, the church would be in danger of losing the skills and courage necessary for her mission in the world. But it is also obvious why the church might be reluctant or even unable to engage in the conversation about martyrs in a lively and ongoing way. For doing so involves accepting and welcoming the threat martyrs offer. In many ways, the church is much "safer" without the stories of the martyrs. And yet, as I have shown, without martyrs the church would not be able to remember her call and mission as maiden of peace in a violent world. Moreover, she would not be able to see that living out that call involves a life of constant vigilance, nonviolent struggle and commitment to peacemaking, and practices of everyday "resurrected living" in the midst of violence.

But an appreciation of the hope that martyrs represent has to do not only with the practice of naming martyrs, but also with the rich tradition of remembering their lives. Such remembering takes many forms: vigils, celebration of feast days, assuming martyrs' names, storytelling, and so on. While all these practices might happen outside the context of worship, they point to the church's worship as the primary context and practice through which the memory of martyrs is shaped and relived. In the end, worship becomes the primary theater and drama within which the church gives—nay, becomes—"an account of hope." But if our discussion in this study has proved anything, it is the realization that the church's worship is not mere worship, certainly not for a church that has a lively memory of martyrs. For, like Rachel, in remembering her "children who are no more," the church refuses to be comforted by any cheap promises of peace. In holding onto the memory of these children, she is drawn into their ceaseless lament, their cry of "how long, O God?" But that cry is a breaking point that invites, draws, and threatens the church into a life of vigilance, of nonviolent struggle, and of practical ways of living that reflect the shalom of God's peace. This is what makes the memory of martyrs a dangerous memory, a practice of dangerous hope.

32. Therefore, I find Robert Royal's book *The Catholic Martyrs of the Twentieth Century: A Comprehensive World History* (New York: Crossroad, 2000) very helpful in engaging in this conversation, not only because of its attempt to provide a global map for martyrdom in our time, but also for the stories and lives he names as martyrs, some of them controversial.

"Une herbe qui brûle" (The Grass That Burns)

> *How could we tire of hope?*
> *—so much is in bud . . .*
> *there is too much broken*
> *that must be mended*
> *too much hurt we have done*
> *to each other*
> *that cannot yet be forgiven . . . .*
> *So much is unfolding that must*
> *complete its gesture,*
> *so much is in bud.*

Denise Levertov

In a continent beset by seemingly never-ending civil wars, dictatorships, poverty, and other forms of violence that kill millions of Africans, how can we talk about hope? What is hope—and what does it look like? These are the questions that have been at the heart of this book. I have provided different portraits of hope through stories of Christian activists for nonviolent change from the Great Lakes Region of Eastern Africa. Our exploration of these various narratives has been one way of responding to Peter's exhortation to give an account of hope (1 Pet. 3:15), the hope that is in Africa. Concretely responding to Peter's invitation has required us to locate the agency of Christian social activists within the context of Africa's cultural, political, and economic history. But it has also meant reading in their agency the pattern of Christ's suffering, death, and resurrection. This has meant that in trying to get "inside" their historical agency, I have not only been listening to their stories; I have also been listening for a particular story. In that process a number of interrelated conclusions have emerged.

First, lament is agency. The ground on which the faith activists stand is a ground of immense pain and suffering, a reality that has been captured through a number of poems, songs, and other cultural expressions from Congo and Northern Uganda. These activists are caught up within this vortex of suffering. Their agency is in the first place a cry of lament. But this cry of anguish is as much a way of naming and mourning what is lost as it is a way of standing in the midst of suffering. This study has confirmed that, far from passively acquiescing to suffering, lament is an active engagement with the world of suffering. Far from distracting us from practical engagement, the practice of lament deepens and intensifies engagement with the world of suffering. Lament invites us into deeper political engagement, while at the same time reframing and reconstituting the very nature and meaning of politics.

Second, lament is a way of engaging God in the midst of suffering. Angelina spoke of it as a way of "wrestling" or "arguing" with God. The language I have been using is the language of "turning": lament as a way of turning toward and around God in suffering. A significant conclusion that has emerged from the study is that the faith activists discover that the God they turn to in their suffering is a God who is already turned toward suffering humanity. The God they turn to is an incarnate God ("born in the gash of human history") and a "crucified God"—a God, therefore, who stands in solidarity with suffering humanity. They also discover that God's suffering is not simply a form of passive endurance, but an active divine agency by means of which God responds to evil and violence through an excess of love. Thus, for Kataliko, the church's liturgical seasons are at once an invitation into and a reenactment of the story of God's excessive love. Munzihirwa spoke of this way of responding to violence through suffering love as "the way of Christ," into which he constantly invited the suffering population of Bukavu. Nyirumbe countenanced this suffering but compassionate God in her devotion and life as a sister of the Sacred Heart. Maggy encountered the love, compassion, and forgiveness of this God who hangs on the cross, especially during her breakdown and retreat at the Carmelite monastery, but also in her continuous visits to the gravesites of those slaughtered in the 1993 massacre, as well as in her daily adoration before the cross and the blessed sacrament.

Third, involved in this turning toward God is the sense of "being carried"—and thus of being drawn into—the drama of God's saving engagement with the world, at the heart of which is the mystery of Christ's suffering, death, and resurrection. This is the drama into which the faith activists feel they are drawn as participants, and within which God remains the key actor. Thus it was the "love affair" with God that set Kasali on his journey, which involves a posture of constantly discerning, listening, and obeying God. The Université Chrétienne Bilingue du Congo and the Congo Initiative can thus be understood as the result of this "obedience."

Maggy speaks about her life as such a journey—a calling from God. At one workshop, after listening to Maggy tell her story, an obviously moved leader asked her how she would like to be known. Maggy responded: "I never thought every person must be known." When the leader persisted and wanted to know how she would like to be remembered, she answered simply: "That God is God." Then she added, "We are merely grass that burns—*une herbe qui brûle*"—an allusion to the metaphor in Psalm 90 that portrays human beings as grass that springs up in the morning but by the evening withers and fades (Ps. 90:6).

Fourth, the sense of "being carried" is reflected in the way a number of the activists portrayed here talked about "being led" to a new place through their experience of suffering. This new place is a form of knowledge, an epistemology confirming that the knowing at stake is not an abstract or detached way of knowing but a kind of *yada'*, an intimate knowledge through which Munzihirwa and other activists understand their lives and their work as a participation in God's reconciling love for the world. But the knowledge into which they are drawn through their suffering is not merely "pious" or "spiritual"; it is a very concrete and practical knowledge. It is, in fact, a revolutionary social vision, a way of seeing and engaging the world from the vantage point of God's nonviolent and self-sacrificing love.

By standing within this vision, the activists are able not only to resist violence (Maggy: "No to the violence and yes to love") but also to discover nonviolent alternatives, as suffering is itself transformed into fiery and compassionate advocacy on behalf of their suffering communities. The advocacy takes many forms: engaging various political actors (Kataliko and Munzihirwa); the imagination of a university in the midst of the war (Kasali); the everyday work of stitching, repairing, and gluing together the shattered lives of girls in Northern Uganda (Nyirumbe) and of children in Burundi (Maggy).

Fifth, the foregoing is why the concern that is revealed in their advocacy is not merely a "humanitarian" concern for those who are suffering; it is the shape of a new politics in the midst of Africa's politics of greed and self-seeking power. Their advocacy does not simply have political ramifications; it is decisively political. Moreover, it is not simply political reform that they are interested in, but a thorough theological reinvention of politics. They are not simply calling for law and order, nor simply for some justice and reconciliation. They would not be satisfied with mere legal and administrative adjustments within the framework of the current politics. They have been led to—and they invoke—a totally new vision of society. Their advocacy and initiatives reflect the shape of the new world, which now breaks forth within the shell of the old world as both a radical critique of and an alternative to the politics of military alliances and economic greed. The faith activists understand themselves as both the agents and fruits of that new world.

Sixth, since the faith activists portrayed here see themselves as already participating in the new and alternative vision of society, a sense of "newness" and "freedom" marks their own lives. What one priest remarked about Munzihirwa's simplicity—"he was completely free, simple, and unafraid"—can be said of the others. This radical sense of freedom also means that, even as the various forms of advocacy and practical engagements require sacrifice, hard decisions, and disciplined commitment, a sense of gift and surprise is at the heart of their agency. The memory of Rachel's weeping explodes with rich resonance through the various portraits. For the memory of Rachel is the story of her tears turned into guideposts for a new future, as God promises a new thing in the world. The story of Kasali and the new university in Beni also testifies to this logic of gift and surprise. So do the story and work of Maggy with Maison Shalom, where tears, with time, turn into a Magnificat. So does the witness of martyrs, whose lives and stories constantly "threaten" the church with the painful yet joyful gift of resurrection. Angelina would describe the miraculous return of her daughter as "painfully sweet."

Seventh, Africa is a continent of hope. While *Dancing in the Glory of Monsters* (and other similar accounts) might give credence to the idea of a hopeless continent, what this book has confirmed is that, in the midst of Africa's turbulent history, God continues to plant seeds of hope through the lives of activists like the ones portrayed here. Accordingly, this book is a confirmation that we cannot give up hope. In her poem "Beginners," Denise Levertov speaks about "too much pain," "too much hurt," and "too much that is broken." While she is not speaking directly of Africa, that "too much" speaks particularly to the reality of Africa. But Levertov also speaks about the reality of "so much that is unfolding" and "so much that is in bud." In many ways this is the historical reality of Africa: it is located at the intersection of "too much broken" and "so much in bud." The theological task, in response to Peter's exhortation, is how to give an account of that "so much that is unfolding" in the midst of Africa's "too much suffering." In responding to this exhortation, what I have tried to show in this book is that capturing the unique logic of that intersection requires a theological lexicon and grammar. This is the grammar of hope that I have sought to display as a theologically rich discipline, internally and dynamically related with another theologically thick discipline—the discipline of lament.

Eighth, what I have tried to show in this book is that an account of that intersection requires the reality of the church as the body of Christ: a body that is able to experience the reality of "too much pain" without, however, being consumed by it. The faith activists portrayed here assume this ecclesiological reality. They see and understand themselves as part of this corporeal "we" that is born in God's self-sacrificing love on the cross. Therefore, their lives and agency provide an exceptionally lucid rumination on the church as a "field hospital" (Pope Francis). As a field hospital, the church strives to "repair" the brokenness of the "yet to be mended" and to heal that which is "yet to be forgiven." True, the church is neither the sole actor at this intersection nor the only effort that seeks to repair the brokenness. Different agencies and programs engage this effort. From international bodies such as the United Nations to grassroots counseling ministries and trauma-healing programs, from government to nongovernment programs, the range of peacebuilding programs and efforts is broad and multisectional.

What the church uniquely offers, and what the lives and work of the faith activists illuminate, is the theological grammar of hope. The church's unique calling and mission at the intersection of social brokenness and repair is to be a *sacrament* of God's ongoing work of social repair. What this means is that the church's life and work at this intersection are not grounded in the conviction that she has something to bring, something to give to those who are suffering, but in the conviction that, by standing with those who are suffering, she participates in the mystery of God's own suffering, death, and resurrection. It is this participation that mysteriously releases, in the words of Bishop Mazzoldi, "a gentle but great force, which does not kill but renews and restores." This is the hope, which is made possible by the death and resurrection of Christ, and which the church reenacts in the midst of suffering. Accordingly, as ecclesial radiances, the portraits of the various activists in this book illuminate different faces of the church as a sacrament of hope in Africa.

Finally, the African church is a unique gift to world Christianity. Given her unique location at the intersection of "too much pain" and "so much in bud" of the African continent, the African church is a rich laboratory of hope. As a laboratory of hope, the African church provides a constant reminder to the universal church that, in the words of Levertov, "we can never tire of hope." Moreover, through the stories that I have told here, the African church provides a living witness of what hope looks like in the context of violence and war. In a world that so often despairs of nonviolent peace, this is a much-needed reminder. Moreover, at a time when the church's own witness to God's nonviolent peace is quite often ambiguous, or seems to wane and grow faint, the African church's witness of hope can reinvigorate and rekindle the global church's mission as a sacrament of peace in the world.

This gift of the African church to world Christianity is well captured by a final story. On October 20, 2002, Daudi Okello and Jildo Ilwa, former catechists from Gulu, Northern Uganda, were canonized by Pope John Paul II as martyrs. But at the ceremonial signing of the statute of the martyrs—to add their names to the universal communion of saints—the pope's pen ran out of ink. Pope John Paul II then borrowed a pen from Archbishop Odama of Gulu and signed the document. This story has a number of lessons. One is that, when the final story of world Christianity is told as the story of hope, my hope is that the stories of hope from Africa will be spoken of as those that provided the ink, the much-needed energy, and the fresh vitality to bolster the waning prospects of global Christianity in the twenty-first century. But even as we await that final reckoning, the theological task before us now, as it has always been, is "to give an account" of the hope we see in the various local histories within which the church finds herself. *Born from Lament* has been one attempt to do precisely this in the context of Africa's turbulent history.

Works Cited

Abim, Paul Peter Rom. *The Spill of Blood and Lamentations of Lamalo*. Rossendale, UK: Rossendale Books, 2011.

Achebe, Chinua. *Arrow of God*. New York: Anchor, 1969.

Adam, Margaret B. *Our Only Hope: More than We Can Ask or Imagine*. Eugene, OR: Pickwick, 2013.

Adetunji, Jo. "Forty-eight Women Raped Every Hour in Congo, Study Finds." *The Guardian*, May 12, 2011. Online: http://www.theguardian.com/world/2011/may/12/48 -women-raped-hour-congo (accessed Apr. 8, 2014).

Ahearne-Kroll, Stephen A. *The Psalms of Lament in Mark's Passion: Jesus' Davidic Suffering*. Society for the Study of the New Testament Series. Cambridge, UK: Cambridge University Press, 2007.

Allen, John. *The Global War on Christians: Dispatches from the Front Lines of Anti-Christian Persecution*. New York: Image, 2013.

———. *Rabble-rouser for Peace: The Authorized Biography of Desmond Tutu*. New York: Free Press, 2006.

Anderson, Allan H. *African Reformation: African Initiated Christianity in the 20th Century*. Trenton, NJ: Africa World Press, 2001.

Appleby, Scott. *The Ambivalence of the Sacred: Religion, Violence, and Reconciliation*. Lanham, MD: Rowman and Littlefield, 2000.

Atkinson, Judy. *Trauma Trails, Recreating Song Lines: The Transgenerational Effects of Trauma in Indigenous Australia*. North Melbourne: Spinifex, 2002.

Augustine. *Expositions on the Book of Psalms*. Vol. 1. New York: Augustinian Heritage Institute, 2000.

Baaz, Maria Eriksson, and Maria Stern. *Sexual Violence as a Weapon of War: Perceptions, Prescriptions, Problems in the Congo and Beyond*. London: Zed Books, 2013.

Baraka, Joël. *My Loves My Sorrows*. Youth poetry, 2012.

Benedict XVI. *Africae Munus*. 2011. Online: http://w2.vatican.va/content/benedict-xvi

/en/apost_exhortations/documents/hf_ben-xvi_exh_20111119_africae-munus.html (accessed December 8, 2015).

Bergant, Dianne. *Lamentations*. Abingdon Old Testament Commentaries. Nashville, TN: Abingdon, 2003.

Berry, Wendell. "Manifesto: The Mad Farmer Liberation Front." *Reclaiming Politics* (Fall/ Winter 1991).

Billman, Kathleen B., and Daniel L. Migliore. *Rachel's Cry: Prayer of Lament and Rebirth of Hope*. Cleveland: United Church Press, 1999.

Black, C. Clifton. "The Persistence of Wounds." In *Lament: Reclaiming Practices in Pulpit, Pew, and Public Square*, edited by Sally A. Brown and Patrick D. Miller. Louisville: Westminster John Knox, 2005.

Blount, Brian K. "Breaking Point: A Sermon." In *Lament: Reclaiming Practices in Pulpit, Pew, and Public Square*, edited by Sally A. Brown and Patrick D. Miller. Louisville: Westminster John Knox, 2005.

Boff, Leonardo. *Cry of the Earth, Cry of the Poor*. Maryknoll, NY: Orbis, 1997.

Bonhoeffer, Dietrich. *Letters and Papers from Prison*. New York: Macmillan, 1972.

Brueggemann, Walter. "The Costly Loss of Lament." *Journal of the Study of the Old Testament* 11, no. 36 (1986): 57–71.

———. *The Prophetic Imagination*. Philadelphia: Fortress, 1978.

———. *The Psalms and the Life of Faith*. Minneapolis: Augsburg Fortress, 1995.

———. *Texts That Linger, Words That Explode: Listening to Prophetic Voices*. Minneapolis: Fortress, 2008.

Bukuru, Zacharie. *Les quarante jeunes martyrs de Buta (Burundi 1997): Frères à la vie, frères à la mort*. Paris: Karthala, 2004.

———. *We Are All Children of God: The Story of the Forty Young Martyrs of Buta-Burundi*. Translated by Jodi Mikalachki. Nairobi: Paulines, 2015.

Campbell, D. Keith. "NT Scholars' Use of OT Lament Terminology and Its Theological and Interdisciplinary Implications." *Bulletin for Biblical Research* 21, no. 2 (2011): 213–26.

Casey, Sara E., et al. "Care-Seeking Behavior by Survivors of Sexual Assault in the Democratic Republic of Congo." *American Journal of Public Health* 101 (June 2011): 1054–56.

Catholic Online. "Saint Christopher." Online: http://www.catholic.org/saints/saint.php?saint_id=36#wiki (accessed Dec. 6, 2015).

Cavanaugh, William T. *Field Hospital: The Church's Engagement with a Wounded World*. Grand Rapids: Eerdmans, 2016.

———. *The Myth of Religious Violence: Secular Ideology and Roots of Modern Conflict*. Oxford: Oxford University Press, 2009.

Chenoweth, Erica, and Maria J. Stephan. *Why Civil Resistance Works: The Strategic Logic of Nonviolent Conflict*. New York: Columbia University Press, 2012.

Cigwira, Joseph Mukabalera. "Monseigneur Munzihirwa Christophe, Romero du Congo?

Les concepts de Martyre de Béatification et de Canonization revisités à lumière de l'histoire religieuse contemporaine." PhD diss., L'Université Libre de Bruxelles, 2003.

Claassens, L. Juliana M. "Calling the Keeners: The Image of the Wailing Woman as Symbol of Survival in a Traumatized World." *Journal of Feminist Studies in Religion* 26, no. 1 (2010): 63–77.

Comboni Missionaries. "The Cross as Bride." Online: http://www.comboni.org.uk /combonis_writings.html (accessed Mar. 27, 2015).

Congo Initiative. Online: http://www.congoinitiative.org/ (accessed Dec. 17, 2015).

Cross, Karie. "Mapping Exercise: Gender and Grassroots Perspectives." Unpublished term paper, Kroc Institute for International Peace Studies, University of Notre Dame, Notre Dame, IN (2014).

"David M. Kasali: Being Transformed to Transform." *Faith and Leadership,* September 19, 2010. Online: http://www.faithandleadership.com/multimedia/david-m-kasali -being-transformed-transform (accessed Dec. 9, 2015).

Davis, Ellen. "Jeremiah: Master of Lament." Sermon delivered at Duke Divinity School Summer Institute, May 29, 2013.

De Chergé, Christian. "Last Testament: A Letter from the Monks of the Tibhirine." *First Things,* August 1996. Online: http://www.firstthings.com/article /1996/08/006-last-testament (accessed Dec. 11, 2015).

Decker, Christian. "Voices from the Grave." Online: http://jloughnan.tripod.com/zaire .htm (accessed Apr. 3, 2015).

DeYoung, Curtiss Paul. *Living Faith: How Faith Inspires Social Justice.* Minneapolis: Fortress, 2007.

Dobbs-Allsopp, F. W. *Lamentations.* Interpretation: A Bible Commentary for Teaching and Preaching. Louisville: John Knox, 2002.

Dusengumuremyi, Jean d'Amour. *No Greater Love: Testimonies on the Life of Felicitas Niyitegeka.* Lake Oswego, OR: Dignity, 2015.

Eklund, Rebekah Ann. "Lord, Teach Us How to Grieve: Jesus' Lament and Christian Hope." ThD diss., Duke University, 2012.

Ellington, Scott A. *Risking Truth: Reshaping the World through Prayers of Lament.* Eugene, OR: Pickwick, 2008.

English, Fenwick D. "A Critical Appraisal of Sara Lawrence-Lightfoot's *Portraiture* as a Method of Educational Research." Online: http://edr.sagepub.com/content/29/7/21 .full.pdf (accessed Dec. 2, 2015).

Esquivel, Julia. *Threatened with Resurrection: Prayers and Poems from an Exiled Guatemalan,* 2nd ed. Elgin, IL: Brethren, 1994.

Featherstone, Joseph. "To Make the Wounded Whole." *Harvard Educational Review* 59 (1989): 367–78.

Fletcher, Laurel E. "Violence and Social Repair: Rethinking the Contribution of Justice to Reconciliation." *Human Rights Quarterly* 24 (2002): 573–639. Online: http://scholarship .law.berkeley.edu/cgi/viewcontent.cgi?article=1544&context=facpubs (accessed Dec. 17, 2015).

Fork Films. *Pray the Devil Back to Hell.* 2008.

Francis I. "Address to Journalists." March 16, 2013. *Zenit.* Online: http://www.zenit.org /en/articles/pope-francis-address-to-journalists (accessed Dec. 17, 2015).

———. "A Big Heart Open to God." Interview with Antonio Spadaro, SJ. *America,* September 30, 2013. Online: http://americamagazine.org/pope-interview (accessed Dec. 6, 2015).

———. *Evangelii Gaudium*: Apostolic Exhortation, 2013.

Frisk, Bruce N. "See My Tears: A Lament for Jerusalem (Luke 13:31–35; 19:41–44)." In *The Word Leaps the Gap: Essays on Scripture and Theology in Honor of Richard B. Hays,* edited by J. Ross Wagner, C. Kavin Rowe, and A. Katherine Grieb. Grand Rapids: Eerdmans, 2008.

Galtung, Johan. "Cultural Violence." *Journal of Peace Research* 27, no. 3 (1990): 291–305.

Gbowee, Leymah. *Mighty Be Our Powers: How Sisterhood, Prayer, and Sex Changed a Nation at War—A Memoir.* New York: Beast Books, 2011.

Goatley, David Emmanuel. *Were You There? Godforsakenness in Slave Religion.* Maryknoll, NY: Orbis, 1996.

Gutiérrez, Gustavo. *On Job: God-talk and the Suffering of the Innocent.* Maryknoll, NY: Orbis, 1987.

———. *A Theology of Liberation: History, Politics, and Salvation.* Maryknoll, NY: Orbis, 1988.

Hall, Douglas John. *Lighten Our Darkness: Toward an Indigenous Theology of the Cross.* Philadelphia: Westminster, 1976.

Harasta, Eva, and Brian Brock, eds. *Evoking Lament: A Theological Discussion.* New York: T&T Clark, 2009.

Hart, David Bentley. *The Doors of the Sea: Where Was God in the Tsunami?* Grand Rapids: Eerdmans, 2005.

Hauerwas, Stanley. *With the Grain of the Universe: The Church's Witness and Natural Theology.* Grand Rapids: Brazos, 2001.

Heal Africa. "History." Online: http://www.healafrica.org/history (accessed Dec. 17, 2015).

Heschel, Abraham Joseph. *The Prophets.* 2 vols. New York: Harper and Row, 1969–71.

Hochschild, Adam. "Explaining Congo's Endless Civil War." *The New York Times,* April 1, 2011. Online: http://www.nytimes.com/2011/04/03/books/review/book-review -dancing-in-the-glory-of-monsters-the-collapse-of-the-congo-and-the-great-war -of-africa-by-jason-k-stearns.html (accessed Dec. 16, 2015).

Holst-Warhaft, Gail. *Dangerous Voices: Women's Laments and Greek Literature.* London: Routledge, 1992.

"A Hopeful Continent." *The Economist,* February 28, 2013. Online: http://www.economist .com/news/special-report/21572377-african-lives-have-already-greatly-improved -over-past-decade-says-oliver-august (accessed Dec. 2, 2015).

"Hopeless Africa." *The Economist,* May 11, 2000. Online: http://www.economist.com /node/333429 (accessed Dec. 2, 2015).

"The Hopeless Continent." *The Economist,* May 13, 2000. Online: http://www.economist
.com/printedition/2000–05–13 (accessed Dec. 17, 2015).

Hoskins, Judith Debetencourt. *Hummingbird, Why Am I Here? Maggy's Children.* Charleston, SC: CreateSpace, 2012.

Human Rights Watch. *The War within the War: Sexual Violence against Women and Girls in Eastern Congo.* New York: Human Rights Watch, 2002.

Iafrate, Michael. "Rock as 'Interruption' and Bearer of Dangerous Memories." *Rock and Theology,* July 4, 2010. Online: http://www.rockandtheology.com/?p=2171 (accessed Apr. 29, 2015).

Ilo, Stan. "The Church of the Poor: Towards an Ecclesiology of Vulnerable Mission." *Ecclesiology* 10 (2014): 229–50.

John Paul II. *Ecclesia in Africa.* 1995. Online: http://w2.vatican.va/content/john-paul-ii/en/apost_exhortations/documents/hf_jp-ii_exh_14091995_ecclesia-in-africa.html (accessed December 10, 2015).

———.*Tertio Millennio Adveniente.* 1994. Online: https://w2.vatican.va/content/john-paul-ii/en/apost_letters/1994/documents/hf_jp-ii_apl_19941110_tertio-millennio-adveniente.html (accessed Dec. 10, 2015).

Johnson, Elizabeth A. *She Who Is: The Mystery of God in Feminist Theological Discourse.* New York: Crossroad, 1992.

Johnson, William Stacy. "Jesus' Cry, God's Cry, and Ours." In *Lament: Reclaiming Practices in Pulpit, Pew, and Public Square,* edited by Sally A. Brown and Patrick D. Miller. Louisville: Westminster John Knox, 2005.

Kataliko, Emmanuel. *Lettres Pastorales et Messages de Monseigneur Emmanuel Kataliko (18 mai 1997–Octobre 2000).* Editions Archevêché de Bukavu.

Katongole, Emmanuel. "Christianity, Tribalism, and the Rwanda Genocide." In *A Future for Africa: Critical Essays in Christian Social Imagination.* Scranton, PA: University of Scranton Press, 2005.

———. "Justice, Forgiveness, and Reconciliation in the Wake of Genocide: The End of Words." *The Other Journal,* August 16, 2012. Online: http://theotherjournal.com/2012/08/16/justice-forgiveness-and-reconciliation-in-the-wake-of-genocide-the-end-of-words/ (accessed Dec. 2, 2015).

———. *Mirror to the Church: Resurrecting Faith after Genocide in Rwanda.* Grand Rapids: Zondervan, 2009.

———. "Mission and the Ephesian Moment of World Christianity: Pilgrimages of Pain and Hope and the Economics of Eating Together." *Mission Studies* 29, no. 2 (2012): 183–200.

———. "Odd Bodies—A Sermon." Capital Christian Fellowship, Washington, DC (May 22, 2011). Online: http://emmanuelkatongole.com/wordpress/wp-content/uploads/2013/11/ODD-BODIES-CCF.pdf (accessed Dec. 11, 2015).

———. "Of Coffins and Churches: Seven Marks of an Emerging African Ecclesiology." In *The Church We Want: Foundations: Theology and Mission of the Church in Africa,* edited by Agbonkhianmeghe E. Orobator. Nairobi: Paulines, 2015.

———. "On Learning to Betray One's People: The Gospel and a Culture of Peace in Africa." The Luzbetak Lecture in Mission and Culture delivered at Catholic Theological Union, Chicago (September 29, 2014). Online: http://learn.ctu.edu/luzbetak _lecture_2014 (accessed Dec. 11, 2015).

———. *The Sacrifice of Africa: A Political Theology for Africa.* Grand Rapids: Eerdmans, 2011.

———. "'Threatened with Resurrection': Martyrdom and Reconciliation in the World Church." In *Witness of the Body: The Past, Present, and Future of Christian Martyrdom,* edited by Michael Budde and Karen Scott. Grand Rapids: Eerdmans, 2011.

———. "Violence and Christian Social Reconstruction in Africa: On the Resurrection of the Body (Politic)." *The Other Journal,* August 8, 2005. Online: http://theother journal.com/2005/08/08/violence-and-christian-social-reconstruction-in-africa -on-the-resurrection-of-the-body-politic/ (accessed Dec. 10, 2015).

Kiess, John. "When War Is Our Daily Bread: Congo, Theology, and the Ethics of Contemporary Conflict." PhD diss., Duke University, 2011.

King, Martin Luther, Jr. *Why We Can't Wait.* New York: Harper and Row, 1964.

Kobia, Samuel. *The Courage of Hope: The Roots for a New Vision and the Calling of the Church in Africa.* Geneva: World Council of Churches, 2002.

Krieg, Robert. *Story-Shaped Christology: The Role of Narratives in Identifying Jesus Christ.* New York: Paulist, 1988.

Lacey, Marc. "Rwandan Priest Sentenced to 15 Years for Allowing Deaths of Tutsi in Church." *The New York Times,* December 14, 2006. Online: http://www.nytimes .com/2006/12/14/world/africa/14rwanda.html?_r=0 (accessed Dec. 10, 2015).

Lambelet, Kyle. "'How Long, O Lord?' Practices of Lamentation and the Restoration of Political Agency." Unpublished paper. Duke Graduate Conference in Theology, Fall 2014.

"Lamentations: The Prayer of the Desperate." In *The African Bible.* Nairobi: Pauline Publications, 1999.

Lanahan, William F. "The Speaking Voice in the Book of Lamentations." *Journal of Biblical Literature* 93, no. 1 (1974): 41–49.

Lang, David. "Why Is Rachel Weeping at Ramah?" Online: http://www.accordancebible .com/Why-Is-Rachel-Weeping-At-Ramah (accessed Apr. 20, 2015).

La Salle, Donald G. "Liturgical and Popular Lament: A Study for the Role of Lament in Liturgical and Popular Religious Practices of Good Friday in Northern Italy from the Twelfth to Sixteenth Centuries." PhD diss., Catholic University of America, 1997.

Lawrence-Lightfoot, Sara, and Jessica Hoffman Davis. *The Art and Science of Portraiture.* San Francisco: John Wiley, 1997.

Leatherman, Janie. *Sexual Violence and Armed Conflict.* Cambridge, MA: Polity, 2011.

Lederach, John Paul, and Angela Jill Lederach. *When Blood and Bones Cry Out: Journeys through the Soundscape of Healing and Reconciliation.* Oxford: Oxford University Press, 2010.

Lemarchand, René. *The Dynamics of Violence in Central Africa*. Philadelphia: University of Pennsylvania Press, 2009.

Long, D. Stephen, and Geoffrey Holdsclaw. "Is Anything Worth Dying For? Martyrdom, Exteriority, and Politics after Bare Life." In *Witness of the Body: The Past, Present, and Future of Christian Martyrdom*, edited by Michael Budde and Karen Scott. Grand Rapids: Eerdmans, 2011.

Maathai, Wangari. *The Challenge for Africa*. New York: Pantheon, 2009.

Magesa, Laurenti. *What Is Not Sacred? African Spirituality*. Maryknoll, NY: Orbis, 2014.

Mana, Kä. *Christians and Churches of Africa Envisioning the Future: Salvation in Jesus Christ and the Building of a New African Society*. Akropong-Akuapen, Ghana: Regnum Africa, 2002.

Marsh, Charles. *The Beloved Community: How Faith Shapes Social Justice*. New York: Basic Books, 2005.

Martin, Christel. *La haine n'aura pas le dernier mot: Maggy la femme aux 10000 enfants*. Paris: Albin Michel, 2005.

Maxwell, David. "'Delivered from the Spirit of Poverty?' Pentecostalism, Prosperity and Modernity in Zimbabwe." *Journal of Religion in Africa* 28, no. 3 (1998): 350–73.

McClendon, James William. *Biography as Theology: How Life Stories Can Remake Today's Theology*. Eugene, OR: Wipf and Stock, 2002.

Meger, Sara. "Militarized Masculinities and the Political Economy of Wartime Sexual Violence in the Democratic Republic of Congo." In *Engaging Men in the Fight against Gender Violence: Case Studies from Africa*, edited by Jane Freedman. New York: Palgrave Macmillan, 2012.

Metz, Johannes. *Faith in History and Society: Toward a Practical Fundamental Theology*. New York: Crossroad, 2011.

Meyer, Birgit. "'Make a Complete Break with the Past.' Memory and Post-Colonial Modernity in Ghanaian Pentecostalist Discourse." *Journal of Religion in Africa* 28, no. 3 (1998): 316–49.

Milbank, John. *Theology as Social Theory: Beyond Secular Reason*. Oxford: Blackwell, 2006.

Mirindi Ya Nacironge, Deogratias. *Père Evêque Christophe Munzihirwa Mwene Ngabo, prophète et Martyr en notre temps*. Center Interdiocésain de Pastorale, Catéchèse et Liturgie, Bukavu, July 2003.

Moltmann, Jürgen. *The Crucified God: The Cross of Christ as the Foundation and Criticism of Christian Theology*. New York: Harper and Row, 1974.

Morris, Leon. *The Gospel According to John*. Revised ed. New International Commentary on the New Testament. Grand Rapids: Eerdmans, 1995.

Moteiro, Fabrice. *Wind of Change*. Online: http://fabricemonteiro.viewbook.com/wind-of-change (accessed Dec. 8, 2015).

Mukegwe, Denis Mukengere, and Cathy Nangini. "Rape with Extreme Violence: The New Pathology in South Kivu, Democratic Republic of Congo." *Plos Medicine* 6, no. 2

(December 2009). Online: http://www.ncbi.nlm.nih.gov/pmc/articles/PMC2791171/ (accessed Feb. 2, 2015).

Mulombe, Sébastien Muyengo. *Christophe Munzihirwa: La Sentinelle des Grands Lacs.* Kinshasa: Afriquespoir, 2011.

Munzihirwa, Christopher. Advent Pastoral Letter, Bukavu. November 18, 1995.

———. Letter, September 27, 1996.

———. "Stand Firm in Charity." October 27, 1996.

———. "L'Université de Bukavu et la paix." Bukavu, October 19, 1996. In Joseph Mukabalera Cigwira, "Monseigneur Munzihirwa Christophe, Romero du Congo? Les concepts de Martyre de Béatification et de Canonization revisités à lumière de l'histoire religieuse contemporaine." PhD diss., L'Université Libre de Bruxelles, 2003.

Muwazé, David. "Spate of Village Chief Killings Hits Northeast DR Congo." *The Observer,* January 17, 2014. Online: http://observers.france24.com/content/20140117-village -chief-killings-congo-kivu (accessed Dec. 2, 2015).

Myers, Ched, and Elaine Enns. *Ambassadors of Reconciliation.* Vol. 1. Maryknoll, NY: Orbis, 2009.

Ndeykosi, Stephen. *A Cry for Life: Ituri Drama.* Bunia: Peace House, 2005.

Nepstad, Sharon Erickson. *Nonviolent Struggle: Theories, Strategies, and Dynamics.* Oxford: Oxford University Press, 2015.

Nyamiti, Charles. *African Tradition and the Christian God.* Eldoret, Kenya: Gaba Publications, 1976.

O'Connor, Kathleen M. *Jeremiah: Pain and Promise.* Minneapolis: Fortress, 2011.

———. *Lamentations and the Tears of the World.* Maryknoll, NY: Orbis, 2002.

Olopade, Dayo. *The Bright Continent: Breaking Rules and Making Change in Modern Africa.* Boston: Houghton Mifflin Harcourt, 2014.

Omeje, Kenneth. "Understanding the Diversity and Complexity of Conflict in the Africa Great Lakes Region." In *Conflict and Peacebuilding in the African Great Lakes Region,* edited by Kenneth Omeje and Tricia Redeker Hepner. Bloomington: Indiana University Press, 2013.

Omenyo, Cephas N. "From the Fringes to the Centre: Pentecostalization of the Mainline Churches in Ghana." *Exchange* 34, no. 1 (2005): 39–60.

"The 100 Most Influential People in the World." *Time,* 2014. Online: http://time.com /time100–2014/ (accessed Dec. 4, 2015).

Onyumbe, Jacob. "Why Must I Go about Mourning?" *Duke Divinity Magazine* 12, no. 2 (2013). Online: https://divinity.duke.edu/community-student-life/divinity -magazine/spring-2013/why-must-i-go-about-mourning (accessed Dec. 2, 2015).

Opiyo, Lindsay McClain. "Artistic Suggestions for Peaceful Transition in Northern Uganda: What Youth Are Saying." *African Conflict and Peacebuilding Review* 2, no. 1 (April 2012): 152–63.

———. *Bed Ki Gen: Northern Uganda's Creative Approaches to Peace and Healing.* Knoxville, TN: Self-published, 2009.

———. "Community Peacebuilding through the Arts: Addressing the Past in Post-conflict Northern Uganda." Paper presented at "Engaging the Other" Conference, University of Free State, Bloemfontein, South Africa (December 2012).

Palmer, Parker J. *The Active Life: A Spirituality of Work, Creativity, and Caring.* San Francisco: Jossey-Bass, 1990.

Paris, Peter. "When Feeling like a Motherless Child." In *Lament: Reclaiming Practices in the Pulpit, Pew, and Public Square,* edited by Sally A. Brown and Patrick D. Miller. Louisville: Westminster John Knox, 2005.

Pemberton, Glenn. *Hurting with God: Learning to Lament with the Psalms.* Abilene, TX: Abilene Christian University Press, 2012.

Perkinson, Jim. "Theology and the City: Learning to Cry, Struggling to See." *Cross Currents* 51, no. 1 (2001): 95–114.

Philpott, Daniel. *Just and Unjust Peace: An Ethic of Political Reconciliation.* Oxford: Oxford University Press, 2012.

Pogrund, Benjamin. *How Can Man Die Better? Sobukwe and Apartheid.* London: Peter Halban, 1990.

Price, Richard. "The Voice of Christ in the Psalms." In *Meditations of the Heart: The Psalms in the Early Christian Thought and Practice,* edited by Andreas Andreopoulos, Augustine Casiday and Carol Harrison. Turnhout, Belgium: Brepols, 2011.

Prunier, Gérard. *Africa's World War: Congo, the Rwandan Genocide, and the Making of a Continental Catastrophe.* Oxford: Oxford University Press, 2009.

——— ."The Catholic Church and the Kivu Conflict." *Journal of Religion in Africa* 31, no. 2 (May, 2001): 139–62.

"Rachel's Tomb." *Life in the Holy Land.* Online: http://www.lifeintheholyland.com /rachel_tomb_bethlehem.htm (accessed Dec. 9, 2015).

Rah, Soong-Chan. *Prophetic Lament: A Call for Justice in Troubled Times.* Downers Grove, IL: InterVarsity, 2015.

Raitt, Thomas. *A Theology of Exile: Judgment/Deliverance in Jeremiah and Ezekiel.* Philadelphia: Fortress, 1977.

Roberts, Bayard, et al. "Factors Associated with Post-traumatic Stress Disorder and Depression amongst Internally Displaced Persons in Northern Uganda." *BMC Psychiatry* 8, no. 38 (2008). Online: http://www.biomedcentral.com/1471–244X/8/38 (accessed Dec. 16, 2015).

Roberts, J. J. M. "The Motif of the Weeping God in Jeremiah and Its Background in the Lament Tradition of the Ancient Near East." In *The Bible and the Ancient Near East: Collected Essays.* Winona Lake, IN: Eisenbrauns, 2002.

Robertson, Charles. "Africa's Next Boom." Ted Talk, June 2013. Online: https://www.ted .com/talks/charles_robertson_africa_s_next_boom?language=en (accessed Dec. 2, 2015).

Romero, Oscar. *The Violence of Love.* San Francisco: Harper and Row, 1988.

Royal, Robert. *The Catholic Martyrs of the Twentieth Century: A Comprehensive World History.* New York: Crossroad, 2000.

Scarry, Elaine. *The Body in Pain: The Making and Unmaking of the World*. New York: Oxford University Press, 1985.

Shah, Bruno M., OP. "The Apocalyptic Wound of Lament: The Cry and Call of Hope." Unpublished PhD term paper, University of Notre Dame (Fall 2015).

Shehan, Sharon Atkinson. *This Is for You: The Story of David Kasali and the Congo Initiative*. Self published.

Snagfilms. *Sewing Hope*. 2013.

Snarr, C. Melissa. *Social Selves and Political Reforms: Five Visions in Contemporary Christian Ethics*. New York: T & T Clark, 2007.

Sobrino, Jon. "Jesus of Galilee from the Salvadoran Context: Compassion, Hope, and Following the Light of the Cross." *Theological Studies* 70, no. 2 (2009): 437–60.

———. *The Principle of Mercy: Taking the Crucified People from the Cross*. Maryknoll, NY: Orbis, 1994.

———. *Witnesses to the Kingdom: The Martyrs of El Salvador and the Crucified Peoples*. Maryknoll, NY: Orbis, 2003.

Sölle, Dorothée. *Suffering*. Translated by Everett R. Kalin. Philadelphia: Fortress, 1975.

Song, Choan-Seng. *Jesus, the Crucified People*. Minneapolis: Fortress, 1996.

"Songs and the Civil Rights Movements." Martin Luther King Jr. and the Global Freedom Struggle. Online: http://mlk-kpp01.stanford.edu/index.php/encyclopedia/encyclopedia/enc_songs_and_the_civil_rights_movement (accessed Dec. 3, 2015).

Stearns, Jason K. *Dancing in the Glory of Monsters: The Collapse of the Congo and the Great War of Africa*. New York: PublicAffairs, 2012.

Taylor, Charles. *A Secular Age*. Cambridge, MA: Belknap, 2007.

Townes, Emilie Maureen. *Breaking the Fine Rain of Death: African American Health Issues and a Womanist Ethic of Care*. New York: Continuum, 1998.

———. *In a Blaze of Glory: Womanist Spirituality as Social Witness*. Nashville: Abingdon, 1995.

———. "Searching for Paradise in a World of Theme Parks: Toward a Womanist Ethic of Care." *Lexington Theological Quarterly* 33 (Fall 1998): 131–50.

Tracy, David. "The Hidden God: The Divine Other of Liberation." *Cross Currents* (Spring 1996): 6–16.

———. "The Role of Theology in Public Life: Some Reflections." *Word & World* 4, no. 3 (1984): 230–39.

Trible, Phyllis. "The Gift of a Poem: A Rhetorical Study of Jeremiah 31:15–22." *Andover Newton Quarterly* 17 (1977): 271–80.

Tutu, Desmond, and Mpho Tutu. *Made for Goodness: And Why This Makes All the Difference*. New York: Harper One, 2010.

Umutesi, Maria Beatrice. *Surviving the Slaughter: The Ordeal of a Rwandan Refugee in Zaire*. Madison: University of Wisconsin Press, 2004.

United States Conferences of Bishops. "1 Peter—Introduction." Online: http://www.usccb.org/bible/1peter/0 (accessed Feb. 2, 2015).

Uvin, Peter. "Global Dreams and Local Anger: From Structural to Acute Violence in a

Globalizing World." In *Rethinking Global Political Economy: Emerging Issues, Unfolding Odysseys*, edited by Mary Ann Tétreault, Robert A. Denemark, Kenneth P. Thomas, and Kurt Burch. Routledge/RIPE Series in Global Political Economy 11. London: Routledge, 1990.

Van de Walle, Nicolas. "Review: *Dancing in the Glory of Monsters: The Collapse of the Congo and the Great War of Africa.*" *Foreign Affairs* (May-June 2011).

Verhoeven, Harry. "Review." *African Arguments,* August 2, 2011. Online: http://african arguments.org/2011/08/02/when-an-african-giant-falls-apart-review-of-dancing -in-the-glory-of-monsters-the-collapse-of-the-congo-and-the-great-war-of-africa -by-jason-stearns/ (accessed Jan. 27, 2015).

Volf, Miroslav. *The End of Memory: Remembering Rightly in a Violent World.* Grand Rapids: Eerdmans, 2006.

Voorwinde, Stephen. *Jesus' Emotions in the Gospels.* London: T&T Clark, 2011.

———. "Jesus' Tears—Human or Divine?" *The Reformed Theological Review* 56, no. 2 (May 1997): 68–81.

Wall, Richard. "Entering into the Passion of This World." Review of Jürgen Moltmann's *The Crucified God.* Online: http://www.amazon.com/The-Crucified-God-Founda tion-Criticism/dp/0800628225 (accessed Dec. 4, 2015).

Walls, Andrew. "The Ephesian Moment: At a Crossroads in Christian History." In *The Cross-Cultural Process in Christian History: Studies in the Transmission and Appropriation of Faith.* Maryknoll, NY: Orbis, 2002.

Wansink, Craig. *Chained in Christ: The Experience and Rhetoric of Paul's Imprisonments.* Sheffield: Sheffield Academic Press, 1996.

Weigert, Kathleen M. "Structural Violence." In *Stress of War, Conflict and Disaster*, edited by George Fink. Amsterdam: Elsevier/Academic Press, 2010.

Westermann, Claus. *Praise and Lament in the Psalms.* Atlanta: John Knox, 1981.

Whitten, Reggie, and Nancy Henderson. *Sewing Hope: Joseph Kony Tore These Girls' Lives Apart. Can She Stitch Them Back Together?* Oklahoma City, OK: Dust Jacket, 2013.

Wrong, Michela. *In the Footsteps of Mr. Kurtz: Living on the Brink of Disaster in Mobutu's Congo.* New York: HarperCollins, 2001.

Index of Names and Subjects

Index of Scripture References